Dear Reader,

Interest in the paralegal field is growing. Job opportunities are up, colleges and universities are developing or expanding paralegal education programs, and proprietary institutions compete for students through Internet classes and shortened courses of study. As they become aware of these trends, more and more students are investigating whether a paralegal career is right for them.

Whenever I have conversations with prospective students, they always ask two questions: "What is a paralegal?" and "What do paralegals do?" These are natural questions, but I always hesitate before I answer because the answer to these questions depends, truthfully, on the individual legal employer and the needs of the specific client. There is no "one size fits all" answer; there are endless ways in which a paralegal can improve the delivery of legal services to the client.

I hope this book conveys the sense of variety and possibility that permeates the paralegal field. Whether you are a prospective student, or just curious about paralegals, this book is your guide to what a paralegal "is," and what paralegals "do."

Steven W. Schneider

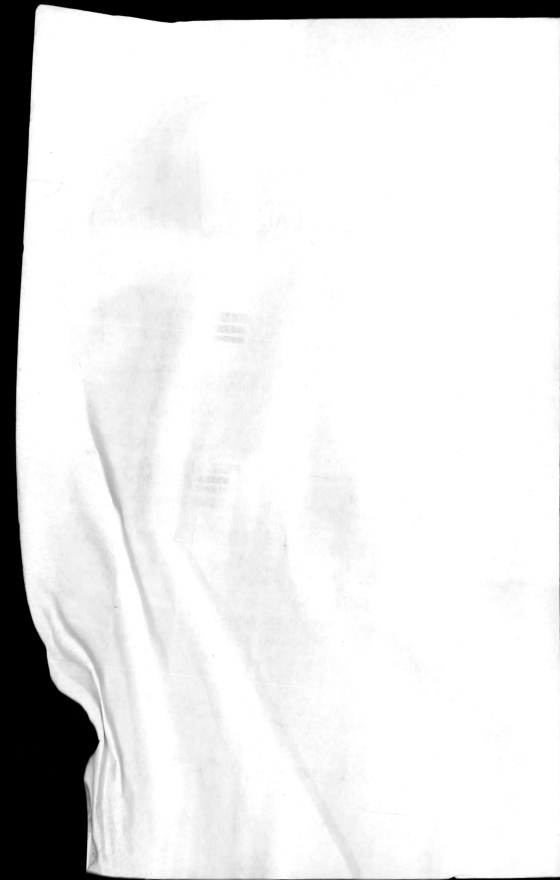

THE
EVERYTHING®
GUIDE TO BEING A
PARALEGAL

Secrets to a successful career!

Steven W. Schneider
Practicing Attorney

Adams Media
Avon, Massachusetts

Dedication

To my family, my colleagues, and my students, from who I have learned much more than can be included here.

• • •

Publishing Director: Gary M. Krebs
Associate Managing Editor: Laura M. Daly
Associate Copy Chief: Brett Palana-Shanahan
Acquisitions Editor: Kate Burgo
Development Editor: Katie McDonough
Associate Production Editor: Casey Ebert

Director of Manufacturing: Susan Beale
Associate Director of Production: Michelle Roy Kelly
Cover Design: Paul Beatrice, Erick DaCosta, Matt LeBlanc
Layout and Graphics: Colleen Cunningham, Sorae Lee, Jennifer Oliveira

An Everything® Series Book.
Everything® and everything.com® are registered trademarks of F+W Publications, Inc.

Published by Adams Media, an F+W Publications Company
57 Littlefield Street, Avon, MA 02322 U.S.A.
www.adamsmedia.com

ISBN 10: 1-59337-583-2
ISBN 13: 978-1-59337-583-6
Printed in the United States of America.

J I H G F E D C B

Library of Congress Cataloging-in-Publication Data
Schneider, Steven W.
The everything guide to being a paralegal / Steven W. Schneider.
p. cm. — (An everything series book)
ISBN 1-59337-583-2
1. Legal assistants—United States. I. Title. II. Series: Everything series.
KF320.L4S365 2006
340.023'73—dc22
2006004162

This publication is designed to provide accurate and authoritative information with regard to the subject matter covered. It is sold with the understanding that the publisher is not engaged in rendering legal, accounting, or other professional advice. If legal advice or other expert assistance is required, the services of a competent professional person should be sought.
—From a *Declaration of Principles* jointly adopted by a Committee of the American Bar Association and a Committee of Publishers and Associations

Many of the designations used by manufacturers and sellers to distinguish their products are claimed as trademarks. Where those designations appear in this book and Adams Media was aware of a trademark claim, the designations have been printed with initial capital letters.

This book is available at quantity discounts for bulk purchases.
For information, please call 1-800-289-0963.

Visit the entire Everything® series at *www.everything.com*

Contents

Top Ten Reasons to Become a Paralegal

1. Paralegals are an indispensable part of the delivery of quality, cost-efficient legal services.

2. The paralegal field is one of the fastest-growing fields of employment in the country, and that trend is projected to continue.

3. Paralegals have unlimited career growth potential.

4. Paralegals have the opportunity to work directly with clients.

5. Paralegals work on a wide variety of assignments and have the opportunity to learn about the legal profession.

6. Paralegals are able to work independently.

7. Paralegals can help people who need legal representation in order to protect their rights.

8. Paralegals are responsible for significant aspects of client service.

9. Paralegals work with current information management technology.

10. Paralegals experience daily intellectual challenges.

Introduction

When I started practicing law, paralegals—broadly defined as specially trained assistants to lawyers—were few and far between. The general consensus in the legal community then was that there was no need to have paralegals doing what associate lawyers could do. As an associate, I spent many hours summarizing documents, digesting depositions, contacting witnesses, and generally doing the kinds of things that are now commonly accepted as paralegal duties. It was part of the training of many new lawyers at the time.

Several years later, the first boom in paralegal employment arrived. This increase in the use of paralegals was not caused by some shift in the thinking of practicing lawyers—in fact, many of them resisted the move toward using paralegals. Instead, lawyers began to use paralegals because their *clients* demanded it. Clients who had been paying their legal bills without complaint began to pay attention to the bottom line. If the law firm would not lower their fees, clients would find a law firm that would. Furthermore, many corporations took their legal work "in house" to reduce fees.

The downward pressure on legal fees came in the form of a single edict from clients: "We will not pay for qualifications that are not necessary to the legal task at hand." This meant that associates could no longer summarize depositions at the hourly rate charged by a lawyer when a paralegal could do the same task for about half the cost. Law firms that did not employ paralegals could not lower prices and, as a result, lost clients.

Today, there is the same downward pressure on legal fees. The difference is that lawyers have come to accept paralegals as a part of the legal services landscape. Paralegals allow lawyers to lower legal costs without lowering the quality of service to the client. I know many lawyers who swear by paralegal assistance—as the factor that allows them to practice law efficiently and effectively.

The first paralegals were trained on the job. I was involved in the education of some of those paralegals, and I can attest to the fact that initially, training of paralegals was somewhat haphazard. It was usually directed to the task at hand. Paralegals learned by doing and by making mistakes. This process was sometimes slow and painstaking, but that gradually changed. Now paralegals often come to law firms from schools and institutions dedicated to providing these legal professionals with the knowledge and skills required to be successful immediately.

For all its popularity, there is still much confusion about paralegalism. Much of the information about the profession is targeted to those who have already decided on a career as a paralegal. Students therefore enter paralegal programs with only a vague idea of what a paralegal does. This book tries to fill that gap. I have tried to provide information that you will find useful in deciding on whether to pursue this fascinating profession. Good luck!

Chapter 1

What Is a Paralegal?

Being a "paralegal"—working beside those in the high-profile legal profession—sounds challenging, exciting, putting one in the middle of the action. The paralegal field is all of that and more—it is client relations, teamwork, and problem solving. Simply put, a paralegal is a lawyer's assistant. Paralegals are specifically educated and trained to perform legal tasks delegated to them by a lawyer, tasks that require specific legal knowledge greater than that possessed by the typical legal secretary. Understanding the key aspects of the paralegal profession is the first step in determining if becoming a paralegal is right for you.

Why Consider Becoming a Paralegal?

If you are considering the paralegal field as a career choice, you probably want to know why others have become paralegals, and whether their expectations were fulfilled. While every paralegal has their own personal reasons for entering the field, three of the most common reasons are job growth, job satisfaction, and variety of work.

Job Growth

The paralegal field offers one of the fastest-growing employment opportunities in the United States. A 2002 Bureau of Labor Statistics report estimated that there are more than 200,000 practicing paralegals in the United States. The same report projected a ten-year increase in the number of paralegals by 28.7 percent. By the year 2012, there will be more than 257,000 practicing paralegals.

The projected growth in the paralegal field is the outgrowth of an ever-increasing demand for the use of paralegals from clients. Over the last fifty years, the hourly rate has become the standard for legal billing. At the same time, clients have experienced an increase in the overall cost of legal services. As the cost of legal services continued to rise, clients looked for ways to save money. A properly trained paralegal is able to deliver many of the same legal services as a lawyer, but at a lower cost.

Essential

Hourly rates for paralegals are approximately 50-75 percent of the supervising lawyer's hourly rate. For example, a paralegal working with a supervising lawyer who charges $150 per hour would normally charge the client between $75 and $110 per hour, depending on the experience of the paralegal.

As word of this discovery got out, large corporations and insurance companies required their lawyers to cut legal costs by using paralegals. Lawyers soon realized that the proper use of paralegals made the practice of law more efficient and less expensive. The use of paralegals has now expanded to nearly every area of the law.

Job Satisfaction

Another reason the paralegal field is so popular is that it offers a high degree of job satisfaction. People who enter the paralegal field are often highly motivated and seek positions that offer a professional challenge. While paralegals work under the supervision of lawyers, they often have a significant amount of independence in performing their assigned tasks. Because paralegals offer a more cost-effective means of gathering information, most paralegals spend a significant portion of their time dealing with clients, the legal representatives of other parties, court personnel, and other persons. As a part of a team providing legal services, a paralegal is often directly involved in identifying and solving the client's legal issues.

Variety of Work

Paralegals often comment on the variety of work activities offered in the paralegal field. Each legal problem presents its own set of facts and legal issues. Even paralegals who specialize in a specific area of the law perform a wide variety of tasks on specific client matters. This variety makes the paralegal field interesting and challenging.

Defining a Paralegal

A paralegal's responsibilities include tasks that would otherwise be performed by a lawyer. There is no universally accepted definition of a paralegal. Some employers create a job description based on the specific educational qualifications and levels of work experience they seek. But there are no formal requirements. Other definitions attempt to provide a comprehensive list of paralegal duties. Still other definitions describe specific skills and competencies required of paralegals.

None of these definitions is completely satisfactory because lawyers and clients use paralegals in many different ways. There is no "one size fits all" definition of a paralegal. In fact, the bar associations in many states have their own definitions, some preferring the term *legal assistant.*

 Fact

Paralegals are sometimes called "legal assistants." The dispute over what to call these legal professionals has divided three of the most influential organizations in the paralegal profession. The National Association of Legal Assistants (NALA) prefers the term *legal assistant.* The National Federation of Paralegal Associations (NFPA) uses the term *paralegal,* while the American Bar Association (ABA) considers the terms interchangeable.

Even with all these variations, the several definitions of paralegal share some important features:

- A paralegal does not practice law, although some administrative agencies allow paralegals to appear before them without a lawyer.

- A paralegal has specific legal knowledge acquired through education, training, or work experience.
- A paralegal uses this legal knowledge to perform substantive legal tasks under the supervision of a lawyer.

What Does a Paralegal Do?

In theory, there is no standard for what a paralegal does. In practice, the ways a paralegal can assist a lawyer in delivering affordable, quality legal services are limited only by the imagination of the lawyer.

Many factors affect the nature of the assignments a paralegal receives, including the experience and education of the paralegal, the complexity of the legal task, and the specific practice setting. In most cases, however, a paralegal performs some or all of the following tasks:

- **Client contact.** Most paralegals assist lawyers by serving as the first line of communication with the client. By designating the paralegal as the primary contact, the lawyer is free to perform other functions. Unless the client has a question or problem that requires legal advice, paralegals are quite effective in keeping the client up to date on the progress of his case.
- **Client interviews.** To provide good legal service, a lawyer needs to know the facts of the client's legal problem. The task of obtaining factual information from the client is often delegated to paralegals. Most paralegals have specific skills in client interviewing and fact identification.
- **Legal investigations.** Paralegals are often assigned the task of gathering, organizing, and summarizing relevant information. A probate matter might require an investigation into the value of a certain piece of personal property; a personal injury lawsuit might be based on photographs of the accident scene taken by the investigating police officer. An experienced paralegal knows where to find relevant information and how to evaluate it.
- **Docket control.** Nearly every legal task has a deadline. A document must be filed with the court, a contract must be

signed, or a response to a request for information is due. In many offices, the paralegal is responsible for tracking deadlines and other important dates for the lawyer.

- **Legal research.** If properly trained, paralegals can often perform routine legal research for the lawyer. Routine legal research tasks include locating the applicable cases, statutes, court rules, and regulations on a specific legal issue. A paralegal might also be asked to analyze and summarize the impact of this research on the client's case.
- **Legal drafting.** A paralegal is able to prepare legal documents under the supervision of a lawyer. Paralegals often prepare drafts of pleadings, contracts, deeds, or wills for review by the lawyer, as well as routine legal correspondence and interoffice memoranda.

This list is not exhaustive. The precise duties of a paralegal depend on the needs of the lawyer and the client. Some paralegals accompany their lawyers to court or to witness depositions, especially if document management is a concern. Other paralegals perform secretarial functions such as typing, filing, and photocopying.

Traits of a Successful Paralegal

Successful paralegals have entered the profession by many different paths. Some are former legal secretaries who became paralegals as their knowledge and experience proved more and more valuable to the clients. Some were employed in some other aspect of the legal system, such as an insurance adjuster or union representative. Still others obtained formal paralegal degrees before entering the profession. (Chapter 2 explores the range of preparatory programs available today.)

There is, at this time, no licensing requirement for paralegals, and paralegals do not have to pass an examination to practice as lawyers do. And since it is not necessary that a paralegal have a specific level of education or work experience, a single firm might employ a paralegal staff coming from a variety of backgrounds and experience. Even so, those paralegals have several personal attributes in common. They all have a high degree of professionalism, they all have an understanding of the importance of confidentiality in the legal profession, and they all have a significant measure of self-confidence. These qualities are essential in any successful paralegal.

Professionalism

A paralegal must exhibit professionalism. Professionalism is not simply a matter of how you behave in front of others or how you dress. These are important, but not as important as how you think. A professional paralegal does not allow emotion or personal biases to affect the service to the client. A professional paralegal is able to set aside outside influences, from worry about a child's illness to a personal dislike of the client, and focus on doing the best job possible on the assigned legal task.

Paralegals must be able to deal with clients in many difficult situations. Some clients are at a crisis point in their lives—dealing with divorce or death of a loved one. These clients must be treated with tact and empathy. Other clients may be extremely demanding or undergoing periods of stress. A successful paralegal is able to deal with these situations in a way that strengthens the client relationship.

A paralegal will not always agree with the positions taken by a client. However, such feelings cannot be allowed to influence the paralegal's approach to assigned tasks. This attribute is so important that there is an ethical rule requiring paralegals to advise their employers if personal feelings might interfere with the quality of service to the client.

Maintaining Confidentiality

A paralegal must understand the importance of confidentiality in the legal setting. Most of us have heard of attorney-client confidentiality. This describes the obligation of a lawyer to never reveal to a third person any information received from a client without the client's permission. Paralegals must observe the same ethical obligation. The duty to protect the confidentiality of client communications is a proactive one.

A successful paralegal is vigilant in ensuring client confidentiality. Keeping client information confidential requires constant watchfulness.

Mislaid papers, overheard telephone conversations, or simple gossip are common breaches of confidentiality. The paralegal must guard against breaches of confidentiality in every situation.

Self-confidence

To be successful, a paralegal must be able to work independently, often with little or no direction. The supervising lawyer will not always be available to answer questions or provide direction.

Self-confidence takes another form as well. Paralegals must deal with other people—clients, other legal representatives, court personnel, and witnesses, to name a few. These persons often expect the paralegal to be knowledgeable about a given subject. A successful paralegal must feel and be able to convey the assurance of competence in order to be effective in these encounters. Self-confidence that you understand the topic is a necessary attribute.

Skills of a Successful Paralegal

Success in the paralegal field is not based solely on legal knowledge. To become an integral part of the legal services team, a paralegal must have certain skills and abilities, in addition to a command of procedural rules and substantive legal principles. These skills are the defining characteristics of the most successful paralegal practitioners.

A successful paralegal is able to apply specific legal knowledge gained through education and experience to assist in solving the client's legal problem. Paralegals operate as part of a team that delivers legal services to the client. This focus on the client's success requires a paralegal to perform quality work in a timely fashion with appropriate attention to detail.

Performing quality work does not mean that the client will always achieve the desired result. No paralegal can control the outcome of a client's case. The best any legal professional can do is to analyze the client's problem as thoroughly as possible and assist the client in selecting the best possible solution to that problem. Quality legal work requires a paralegal to apply skills of writing, communication, analysis, organization, use of computers, and other skills to the client's problem. Paralegals use these skills every day in many different ways.

Writing Skills

Much of the day-to-day communication in a law office is through writing. Assignment memos, investigation reports, interview summaries, deposition summaries, and research memoranda are all common forms of writing required of paralegals. Paralegals are also expected to draft legal documents, such as contracts, articles of incorporation, wills, purchase agreements, and pleadings.

 Fact

Writing for a court is much different from writing internal office memoranda. Court rules often specify such mechanical components as font type and size, line spacing, page margins, use of footnotes, and topic organization. These rules should be tabbed or indexed and reviewed each time the paralegal begins work on a document that will be submitted to the court.

Not all writing prepared by a paralegal stays within the law office. Paralegals write to clients, to other attorneys, and to witnesses. Documents prepared by paralegals are sent directly to clients or filed with the court. A contract or deed prepared by a paralegal might become an exhibit in later litigation over the transaction.

Mechanically Correct Writing

Writing that is mechanically correct is properly punctuated, grammatically correct, and free of typographic errors. Good writing uses legal terminology correctly, follows appropriate formatting requirements, and uses correct citation form. Formatting and citation form are dictated by the court for some types of writing.

These mechanical aspects of writing are more important than most paralegals realize. Lawyers are detail oriented by nature and they expect their paralegals to be attentive to detail as well. Errors in punctuation, grammar, and spelling have a subtle effect on the reader: they create the impression that the writer is not attentive to details.

There are several ways to improve the mechanics of your writing. Most paralegal programs offer courses that deal specifically with legal writing and have a significant writing component to many substantive law courses. A number of books, reference manuals, and Web sites deal with aspects of legal writing or writing in general. A good usage text is an indispensable tool for developing clear, effective writing. In addition to these, most law firms have brief banks or form files that contain examples of good legal writing for you to study and emulate.

Clear and Precise Writing

Like good writing mechanics, clear and precise writing projects an impression of competence. Some commentators describe this effect as the *contract* with the reader. All legal writing presumes a relationship with the reader—writing is a means of imparting information. The contract with the reader assumes that the information will be imparted clearly, precisely, and competently.

E ssential

One way to achieve clarity in writing is to avoid the use of "legalese." Legalese is the use of overly technical and verbose legal terminology when it is not required. For example, it is common for a will to "give, devise, and bequeath," when a simple "give" will do. Instead of writing, "enclosed herein please find," write, "the [document] is enclosed," or "enclosed is." If a simpler phrase does not alter the meaning of your writing, use it.

Writing that includes unnecessary qualifiers, complex sentence structure, or legalese does not effectively impart information. When a writer makes the reader sort through a poorly worded sentence to discover an important fact, the contract with the reader is broken. Unclear and imprecise writing indicates that the writer does not know what is important and is willing to leave it to the reader to figure out. When the writer does not live up to the contract, the reader will assume this is because the writer is incompetent.

Writing with Attention to Purpose

Successful paralegals make sure their writing has an identifiable purpose. They develop their writing skills so they produce the best possible product. Your writing habits should fall into three categories.

- **Prewriting.** Successful paralegals never begin a writing project without answering two questions about the document. First: Who is the intended reader of the document? Knowing your audience allows you to write according to that audience's expectations. Second: What is the purpose of the document? Decide on the best way of accomplishing that purpose.
- **Writing.** Converting the purpose of the writing into words is often the most troublesome aspect of preparing a document. Important information must be separated from unimportant information. It is often useful to work from an outline or some form of organized notes when writing longer documents.
- **Postwriting or editing.** Editing involves both proofreading and revision. The writing must be checked for spelling errors and mistakes in grammar. The proper use of legal terminology should be verified. Punctuation errors should be corrected. Revision involves changing or rewriting any part of the document that does not fulfill the purpose of the document.

 **Alert**

Legal writing is of two kinds: objective or persuasive. *Objective writing* is intended to communicate. It should be as factual as possible and avoid emotional or inflammatory language. A legal opinion letter is an example of objective writing. *Persuasive writing* is intended to persuade. Persuasive writing should be based in fact, but it can appeal to emotion. A settlement demand letter is an example of persuasive writing.

Oral Communication Skills

Developing good oral communication skills involves improving in three areas. First, know your subject. Oral communication is a means of imparting information. Incorrect information can have grave consequences for the client. When you speak with a client about a legal matter, the client expects that the information you give will be correct. If you tell the client that a court appearance is at 3:00 P.M. when it is actually at 1:30 P.M., you may have damaged the client's case by not knowing your subject. The law firm's relationship with the client will surely be damaged.

Second, good oral communication is precise and clear. Ambiguous oral communication risks being misunderstood. The successful paralegal must use proper grammar when speaking. Slang and colloquialisms should be avoided, especially when discussing complex legal concepts. All oral communication should be as concise as possible. The successful paralegal knows the difference between conversational communication and professional communication.

Third, a successful paralegal must develop the skill of listening. Much of the information in a legal matter comes from oral communication—instructions from a supervising attorney, the statements of a witness, or the description of a legal problem from a client. In each case, the paralegal must possess effective listening skills.

Active listening is usually defined as attentive listening with feedback to the speaker indicating the listener understands what is said. *Passive listening* is attentive listening with feedback that reassures the speaker that the listener is actually listening. Both are valid techniques for establishing a connection with the speaker, but neither requires the listener to be an effective listener.

Effective listening is the process of listening to the speaker and, at the same time, relating the information to the purpose of the conversation. This requires the listener to grasp the significance of what is said. The effective listener is able to ask questions to clarify or expand on important points while keeping the conversation on track. Effective listening not only demonstrates that the paralegal is listening, but that she is also paying attention.

Analytical Skills

In every area of the law, paralegals are asked to identify and sort facts. These facts are then evaluated in light of an applicable rule of law. The traditional acronym for this kind of legal analysis is *IRAC*, which stands for Issue, Rule of Law, Application, and Conclusion. After you have analyzed a legal problem, look back to be sure you have accurately identified each component of good legal analysis. Through practice and repetition, the application of IRAC formula will become second nature.

- **Issue.** A key component in examining any legal problem is to define the issue—the statement of the question to be answered, expressed in legal terms. The statement of the issue must revolve around facts that are important to the application of the legal principle. Facts that have no bearing on the legal principle are irrelevant. If you are trying to determine whether a driver was at fault for an intersection accident, the fact that the driver ran through a red light is an important fact, but the fact that he was driving a blue car is not.
- **Rule of law.** Rules of law come from court opinions, statutes, and regulations. A part of your analytical duties is identifying the proper rule of law in a legal problem. In the example about the driver who ran the red light, the proper rule of law is the statute prohibiting vehicles from entering an intersection on a red light. If you try to analyze the problem using the statute that governs alternate side parking, you are unlikely to come to any useful conclusions.
- **Application.** After the important facts, the issue, and the rule of law are identified, the next step is to apply the law to those facts. The application step requires a careful analysis of the facts to determine if each element is present. If the rule of law states, "It is a violation of law for a bar to sell alcohol at any time before 10:00 A.M. or after 2:00 A.M.," the rule has three elements: there must be a bar, there must be a sale of alcohol, and the sale must occur between 2:00 A.M. and 10:00 A.M. The

absence of factual support for any element means that the rule of law does not apply.

- **Conclusion.** The conclusion is the result of the application of the rule of law to the facts. The conclusion may be that a rule of law does apply or does not apply. It may also address the consequences of applying the rule of law to the facts. The purpose of the conclusion is to address the client's legal problem and to provide an answer.

Computer Skills

Computers are a fact of life in the modern practice of law. Most legal documents are created on a computer. Computers are used to keep track of court deadlines and to organize data for presentation to regulatory agencies. They are used for legal research and for certain kinds of legal investigations. Many courts now require that all pleadings be filed in electronic format. Nearly every law school graduate in the last ten years has basic computer skills.

 Fact

Some courts now require electronic filing of all litigation paperwork. Many courtrooms now accommodate electronic exhibits and some offer real-time transcription of testimony. Instead of struggling with easels and poster boards, lawyers and witnesses now use electronic slide presentations. A paralegal who is not familiar with these basic computer capabilities will soon be left behind.

A beginning paralegal without basic computer skills is virtually unemployable in today's marketplace. At the least, a paralegal must have basic word processing skills. The ability to use advanced database and case management software is desirable. In certain legal practices, the most desirable paralegal positions require familiarity with how computers store and manipulate data; a large part of a paralegal's job is the management of information.

Preparing to Become a Paralegal

If you are already employed in the legal profession or in a closely allied field, you may be able to enter the paralegal profession without any further education. Persons in these fields often make a successful transition to the paralegal profession because they already have knowledge of the legal system and of legal principles. These persons also possess strong skills in analytical thinking and communication from their current jobs. Legal employers are more willing to fill any gaps in knowledge with on-the-job training for these individuals.

E ssential

The local chapter of the state paralegal association is a terrific place to get information about the paralegal field. Working paralegals are very knowledgeable about and interested in the development of the paralegal profession. Many are happy to share their experience and expertise with students and new paralegals.

If you are not employed in one of these fields, the move to becoming a paralegal usually necessitates additional education in the paralegal field. Fortunately, the growing popularity of the paralegal profession has led to an explosion in the number of institutions offering paralegal education. Because the paralegal field is largely unregulated, however, the education offered by these institutions is not standardized. A paralegal student can choose between paralegal programs offering paralegal certificates, two-year degrees, four-year degrees, and advanced degrees. In addition, an increasing number of programs offer students the opportunity to complete their paralegal education through online classes—classes offered over the Internet where a student logs on from a home computer for class lectures, discussions, and assignments.

Chapter 2 offers a comprehensive survey of your options in securing an education for success as a paralegal. Whatever paralegal education program you choose, you can expect to make a significant investment in time and money. On the other hand, a formal paralegal education is increasingly essential for persons hoping to break into the paralegal profession. The sheer number of available paralegal programs can make choosing the right program seem overwhelming. Making a wise choice involves answering four questions:

- **What are the education requirements in your specific job market?** Some employers consider a certificate sufficient and expect that on-the-job training will fill any gaps in the applicant's education. Other legal employers insist on a higher level of formal education. You can obtain this information from working paralegals, the local chapter of the state paralegal association, or the placement office of the educational institution.

- **What is the educational focus of the program?** The day-to-day work of paralegals is practical; the objective is to get the job done. Because of this, the American Bar Association (ABA) strongly recommends that paralegal programs focus on the skills necessary to complete practical, real-life tasks. Nevertheless, many paralegal programs focus on the theoretical aspects of the law.

- **Who teaches the core legal courses in the program?** Ask whether the legal courses are taught by lawyers, paralegals, or other instructors. The specific instructors can tell you a great deal about the quality of education offered by the institution.

- **Does the program offer internships or some other means of gaining practical experience in a real work environment?** Employers are more comfortable hiring paralegals who have some work experience. This often causes an employer to "promote from within," preferring a current employee as a paralegal candidate to an inexperienced graduate of a paralegal program. Internships, legal clinics, and other established opportunities for practical experience allow the newly minted paralegal graduate to overcome the "promote from within" mindset.

Paralegal Salaries and Career Opportunities

Most students interested in becoming paralegals are concerned with how much they will earn. This is understandable since becoming a paralegal involves a significant investment of time and money. Unfortunately, just as with job duties, paralegal earnings vary greatly, so here, too, there is no "one size (rate) fits all."

A number of factors affect what a paralegal earns, including the education and experience of the paralegal, the area in which the paralegal practices, the type of legal specialty, and the nature of the legal practice. The wide range of employment opportunities for paralegals in the public and private sectors also affect levels of compensation. Furthermore, legal business cycles—periods of time when the demand for legal services is either sharply up or sharply down—can affect paralegal salaries.

 **Alert**

All state bar associations expect licensed attorneys to provide legal services, free of charge, to people who are unable to afford those services. This is the lawyer's pro bono service obligation. A common expectation is that a lawyer will devote fifty hours per year to pro bono activities. Both the National Association of Legal Assistants (NALA) and the National Federation of Paralegal Associations (NFPA) have similar expectations of their paralegal members.

How Employee Benefits Affect Paralegal Compensation

The rate of paralegal pay is only part of the compensation story. If you are thinking about entering the paralegal profession or are looking for a paralegal position, here are a few matters you should consider when evaluating paralegal pay:

- **What is the value of the benefits offered by the employer?** Most employers offer some standard benefits—vacation and sick pay; retirement plans; and life, medical, and dental insurance. These benefits increase the total cost of hiring a paralegal. Along with these benefits, consider other common expenses a legal employer might pay—parking, association memberships, attendance at continuing education seminars, or paid time off for pro bono activities.

- **What are the opportunities for advancement?** In some law firms, beginning paralegals often start in secretarial positions. The paralegal works in this position to learn the nature of the law firm's practice, the needs of the clients of the law firm, and to become familiar with a specific area of law. Paralegals in these positions are paid less than other paralegals because these duties are not charged to clients. The compensation rate increases as the paralegal gains experience.
- **What are the employer's billable hour expectations?** Typically, the work of a paralegal is charged to the client based on an hourly rate. Many firms expect paralegals to generate a specified number of billable hours every year. Since not every moment at work is billable to a client, the billable hour requirement may not represent all the work expectations of the employer. A legal employer with a high billable hour expectation is likely to offer a higher starting salary than an employer with lower billable hour expectations.

Compensation Surveys

A major source of information on paralegal salaries is compensation surveys. These surveys collect information from a wide spectrum of legal employers and paralegal professionals. In addition to salary and benefit information, most surveys include questions on job duties, minimum employment requirements, and billable-hour expectations. Three major sources of statistical data on paralegal salaries are the U.S. Department of Labor, the National Federation of Paralegal Associations, and the National Association of Legal Assistants.

The Department of Labor maintains salary information through the Bureau of Labor Statistics. The Bureau of Labor Statistics report deals only with reported salaries; it does not attempt to value benefits or work expectations. In 2002, the Bureau of Labor Statistics reported that the median annual income for a full-time paralegal was $37,950. The Bureau of Labor Statistics uses only national data in its calculations, and so these income statistics may not reflect paralegal salaries in your area.

The National Association of Legal Assistants (NALA) conducts its compensation survey on even-numbered years. The NALA report is available on its Web site, listed in Appendix A. The 2004 NALA survey reports that paralegals responding to the survey earned an average annual salary of $44,373. This figure represents an increase of $19,426 in the average annual salary since the NALA began reporting salary statistics in 1988.

The National Federation of Paralegal Assistants (NFPA) also conducts a biannual salary survey, conducted in odd-numbered years. The results of the current NFPA survey are available for sale on its Web site, listed in Appendix A. In 1999, the NFPA reported an average annual paralegal salary of $38,085.

Use these statistics with caution. Each of the studies has limitations that may affect their usefulness to you. Many paralegals entering the job market have salary expectations colored by survey results that are not accurate for their specific area of the country or experience level. Here are some things to take into account:

- The Bureau of Labor Statistics data weighs heavily toward large metropolitan areas. This is because more of the respondents are in these areas than in nonmetropolitan areas. Because metropolitan areas often have higher salaries, the average salary may not reflect actual salaries in other areas of your state.
- Over 70 percent of the paralegals responding to the NALA survey had advanced certifications. A paralegal who attains an advanced certification has met minimum educational requirements and has a minimum of two years of paralegal experience. The salaries paid to these paralegals are not comparable to the salary paid to a beginning paralegal.

- Only 4 percent of the NALA survey responses came from the New England/MidEast area. This low sample may affect the accuracy of the responses from this area of the country.
- The experience level of the average respondent to the NFPA survey was seven to ten years. Again, salaries tend to rise with experience, so the reported average salary may be higher than what a beginning paralegal can expect to make.

Regulation Versus Evaluation

A lawyer must meet certain educational requirements and pass a test demonstrating knowledge of the law before obtaining a license to practice law. A lawyer maintains this license by complying with the ethical standards of the profession. Many states also require lawyers to meet continuing education requirements as a condition of continued licensure. In all states, lawyers are self-regulated; the determination of whether a person meets the requirements to practice law in the state is made by other lawyers under the supervision of the state supreme court.

E ssential

Do not be fooled by the seeming lack of control over the paralegal profession. Supervising lawyers exercise very strict control over their paralegals and usually have very exacting standards for hiring new paralegals. Just because the profession does not *require* a legal education does not mean there are jobs available for paralegals without this qualification. The better your legal education is, the better your chances of getting a job.

The paralegal profession is not regulated in the same way. Paralegals are not required to meet any specific educational requirements. They do not have to pass a licensing examination—although some proposals have been made to change this. A paralegal cannot be prevented from acting as a paralegal because of unethical behavior. There are no continuing legal education requirements imposed on paralegals. In fact, as you will see later, the only regulation of paralegals is indirect because paralegals work under the supervision of lawyers. They are subject to regulation by the lawyers who employ them.

The lack of regulation might seem beneficial to the paralegal profession. In reality, the absence of regulatory authority is two-edged sword. Without regulation, there is no way to ensure that all paralegals meet minimum competency levels. An unethical paralegal cannot be barred from practicing as a paralegal, except when the legal community refuses to employ that paralegal. And unless their employers demand it, paralegals are not required to expand and deepen their knowledge of the law. Nevertheless, the most successful paralegals are those who are well educated and well trained.

Chapter 2

The Right Paralegal Program

Selecting the right paralegal education program is a daunting task. As mentioned in Chapter 1, you may choose between degree and certificate programs, program lengths ranging from as short as four months to as long as four years, and in-class or online instruction. Which program is right for you depends on your education and employment background and your career goals.

Types of Paralegal Education Programs

There are four basic kinds of paralegal education programs. Each of them offers something different.

Certificate Programs

Certificate paralegal education programs are nondegree programs, usually ranging from six months to eighteen months in length. Class times vary—some programs schedule classes during the day; others offer night classes; still others offer concentrated or accelerated classes on weekends.

The typical certificate paralegal education program focuses entirely on the acquisition of legal knowledge. There are no requirements that the paralegal demonstrate or learn competency in oral and written communication, analytical thinking, or computer proficiency outside the context of core legal courses. Typical core legal courses include real estate law, bankruptcy law, litigation, and probate administration.

Universities, colleges, and community colleges offer certificate paralegal education programs. Proprietary schools—institutions that specialize in concentrated training programs on several different subjects—also offer them. Proprietary schools may or may not be accredited institutions.

The shorter program length of certificate programs attracts some students who are interested in joining the work force as soon as possible. However, the rapid educational pace of certificate programs often overwhelms these students. Most certificate programs are designed for persons with a prior degree or with substantial work experience. Students who enter a program that matches their needs increase their chances of success.

Candidates for paralegal certificate programs are:

- Students who have a prior college degree and need to supplement their education in the legal area in preparation for a career change.
- Students who are currently employed in the legal field and seek to supplement their practical knowledge through formal education.
- Students who want to add a legal component to their education, but do not intend to seek employment in the paralegal field.

Associate Degree Programs

Associate degree paralegal education programs are typically two-year programs. A large number of these programs are offered through community colleges. Some colleges and universities offer associate degree paralegal education programs. These programs often have advisory committees comprised of former students, community employers of paralegals, and other interested community members. They advise the institution on changes and trends in employer demand for paralegal skills. This information helps the institution direct curriculum development, advise students on choice of electives, and determine frequency of course offerings. As a result, these institutions tend to offer a more varied selection of specialty legal courses. Typical courses include a paralegal survey course, legal research, and legal writing. The paralegal student might then be able to choose among courses in real property, business law, bankruptcy, torts and personal injury, civil procedure, criminal law, criminal procedure, and wills and probate.

The nature of the associate degree offered depends on the program requirements. Some of the programs that require course work outside the courses have a business focus. Candidates for these degrees will often take courses in business communication, office software applications, terminology, and other practical skills. Other associate degree paralegal education programs require general education courses in addition to core legal courses. Candidates for these degrees take courses in the humanities to broaden the scope of their appreciation for the role of the law in our society. Many associate degree paralegal education programs offer classes at a variety of times to accommodate traditional and nontraditional students.

 Fact

Generally speaking, the Associate of Applied Science (A.A.S.) degree is appropriate for the student who plans to enter the work force immediately after completing the program. The Associate of Science (A.S.) degree is intended for those students who plan to pursue further education after completion of the paralegal program.

Students who apply for associate degree paralegal education programs must be well qualified. Paralegal course work requires a considerable amount of time and effort to prepare for classes and complete assignments. Legal classes often demand sophisticated analytical thinking that is the product of thorough preparation and study. Some institutions may utilize prescreening, such as standardized test scores, to select students for admission to the program. Other institutions require preadmission interviews or rely on an advising model to ensure that students entering the program are capable of succeeding.

Four-year Programs

Four year paralegal education programs can be found at some colleges and universities. These programs are often minor field of study, although an increasing number of institutions offer Paralegal Studies as a separate major. These fields of study are often found in the Political Science or Business departments.

The four-year paralegal education program offers a longer period of study, giving the paralegal student more options for legal study. Four-year programs typically require the student to meet course requirements in a broad liberal arts curriculum. The paralegal education courses include introductory courses such as terminology and legal research. As the student advances, there are opportunities to choose classes in business organizations, corporate law, employment law, and constitutional law. The longer course of study allows these programs to offer the paralegal student more in-depth study on specific legal topics.

Distance Learning Programs

The traditional method of teaching lawyers and paralegals is through in-person dialogue—a question-and-answer format known as the Socratic method. Many paralegal programs still follow this educational format. Students attending these institutions must attend class at a "brick-and-mortar" location and attend classes at specific times. As this arrangement is often inconvenient for students who must travel long distances to attend class or who are employed and unable to attend class at the scheduled time, paralegal distance education programs are becoming increasingly popular. Some of these programs are offered by proprietary schools and result in a certificate award. Others are associated with community colleges, colleges, and universities and allow the student to obtain any degree offered to a traditional student.

Course offerings for paralegal distance education programs generally duplicate the offerings of on-ground programs. Course materials are delivered through a Web site maintained by the institution. Some programs offer the student an opportunity to interact with the instructor and other students by means of discussion postings, online chats, and group assignments. Other programs offer minimal interaction, relying instead on the student's individual assignments to demonstrate knowledge of the subject.

E ssential

The American Bar Association recommends limiting the number of online legal courses a paralegal student can take. A program that is ABA approved is unlikely to offer as many online courses as other programs. If your job market requires a degree from an ABA-approved program, you will not be able to complete all of your legal coursework online.

A student considering a paralegal distance education program must have certain qualities:

- **Technological proficiency.** Since paralegal distance education programs are offered by computer, the student must be comfortable using technology. Common issues include the ability to navigate a Web site and the ability to create and download documents in a particular format.
- **Organizational skills.** Online courses tend to proceed at a set pace. This set pace often involves sequenced learning: textbook reading followed by online course content, followed by assignments, followed by testing. The student who falls behind in this sequence may find it impossible to catch up.
- **Self-directed learning.** Not every paralegal distance learning programs utilizes online opportunities for group discussion and individualized feedback. Very often, the student is left to explore the subject matter with only the textbook and cues from the online course content as guides. The student must be persistent and resourceful in locating answers to questions that arise.

Which Program Is Right for You?

Paralegal education programs have significantly different approaches to paralegal education, even among programs of the same type. Your selection of a paralegal education program might depend, in part, on practical issues like location, availability of financial aid, and the length of the program. You should never choose a paralegal education program, however, without addressing a few other factors.

Employability

The education requirements of the employers in your area are an important factor in choosing a paralegal education program. You may not want to devote the time to complete a four-year program if local employers only require a two-year degree. Similarly, completion of a certificate program will not maximize your employment options.

The education requirements of the employer may vary with the type of employer. A large law firm that employs fifty paralegals under the supervision of a paralegal manager might require paralegal applicants to possess a four-year degree from an ABA-approved program. A smaller employer in the same town might accept an applicant with a two-year degree. You should consider both the geographic location and type of employer when evaluating the employment opportunities offered by a paralegal education program.

Career Enhancement Opportunities

You should not view your selection of a paralegal education program as a kind of vocational training. Completion of a paralegal education program may be only one step in your legal education. Consider whether the program offers the opportunity to pursue other education opportunities as well.

Paralegal certificate programs usually provide limited access to further education. Some paralegal certificate programs do not even offer college credit for the course work. Even if college credit is offered, the content of a paralegal certificate program is so specialized that transferability is limited.

Two-year associate degree paralegal education programs offer a great deal of flexibility for further education. When offered through a community college, these programs often serve as "feeder" programs to affiliated four-year institutions. The transferability of course work is nearly automatic for these programs. In addition, some programs have agreements with other institutions that ease the way for transferring students by allowing credits from one institution to satisfy course requirements of another.

Four-year paralegal education programs offer the most flexibility for career enhancement. Because four-year degrees require background in subjects other than law, a paralegal with this type of degree can pursue a graduate degree in almost any subject. Some paralegals pursue an M.B.A. after completing their four-year paralegal degree; others continue to law school. In addition, a small number of institutions offer a master's degree in paralegal studies.

Placement Office

The placement office of the paralegal education institution deserves special mention. The best faculty, reputation, and practical experiences in the world do you no good if the institution is not able to help you find a job when you graduate. In addition to placement statistics, you should consider the role of the faculty in placement—they may maintain contacts in the legal community that can be useful for the job seeker. Ask how many requests from employers are received each year. Placement statistics that only show the number of graduates employed only tell half the story—how many employers are seeking out graduates of the institution? You should also talk to former graduates. Find out how long it took them to find a job, what sort of support did they received from the institution, etc.

Practical Experience Opportunities

Because paralegals assist lawyers in performing practical legal tasks, it is necessary that the paralegal student become acquainted with both the theory and the practice of the law. Instruction in practical applications is so important that both the American Bar Association

(ABA) and the American Association for Paralegal Education (AAfPE) include it as a part of their suggested curriculum.

Practical applications include such matters as drafting pleadings, gathering documents to respond to discovery requests, scheduling a deposition or court hearing, and arranging with a court clerk for the issuance of a subpoena. Classroom instruction provides some practice, but there is no substitute for actual work experience. A school that provides the opportunity for such experience can greatly enhance your value to the legal employer.

Paralegal education programs generally provide work experience through internships. Internships often involve working with a legal employer for an entire credit period. Many internships are flexible in terms of the number of hours required; others expect you to devote the equivalent of a full work week to an internship position. This is in addition to your responsibilities for your schoolwork, your family, and any other employment you might have. Because of this, internships are not always a practical solution for all students.

 Alert

Lawyers do not always agree on what tasks should be assigned to paralegals. Some lawyers give paralegals great responsibility; others prefer to do legal research and drafting themselves. Your paralegal education should prepare you to perform a variety of tasks—how that education is used depends on your employer.

Some schools offer other means of obtaining practical experience. *Job shadowing* is one alternative that is more flexible than an internship. The main disadvantage of job shadowing is that it seldom offers the extent of hands-on learning that paralegal students require. Another alternative is part-time employment with a legal employer. Even working as the "office runner" gives the paralegal student exposure to the practical side of paralegal practice.

Other innovative options for the determined paralegal student include local legal aid programs that provide services to the poor;

these programs are chronically understaffed. Locate a program and volunteer to screen cases, file documents, or do whatever is needed. As a volunteer, you can set your own hours and select the type of law that interests you; legal aid programs deal with criminal law, housing, divorce, bankruptcy, sexual assault, and many other areas of the law. Some schools may even give credit for this kind of volunteering.

ABA Approval

There are more than a thousand paralegal education programs in the United States. Of those, approximately 25 percent have the approval of the ABA.

ABA approval is a voluntary process. A paralegal education program must apply for ABA approval, agree to ABA examination of all parts of the program, and participate in a site visit by the approval committee. The standards for ABA approval include matters such as curriculum, qualifications of instructors and program directors, contents of the program's law library, and length of program. These standards are the result of extended study by the ABA's Standing Committee on Legal Assistants. Programs that have received ABA approval have similar curriculum requirements, are of similar length, and strive for similar educational outcomes. Because ABA approval is the "gold standard" of paralegal education programs, graduates of these programs may have a competitive advantage when seeking employment, especially in larger metropolitan areas.

A program that is ABA approved offers certain advantages, yet presents some disadvantages to the paralegal student. The requirements for ABA approval do not change rapidly and sometimes do not reflect changes in the practice of law. For example, ABA approval requires the paralegal education program to maintain a physical law library with specified contents. In this day and age, however, many small law firms operate without any physical law library, relying instead on computer-assisted legal research services. In addition, the ABA places limits on the amount of credit a paralegal student can receive from distance education courses. Many paralegal education programs can never qualify for ABA approval because of the online nature of the program. ABA approval is an indication that the paralegal student will receive a quality education in that program. Lack of ABA approval does not indicate the opposite, however. Many paralegal education programs without ABA approval maintain very high standards of paralegal education.

 Question

Should I eliminate any programs that do not have ABA approval from my program search?
Not necessarily. There are many quality paralegal education programs that do not have ABA approval.

AAfPE Affiliation

Of the more than 1,000 paralegal programs in the United States, about 450 are members of the American Association for Paralegal Education. The AAfPE is an organization of paralegal educators and their institutions dedicated to improving the quality of paralegal education.

About AAfPE

The AAfPE has created standards for paralegal education to ensure that every paralegal student acquires the necessary substantive knowledge and professional skill to be a successful, contributing member of the legal services team. The AAfPE does not approve or disapprove of the education programs of its members, but it serves as a resource for those institutions interested in implementing and maintaining high standards of paralegal education. The AAfPE maintains a Web site listing its affiliates and providing hints and tips for selecting a paralegal education program. While membership in the AAfPE is voluntary, its affiliate institutions are members because of their interest in providing the paralegal student with the best paralegal education possible.

Paralegal Certification

Both the National Association of Legal Assistants (NALA) and the National Federation of Paralegal Associations (NFPA) offer competency certifications to their members. These certifications are responses to the wide variety of paralegal education programs. Competency certification is seen as a means of ensuring that practicing paralegals possess minimum levels of substantive legal knowledge and professional skills.

The NALA examination is the Certified Legal Assistant (CLA) exam. The NALA allows several paths to qualify for the CLA exam, including completion of a variety of paralegal education programs, completion of a bachelor's degree in any field plus one year of working experience, or—if the candidate has no formal paralegal education—a minimum of seven years of working experience and twenty hours of continuing legal education credits. The specific requirements for qualification can be found on the NALA Web site.

The CLA exam is a two-day examination. The topics cover a variety of professional skills, including interviewing techniques, communications, analytical ability, and others. The exam also tests candidates on their substantive legal knowledge in the areas of bankruptcy law, family law, criminal law, criminal procedure, probate, and real estate law. The NALA claims that paralegals who obtain the CLA designation receive higher pay than other paralegals.

 Fact

Paralegal certification is not required for all paralegal positions. Some employers insist that all qualified paralegals be certified; others make no distinction between certified and noncertified paralegals. Check the employment requirements in your job market.

The NFPA offers a competing certification: the Paralegal Advanced Competency Examination (PACE). The PACE exam is actually a part the NFPA's support of universal paralegal licensure. The

NFPA believes the PACE exam can serve as a part of a plan to regulate paralegal practitioners. As a result, the qualifications for the PACE exam are quite stringent. Candidates for the PACE exam must have a bachelor's degree and completion of an accredited paralegal education program (separately or as a part of the bachelor's degree), and at least two years of work experience. Some paralegals who did not meet these qualifications were allowed to take the PACE exam under a global grandfathering exemption that ended on December 31, 2000.

The PACE exam is a tiered exam. Participants must pass the first tier, which tests critical thinking, general legal knowledge, ethics, and problem solving, before taking the tier two test. The second-tier test addresses substantive legal knowledge in a variety of practice areas.

Selecting a Curriculum

Just as paralegal education programs vary in length, they also vary in the kinds of course offered. A paralegal education should include core legal courses and a variety of specialty courses. The institution should also offer the opportunity to pursue general education or other useful courses.

Core Legal Courses

Every paralegal education institution offers a core set of legal courses. These offerings usually include an introductory course in paralegalism or introduction to law and a legal research class. Many programs require a separate course in legal ethics (discussed in detail in Chapter 5). Look for a program that requires at least these courses and carefully compare the content of the courses across institutions.

Legal Specialty Courses

Most programs offer a selection of legal specialty courses. The specific courses may vary depending on the availability of instructors, the fluctuating demands of the legal market, the area of the country, and other factors. At a minimum, the program should offer legal specialty courses in real property, wills and probate, contract law, business law, criminal law, and family law. Other desirable legal specialty courses are bankruptcy, employment law, criminal procedure, civil procedure, and alternative dispute resolution.

General Education Courses

Unless you have a prior postsecondary degree, a program that focuses only on paralegal education may not provide you with the breadth of education necessary to be successful in this demanding field. A paralegal must have a variety of skills that are developed and nurtured through the study of other disciplines. Look for an institution that requires exposure to philosophy (especially logic and critical thinking), language, history, literature, and composition. The most effective paralegals are well-rounded individuals who are able to relate their experiences in the law to a broader social and intellectual context.

Other Useful Courses

Aside from the thinking and communication skills required of a paralegal, you may want to consider a program that allows you to develop other skills. Most legal employers use computers and require their employees to do the same. The use of computers is far beyond word processing in a busy law office. Computer applications are used for maintaining calendars, billing, and managing case information. Some schools offer specific courses in these kinds of computer applications.

Talk to practicing paralegals about their day-to-day duties. Many paralegal students are surprised to find out that a portion of their job duties includes typing from transcription. Again, some schools offer courses on this subject. Other useful courses might include a course in medical terminology and records, basic accounting or bookkeeping courses, and business communication. Your course selection will depend on your abilities and your target job. Try to select a paralegal education program that offers the opportunity to develop as many job useful skills as possible.

Chapter 3

Paralegal Career Options

Today's paralegal enjoys a wide variety of employment options. The traditional employers of paralegals are private law firms, and these firms still employ the majority of paralegals. Over the years, however, the pressure for efficient and low-cost legal services has opened opportunities for paralegals in corporate legal departments, with government agencies, in banks and insurance companies, with title companies, and in the health care field. In fact, there is hardly an aspect of legal services that does not have a place for paralegals.

Planning Your Paralegal Career

No one can look into the future and completely plan a paralegal career. The area of the law that originally drew you to paralegalism may not present employment opportunities—so that you will find yourself in another area of the law. As you develop additional skills and experience, you may seek out new challenges in a different area. Career opportunities that you never thought of may present themselves, or your life circumstances may change what you seek from a paralegal career. A paralegal career is no different from any other—it is a work in progress.

Self-assessment and Short-term Goal Setting

The first step in planning a paralegal career is self-assessment. Why do you want to be a paralegal? Is there a specific aspect of the law that attracts you? What are your strengths and weaknesses, and how do they fit with the career you have chosen? Whether you are just beginning your paralegal career or have several years of experience, a self-assessment will give you insight into your current career path and what you need to do to change it.

Fact

Because so many lawyers specialize in particular areas of the law, it may be difficult to find the one area of the law that interests you right away. Do not be afraid to change direction if the work you are doing does not satisfy you, even if it means changing jobs. Many paralegals shift focus several times in the course of a career.

Short-term goals are the building blocks of a long-term career plan. If you are just entering the field, a short-term goal might be to complete a quality education that includes an internship in an area of the law that interests you. If you are a recent graduate, you might set a short-term goal of getting a paralegal job in your chosen area of the law. An inexperienced paralegal might have a goal of assisting with a trial. You should identify short-term goals that help you develop experience and skills that move you toward a long-term goal.

Securing Employment as a Paralegal

Before you begin your job search, become familiar with the job market and opportunities in your area. Sometimes job opportunities are not well advertised. Legal employers tend to promote from within, preferring to offer positions to existing employees rather than open them to the general public. In other job markets, legal employers place advertisements for open positions and often sift through a number of candidates before hiring a paralegal. Knowing what to expect in your job market is a big part of landing that first paralegal job.

Tricks of the Trade

The hidden job market for paralegals can be discouraging, but don't give up. The addition of a well-trained paralegal is a positive step for most law firms. The market for paralegals continues to grow, fueled by the mobility of the legal work force and the constant pressure for more efficient and cost-effective legal services. Jobs are available, and the following methods will help you find them.

Networking

The term *networking* is overused and sometimes oversold, but the fact remains that many paralegal jobs are the result of being directed to the right person at the right time. Just keeping in contact with the legal community maximizes the chances that you will be aware of potential positions as quickly as possible. Possible sources of information about paralegal job openings include:

- **Fellow paralegal students.** Keep in touch with the friends you made in school. These contacts are often the first to know of available positions, either because they are job-hunting as well or because they are employed and "in the loop" of information about job openings.
- **Paralegal instructors.** Most paralegal programs use practicing lawyers as instructors. They are often aware of unadvertised job opportunities or have suggestions about which employers might be receptive to receiving unsolicited applications from prospective paralegals.
- **Internships.** If your paralegal program offers an internship, consider using this as an opportunity to develop contacts that will help you in your job search. Internships often turn into job opportunities. Even if this is not so, you will have made contacts with lawyers, secretaries, and other paralegals who can help you identify job opportunities in your area.
- **Paralegal organizations.** Join the local paralegal organization. Most organizations have reduced memberships for students. Working paralegals have an excellent sense of the job opportunities available in the field. This information is particularly useful if you are looking for a specific type of position.
- **Volunteering.** Most local legal aid offices and public defenders are chronically short of help. Volunteer your time at one of these agencies, practice your paralegal skills, and make valuable contacts for information about full-time job opportunities.

Trade Journals

When legal employers advertise available paralegal positions, they seldom place these ads in the local newspaper. Legal job opportunities are more likely to be found in publications specifically targeted at the legal profession. Most state bar associations have a monthly publication with a section devoted to employment opportunities. Many of these publications are available at the local bar association library. These publications sometimes maintain a more current set of listing in an online form. Look for a Web site maintained by the state or local bar association.

Local Bar Associations

Local bar associations often maintain a list of job openings that may not be advertised. Even if the openings are published, the publications are usually distributed only to members. The administrative office of the local bar association will usually provide information on job openings to prospective applicants.

Legal Directories

If you are uncertain about what law firms are in your area, a legal directory is a great source of information. Most directories are available at the local bar association library. Legal directories contain information about law firms, including their location, area of practice, number of lawyers, and other data about the firm. The most commonly used legal directories are the *Martindale-Hubbell Law Directory* and *West's Legal Directory*. Both have online versions as well.

Online Job Search Firms

Several job search firms cater specifically to the legal professional. These firms circulate your resume to prospective employers and can arrange for temporary job placements or permanent employment. These agencies usually operate online and post your resume for review by prospective employers. The agency charges a fee that is usually a percentage of your salary if you are hired by one of their employer contacts.

Applying for a Paralegal Position

Once you have identified a potential employment opportunity, you must submit an application to the employer. The application process for legal employment is divided into three distinct phases—the submission of a resume, the interview, and the follow-up—and in some respects differs from that for other kinds of jobs.

Resume Submission

Nearly all legal employers require applicants to submit a resume—a summary of your qualifications for the job. A resume should include your educational background, your work experience, and a list of references. The resume is a snapshot of you as a professional. It has one purpose—to catch the interest of the legal employer. The resume is the first impression you will make on a prospective employer—you should take care to make sure your resume creates a favorable impression.

Do not try to make your resume stand out by making it look markedly different from other resumes. Wildly colored paper, offbeat fonts, or other attention-grabbing tricks should be avoided. You are applying for a position in a field that is professional and traditionally conservative. Your resume should reflect your own professionalism. Print your resume on good-quality bond paper, preferably white or ivory. Use a traditional business font, such as Times New Roman or Courier. Proofread your resume thoroughly, and more than once. Mistakes in spelling, grammar, or punctuation can terminate an application before it has a chance to be considered.

This does not mean that your resume should not be unique. You are unique and your resume should reflect that. In addition, the position is unique. Your resume should show a strong match between the needs of the position and your qualifications as a paralegal. To this end, you will need to think about the skills the specific legal position requires. Think about how your education and background qualify you for the position. Try not to describe your work experience in the terms used by your previous employer. Instead, think about the skills you acquired that are transferable to the position you are applying for.

Many sources provide checklists for the contents of your resume. Consult these to make sure you have not overlooked an important aspect of your qualifications. Do not, however, feel bound by the structure or phrasing suggested by these resume guidelines. If your resume is two pages instead of one, it does not mean that the employer will ignore it. If you list your employment before your education, it simply means that the employer will read about your employment first. Remember that the job of the resume is to pique the employer's interest.

Essential

Different paralegal positions demand different skills. Your background and experiences are not one-dimensional—use your resume to stress the specific demands of the specific position you are applying for. This may well require a separate resume for each type of position you apply for. A one-size-fits-all resume does not stand out to the prospective employer.

The cover letter has a similar function. Again, a *generic* cover letter probably does more harm than good. You will usually have one qualification that sticks out above all the others. Your cover letter is the place to highlight this qualification. You must relate this qualification to the specific job opening. Find a way to relate your qualifications to client service—the very focus of the practice of law.

The Interview

If your resume and cover letter have done their jobs, you will be contacted for an interview. The approach to the interview will vary from employer to employer: some interviews are conducted by a single person, others involve several interviewers. You should be prepared for anything from a panel interview to serial interviews with several separate interviewers.

The questions asked at an interview for a paralegal position depend on the interviewer. Some questions will simply confirm information on your resume. You may be asked to explain some information, but these questions are mainly factual. Other questions may ask you to discuss a specific experience—an especially satisfying experience or an especially frustrating one. Some interviewers ask the interviewee to list strengths and weaknesses. You may be asked to analyze a hypothetical situation. These are all questions you can prepare for in advance. The key is to appear confident and collected. Interviewees who appear excessively nervous or uncomfortable are rarely hired.

Question

What do I do if the interviewer asks an improper question, such as my marital status or whether I have a disability?

These kinds of questions are more common that you would think, even among lawyers. Try to avoid challenging the interviewer if possible. You need not answer the question, but be prepared to change the subject to allow a smooth transition away from these topics. Asking a question about the firm, or stressing an interest or strength, is usually effective in steering the interview in a new direction.

You may be offered the opportunity to ask questions of the interviewee. You should prepare such questions in advance, to be ready if the opening presents itself. While it is likely you have questions about salary and benefits, billable-hour expectations, and other working environment issues, it is best to reserve these questions until later discussions. At the interview, you want to ask questions that highlight your interest in the substance of the job. Ask about the work the lawyer normally does, how a paralegal can assist in performing that work, and the required skills for the position. This gives you an opportunity to stress how your qualifications fit the job and may provide a basis for further discussion. Make notes of this information as soon as possible after leaving the interview. You might consider referencing some of this information in a thank-you letter sent within three days after the interview.

It is likely you will be called in for a second interview before you are hired. Review the notes of your prior interview. This is the time to explore your working environment questions. By the second interview, you are in a select category of a few applicants the employer is interested in hiring. Use this opportunity to stress qualifications that were overlooked in the first interview and gather additional information about the employer.

Reaching Your Career Goals

Getting that first paralegal job is not the end of career goal setting. While you are getting valuable experience in the paralegal field you must be open to the possibilities to advance your career. Career advancement may involve creating your own opportunities within your current job or changing jobs.

Creating Career Opportunities

You may advance in your current position without much effort. As you demonstrate your capabilities, the supervising lawyers will become comfortable with giving you assignments that are more challenging. The paralegal should seek out these assignments. Every memo should end with suggestions for further action. The paralegal should request assignments that expand and test developing skills. If necessary, the paralegal should ask that some duties be reassigned to less experienced employees. If the paralegal demonstrates a willingness to perform tasks that are more complex for the lawyer, the lawyer is likely to think of the paralegal when those opportunities arise.

Alert

Expanding your career opportunities does not require a long, serious conversation with your supervising attorney. Chances for expanded responsibility occur every day; there is always more work to be done on a client matter. Suggest a course of action or offer to handle a task; most lawyers respond positively to paralegals who are genuinely interested in the cases they are assigned.

Changing Jobs or Specialties

Your current job may not meet your career goals. You may want to work in a different environment or to develop a specialty. The mobility of the legal work force allows the paralegal to pursue career development through job change. The process of making a job change is similar to the initial job search process, except that the paralegal now has experience to offer the prospective employer.

A change in specialty may involve additional education. The paralegal can seek out assignments in a specific field, but if the firm does not practice in that area, experience must come from further education or seminars. The paralegal may have to start at the bottom of the seniority list and work up to desired assignments. When making a change of specialty, the paralegal should seek out a small firm with that specialty or a large firm with specialty departments.

Law Firms

Roughly three of four working paralegals are employed by law firms of widely varying size. Employer law firms range from a single lawyer to several hundred lawyers in several cities. While large law firms usually employ many paralegals, the vast majority of law firm paralegals work for law firms with less than ten lawyers.

Small Law Firms

New paralegals often choose small law firms because of the variety of experiences they offer; lawyers in such a firm handle matters in several different areas of the law. Of course, paralegals who do not wish to work in large cities may find a small law firm is their only choice for employment.

A paralegal in a small law firm may be expected to perform secretarial and clerical duties because of the lack of support staff. Salaries in smaller firms are usually lower than in larger firms and fewer employment benefits are offered. Some paralegals find that these disadvantages are outweighed by a less formal working environment, a greater variety of assignments, and greater flexibility in the employment relationship. A small firm is often the ideal employer for a beginning paralegal.

Essential

Large Law Firms

Large law firms are usually found in large cities. A firm with more than twenty lawyers is usually a more formal type of employer. The lawyers in a large law firm often have practice specialties and expect their paralegals to specialize in these areas. This increased structure sometime applies to the paralegals as well—large law firms sometimes use *paralegal managers* to make paralegal assignments. This may limit the opportunity to develop a personal working relationship with a supervising lawyer.

Large law firms offer higher salaries, more employment benefits, and assignments that may be more challenging than those in a small law firm. Paralegals in large law firms may have their own support staff and access to state-of-the-art technology. Offsetting these advantages are a stricter working environment and limited experience with a variety of legal matters.

Corporate Legal Departments

Many corporations have their own legal departments. These departments handle matters ranging from contract negotiation to regulatory compliance to real estate transactions to supervision of litigation. A lawyer with the title of "General Counsel" usually heads the corporate legal department. This lawyer often supervises a staff comprised entirely of paralegals. Larger corporate legal departments may be organized along the same lines as a large law firm. Paralegals in these jobs may draft business documents, analyze financial records, or oversee the maintenance of required corporate records. These positions offer high salaries, good benefits, and regular hours.

The corporate paralegal often works directly with a division or department of the corporation. For example, a paralegal may work closely with the quality assurance department when working on a product liability case, and work with finance and accounting employees when dealing with a merger proposal.

Government

The increasing need for paralegals has resulted in many employment opportunities for paralegals in government service. Some of these jobs are not specifically designed for paralegals, but they call on common paralegal skills. Many of them require knowledge of legal principles as well.

Federal Government

Some estimates indicate that the federal government has more than 300,000 positions that are classified as "law related." The titles of these positions include Foreign Law Specialist, Civil Rights Analyst, and Personnel Management Specialist. The federal government also has a job classification of Paralegal Specialist.

The jobs of paralegals with the federal government are similar to those in a large law firm or corporate law department. Paralegals are employed by several federal government agencies, such as the Department of Justice, the National Labor Relations Board, the Department of Labor, the Social Security Administration, and others. Available positions are listed on the *Federal Jobs Digest* Web site at *www.jobsfed.com*.

Government paralegal jobs offer generous salaries, excellent benefits, a high degree of job security, and a substantial degree of professional recognition. These positions are often difficult to obtain due to an extensive application process. Some paralegals shy away from these positions because of the perceived difficulties of dealing with an extensive bureaucracy.

State and Local Government

The employment opportunities for paralegals in state and local government vary from state to state. Most states have agencies similar to the federal government and employ paralegals in departments responsible for pollution control and fair housing, as well as in positions in the legislative and executive branches. As with the federal government, paralegal positions in state government are subject to strict qualification requirements.

Local governments sometimes hire paralegals. In larger cities, paralegals may work with the city attorney or with zoning, economic development, or departments providing city services, such as water and gas. In some states, public defenders and legal aid offices are funded by local government. Information about employment opportunities with state or local government can usually be obtained through the personnel or human resources department of the branch of government.

Banks and Insurance Companies

Banks and insurance companies often require paralegal assistance. In some cases, paralegals are employed in a general counsel's office as in a corporation; paralegals may also be assigned to specific departments to assist with specific legal issues arising in that department.

The Banking Industry

The banking industry is heavily regulated, with audits and compliance reports required by federal and state agencies. Banks employ paralegals to assemble data for periodic reports, to keep track of regulatory changes, and to provide training for bank employees who must address regulatory issues. These paralegals often work under the supervision of a legal department.

Banks also employ paralegals in trust and mortgage departments. In a trust department, many trust officers are lawyers who are responsible for administering trusts established by clients of the bank. Trust officers also serve as personal representatives for probate estates. Paralegals working within a trust department may be called on to ensure compliance with court-ordered reporting and other administration requirements of the trust. The paralegal might also be involved in the process of calculating distributions from the trust.

Mortgage departments often use paralegals to perform required functions to comply with mortgage lending and foreclosure requirements. A paralegal might inspect title documents and opinions to assure that the mortgage lender acquires priority over other lenders, prepares the necessary promissory note and other loan documents, and ensures the necessary filing of documents with the county recorder. In the event of foreclosure, the paralegal is responsible for assembling the records necessary to demonstrate failure of payment, preparing the required notices and complaints for the court, arranging the sheriff's sale, and providing the required documentation of the sale to the court.

The Insurance Industry

Insurance companies employ paralegals in a variety of positions. Paralegals may assist the company with regulatory compliance—collecting, summarizing, and reporting data required by state agencies that oversee the operation of the insurance company. Paralegals are also employed to assist insurance companies process, evaluate, and respond to claims. A paralegal trained in gathering, organizing, and evaluating factual information provides valuable support to insurance professionals who deal with policy claims. In addition, insurance companies are often involved in legislative activities that require the research skill of a paralegal.

Title and Mortgage Companies

A paralegal experienced in real estate matters need not work for a law firm or a bank. Title companies and mortgage companies, businesses that are privately owned and provide needed support for real estate transactions, present other opportunities.

Mortgage companies are similar to banks—they provide financing for real estate purchases. These lending arrangements are subject to strict regulations designed to protect consumers from predatory practices. Like banks, mortgage companies require paralegals to ensure compliance with the laws governing the creation of a mortgage interest and to protect the lender in the event of a default.

Title companies have two functions: they supply the abstracts that are used to verify the title of the seller and they provide closing services for real estate sales. An *abstract of title* is a summary of the transactions affecting the ownership of a particular piece of property and is based on records maintained at the county recorder's office. Every time an abstract is requested or must be updated, a personal visit to the recorder's office is required. A paralegal skilled at identifying and classifying real property transactions can gather the necessary information to provide a current picture of the title to the property. Then a registered abstracter prepares the document. Title companies also provide *closing services*. At a closing, the buyer and the seller are brought together to complete the real estate transaction. Paralegals prepare closing statements—summaries of the financial costs of the transaction and may verify that the closing documents (deeds, mortgages, etc.) do not have any obvious defects.

Self-employment Opportunities

There are two types of self-employed paralegals: freelance paralegals and independent paralegals. An experienced paralegal may choose to become an entrepreneur—to operate a paralegal business within certain legal and ethical boundaries.

Freelance Paralegals

Freelance paralegals contract with attorneys to perform paralegal services. These paralegal services are similar to the services supplied by paralegals directly employed by the lawyer, but the freelance paralegal is hired on a temporary or task-based basis. The attorney pays a fee to the freelance paralegal, but does not provide any employment benefits. When the specific assignment is complete, the paralegal is free to move on to the next contract opportunity.

Freelance paralegals are more successful in large cities. The freelance paralegal business must be marketed and promoted to ensure a steady supply of assignments. Freelance paralegals may set their own hours, but they are responsible for arranging their own health insurance, business insurance, equipment, and secretarial or clerical support. As with any independent business, the success of a freelance paralegal depends on the ability to generate fees.

Independent Paralegals

Independent paralegals are similar to freelance paralegals, but they do not work under the supervision of an attorney. Independent paralegals concentrate on providing those paralegal services that do not constitute the unauthorized practice of law. Independent paralegals usually provide services that help customers obtain and fill out legal forms. These forms are often court approved and the independent paralegal supplies information about certain legal procedures and filing requirements. Independent paralegals often assist customers with simple divorces, the preparation of simple wills, or the preparation and filing of bankruptcy forms.

 Fact

Some see independent paralegals as a partial answer to lowering the cost of routine legal services. Most proposals would allow an independent paralegal to assist clients interested in a simple will or simple divorce. These proposals are closely related to the ones emerging about licensing paralegals, an issue that has split the profession.

An independent paralegal is subject to the same business advantages and risks experienced by a freelance paralegal. In addition, an independent paralegal must be very careful not to commit unauthorized practice of law. Advice about the selection or legal effect of a particular form is not permitted, nor is providing assistance concerning the information included on the form. The independent paralegal is mainly limited to typing forms with information supplied by the customer and giving directions about the proper means of filing the document with the court. Independent paralegals are not permitted in all states; in California, these paralegals must hold a specific license to conduct this type of business.

Chapter 4

Working with Lawyers

As we have seen, paralegals work with lawyers in many different settings, including private law firms, government "law firms" such as a prosecuting attorney's office, government regulatory agencies, and a variety of corporate or other nonlaw firm settings. However, since over 70 percent of all paralegals work for private law firms, this chapter will focus on that setting and the significant differences in the ways law firms are organized and operate.

The Paralegal Working Environment

Practicing law is a profession: lawyers use their years of education and experience to serve the interests of their clients. The practice of law is also a business: law firms must generate revenue, pay overhead expenses, and generate a profit for the owners. As the number of lawyers in this country increases, the competition for clients becomes more intense. This competition has fueled the expansion of the paralegal profession, but it also has consequences for the paralegal working environment.

To satisfy the demands of increasingly sophisticated consumers of legal services, lawyers must control the costs of those services. Controlling the costs of services requires more active management of the business of running a law firm. A typical law firm might attempt to manage its business in several different ways, including the financial aspects of the business, the areas of legal practice the firm engages in, the types of internal systems the law firm follows, employee management, and strategic planning. The degree to which the law firm manages these aspects of its business depends on the law firm. Some firms have very involved structures; others address these issues on an ad hoc basis. Knowing how the law firm manages these business issues can tell the paralegal a great deal about the culture of the law firm.

Law Firm Management

Few law firms are managed by professional managers. In a small law firm, the expense of a professional manager is prohibitive. Extremely large law firms sometimes employ professional managers, but ethical rules prevent those managers from having an ownership interest in the law firm. The result is that lawyers make nearly all management decisions about the business of a law firm.

Most lawyers are not trained business or management professionals. They went to law school, not business school. Lawyers are trained to solve the problems of other people and this is how they earn a living. Because of these factors, law firm management is sometimes like the cobbler's children; the lawyer is too busy practicing law to pay attention to the *business* of practicing law.

Financial Management

To survive, law firms clearly must generate revenue—which comes from clients, usually in the form of hourly fees. All law firms have expenses. In addition to employee expenses, there are expenses associated with office space, office supplies, office equipment, maintaining a law library, and continuing legal education. As with any business, these expenses must be paid before the owners of the law firm receive a profit.

The expenses of the law firm are similar to the costs of producing any product. If the cost of producing one hour of legal services exceeds the price that can be charged for that hour of legal service, the law firm will lose money. The financial management of a law firm requires that close attention be paid to controlling overhead costs and setting hourly fees. In addition, the overall overhead costs must be allocated among the income generators of the firm. The method of allocation varies depending on the law firm's approach to cost management.

Not all law firm employees are income generators. Lawyers generate income because they can charge fees to clients. Paralegals generate income for the same reason. Legal secretaries, reception-ists, and office assistants do not generate income. In some offices, all overhead costs are divided equally among the income generators. This is the simplest method of allocation. In others, the allocation is based on the relative cost or use of the overhead item. This allocation method is more complicated, but it is usually a more accurate reflec-tion of the responsibility for overhead costs. Whichever method is used, the allocated costs affect the determination of the hourly rate for that income producer's services.

 Fact

The financial pressures on law firms have a direct effect on the work-ing conditions of paralegals. Client demands for efficiency and lower costs result in increased demands for productivity and increased responsibility for paralegals. The paralegal has a responsibility to ensure that these financial pressures do not adversely affect the quality of the service to the client.

Practice Management

The "law" is a large and sometimes overwhelming field. It includes the statutes and regulations of the federal government and all fifty states, the court decisions in each state, all of the federal courts, and the United States Supreme Court. It includes everything from regula-tions governing the approval of new drugs to the effect of interna-tional treaties on the rights of fishermen. It is broad and varied and no one lawyer can know all the law.

Most lawyers in private practice tend to limit their practice to a few areas of the law known as "practice areas." Just as medical patients often seek out a specialist physician, clients tend to hire law-yers who have specific expertise and experience with their type of legal problem. Lawyers will often decline to represent clients whose problems are outside their expertise. On occasion, those clients are referred to other lawyers with the expertise the client requires.

When a law firm has more than one lawyer specializing in a specific area of the law, it may designate those lawyers as a practice group or department. In very large firms, each department will include paralegals, associates, partners, and a department chair.

Alert

Even if there is some aspect of the law that attracted you to the field initially, do not confine yourself to a specific area of the law in the early stages of your career. Seek a broad range of experience in a variety of legal fields. This will maximize your opportunities for employment and provide valuable background that is attractive to prospective employers. Many paralegals work for several years before choosing a legal specialty.

Knowing the practice management approach of a law firm can influence the job choice of a paralegal. Paralegals in very large firms tend to specialize as lawyers do. A paralegal employed in the real estate department may never have the opportunity to assist with drafting a will or handling an adoption. In general, paralegals who prefer assignments in several different aspects of the law gravitate to smaller law firms.

Systems Management

Each law firm must develop approaches to the practice of law that facilitate that firm's ability to meet their client's objectives. These approaches must be consistent within the law firm so that the same management issue is approached in the same way for every client. These approaches, or systems, must be monitored to ensure compliance and to respond to problems.

Systems management concerns itself with *procedures*, such as how new client files are opened, how client conflict information is stored, how client expenses are incurred and paid, and what deadline docketing procedures are followed. In some firms, these systems are meticulously documented in a procedure manual. In others, established procedures are handed down from employee to employee. A paralegal must understand and follow the systems procedures of the law firm. Most often, such systems are the product of much thought and planning by experienced lawyers. In some law firms, the procedural systems are designed and maintained by paralegals.

Employee Relations Management

The managers of law firms must ensure that every employee of the law firm is dedicated to providing quality legal services to clients. New employees must be hired and trained. Existing employees must receive assignments and performance evaluations. Changes in the law, additional client needs, or shifts in technology may require additional training or education for some employees.

To compensate their employees, law firms must decide on a salary structure and determine the availability of benefits. Some firms opt for a rigid salary and benefit structure, while others prefer greater flexibility. Committees most often make decisions about employee compensation.

Strategic Planning

Increased competition for clients means that law firms cannot wait for clients to come to them. Careful planning allows a law firm to increase in size and profitability. A comprehensive strategic plan might also include professional development for staff or the expectation of increased salaries. A well-developed strategic plan should begin by defining expected client needs for legal services. The strategic plan should include specific approaches to meet those needs. A law firm without a defined strategic plan has not maximized its chances for ongoing success.

Organization of a Law Office

The business structure of a law firm is usually dictated by the size of the law firm. Smaller law firms tend to utilize simpler business structures than do larger law firms. The choice of business entity offers some clues about the working environment within the law firm. Law firms typically choose one of four business entities: sole proprietorship, partnership, professional corporation, or limited liability entity. Each business entity has specific legal consequences (discussed in Chapter 15) and may affect the duties of the paralegal.

Sole Proprietorships

A lawyer practicing alone is usually practicing as a sole proprietor. Paralegals who work for sole proprietors must perform a variety of tasks. A paralegal may be asked to perform legal research on one file, type a real estate deed for a client in another matter, and balance the law firm's checking account. These paralegals are often given significant file management and law office systems responsibilities. Paralegal salaries in a sole proprietorship law firm are usually lower than at other legal employers.

Partnerships

Lawyers often practice together in groups of two or more. The simplest form of a multiple lawyer practice is the partnership. A law firm operating as a partnership can be of any size. Paralegals employed by partnerships sometimes have the opportunity to specialize in a field of law. Assignments from multiple lawyers are common and the paralegal must be able to balance fluctuating workloads and the different supervisory personalities of the partners.

Professional Corporations

A law firm may be incorporated as a professional corporation that is owned by its shareholders. The shareholders are senior lawyers who are responsible for the management of the business. Law firms organized as professional corporations are usually organized according to practice area. A beginning paralegal will have the opportunity to specialize in a field of law and to draw on the experience of other paralegals within the firm. Paralegal salaries offered by law firms organized as professional corporations are usually competitive with those paid by other legal employers.

Timekeeping

Nearly all private law firms require paralegals to keep track of the time they spend on specific tasks. The timekeeping record ordinarily shows the date of the legal service, the client for whom the service was performed, the specific legal service performed, and the amount of time spent performing the legal service. The time a paralegal devotes to a task will determine how much the client is billed for the service. Even for law firms that do not charge clients by the hour, as in a traditional plaintiff's personal injury law practice, timekeeping provides the managing lawyers with useful information.

ssential

> The daily routine of a paralegal often involves working on several different client matters, including taking telephone calls, responding to e-mails, receiving assignments, etc. To make sure you capture all of the billable time in a day, you should allow yourself several opportunities to record the time you spend on client matters.

Importance of Timekeeping

Timekeeping is one of the most important aspects of a paralegal's job. The usefulness of time records is not limited to client billing. The time record provides valuable information about several aspects of a law firm's practice:

- Time records document the progress of a client's legal matter by showing what service was provided and when it was provided.
- Time records show who is working on what aspect of a client's legal problem and provide a means of ensuring appropriate staffing decisions.
- Time records show the time spent on specific tasks, providing information about the competency and efficiency of the timekeeper.

In addition to providing managerial information, time records play a crucial role in the economics of a law firm. Time records allow a firm to determine the profitability of specific client matters by comparing the total fee collected with the time spent to generate that fee. If time records show that a practice area or type of case is consistently unprofitable, the law firm can decline those cases in the future.

Time records are of great assistance in preparing attorneys' fees applications for the court. In some types of lawsuits, the winning party may recover attorneys' fees from the losing side, subject to court approval. In these cases, the winning lawyers often submit time records as in support of a request for attorneys' fees.

Time records are also the primary method of measuring productivity in a law firm. In an hourly billing system, the amount of time spent on a matter governs the charge for the legal service to the client. The amount of money billed to the client by each income generator in the law firm is a measure of the productivity of that person.

Mechanics of Timekeeping

The information on a time record usually includes the date, the client, a file number, a description of the service, the identity of the person performing the task, and the amount of time spent on the task. Time is recorded in parts of an hour. Most clients now require that time be recorded in tenths of an hour. Under this system, a task that takes thirty minutes is recorded as 0.5 of an hour. The minimum recordable time is 0.1 of an hour, or six minutes. If the timekeeper bills the client $100 per hour, the client is charged $10 for each six minutes spent on his legal problem.

Time records can be kept manually. There are several different manual timekeeping systems available, but each operates on the same principle. In a manual system, the timekeeper writes the timekeeping information on perforated sheets. When a timesheet is complete, it is turned into the law firm's billing department. Each section of the sheet, or time slip, is matched to the specific client matter and later used to prepare a bill.

Computerized timekeeping systems can be a stand-alone time and billing system or an integrated part of a more complex case management system. Computerized timekeeping systems record the same information as a manual system. Some software provides automatic time calculations—the user starts the clock when beginning a task and stops it when finished. Most software also feature automatic fee calculations, which can be useful if the client has imposed a legal budget.

Billable Versus Nonbillable Hours

An hourly billing system places a premium on the time spent performing some legal service for the client. This time is known as *billable time.* Time spent on matters that cannot be billed to the client is nonbillable. Every law firm naturally seeks to maximize the billable time of its employees and minimize the nonbillable time. Indeed, most law firms pay so much attention to this it has become known as "the tyranny of the billable hour."

Understanding billable time is an important factor in managing the expectations between a legal employer and a paralegal. As mentioned, the legal employer calculates the hourly billing rate for employees based on the allocated overhead cost. By multiplying the hourly rate by the number of hours the employee is expected to bill in a year, the employer can estimate the total return from each employer. This process produces a yearly billable-hour requirement. Billable-hour requirements for paralegals typically range from 1,400 to 1,600 billable hours per year. A paralegal who bills more than the billable hour requirement increases the profits of the law firm.

 Fact

When a paralegal reports an amount of nonbillable time that is disproportionate to the amount of billable time, the discrepancy may indicate an imbalance in billable assignments, a lack of client work for that paralegal, or some type of employee problem. Keeping track of your own nonbillable time, even if not required by the employer, allows you to be proactive in reaching your billable time goal.

Nonbillable time is not included in the billable hours requirement. It is "lost" time as far as the law firm is concerned. Nonbillable time includes time spent on personal matters—eating lunch, running errands, or receiving personal phone calls. It also includes "watercooler" time—the time spent talking with other law firm employees about things that are not directly client related.

All client matters require some nonbillable time. Also known as administrative time, this is time spent on the client's legal matter that is not chargeable as a professional service. Examples include opening a client file and organizing documents. These activities are not billable because they do not result in a product for the client. Additional administrative time may be required by the law firm due to required attendance at staff meetings, marketing activities, or library maintenance.

The final large category of nonbillable time is pro bono activities. All lawyers are under an ethical obligation to provide pro bono, or uncharged, legal services. Both the NALA and the NFPA suggest that paralegals provide pro bono services as well.

Billing

Client fees are collected through bills for legal services. These bills are generated according to the style and format preferred by the law firm. Although the format of the billing may change from law firm to law firm and even from client to client, virtually all legal billing is itemized. That is, the information from the time record about what legal service was performed is reflected on the bill together with the charge for that service. If the time record fails to adequately describe the legal service, the client may not pay.

The frequency of client billing varies from matter to matter and from client to client. Some matters are billed only when the legal work is complete. In other cases, the client might request periodic billing at six-month intervals. The billing frequency for each client matter should be recorded in the file information.

Ethical restrictions prevent paralegals from setting fees with a client and from billing clients directly. For this reason, paralegals are seldom directly involved in the billing process. Nevertheless, all paralegals should be generally familiar with the process for two reasons. First, client satisfaction with the legal services provided is directly tied to the amount of the bill. A paralegal can do a great deal to diffuse client complaints by making sure the client is informed of the progress of the legal matter and the reasons for all significant activity. Second, a paralegal who understands the billing process will not be an impediment to timely billing because of inadequate descriptions of legal services or failure to submit time sheets.

E ssential

In some legal matters, the law firm may incur expenses related to the representation of the client. These costs, or disbursements, may be billed to the client if they are directly related to the client's matter. For example, a client is expected to reimburse the law firm for court filing fees paid on the client's behalf. A client is not expected to pay for costs that are merely overhead, such as paper usage.

An ordinary billing process begins with the preparation of a *draft bill*. This is a compilation of the time records and disbursements showing the time spent by each timekeeper, the charges for that timekeeper, and any expenses paid by the law firm. The supervising attorney reviews the draft bill for errors and to determine if adjustments are necessary. These adjustments are made so that the bill will accurately reflect the value of the legal services provided.

Once the draft bill is finalized, it is sent to the client. Most law firms track unpaid bills by the length of time the bill remains unpaid. If the client does not pay in a timely fashion, the law firm may consider terminating its relationship with that client.

Client Trust Accounts

Client trust accounts are required when a lawyer handles money for a client. The lawyer must keep money that belongs to a client separate from money that belongs to the lawyer. Fees paid to the lawyer belong to the lawyer and can be placed in the law firm's account. All funds belonging to the client must be placed in a separate account designated for that purpose.

E ssential

The distribution of client trust account funds for personal or office expenses is never appropriate and is a serious ethical violation. A paralegal who exercises responsibility over a client trust account should always insist on seeing a written accounting to the client before distributing any trust account funds.

The proper use of a client trust account is an ethical obligation of the lawyer. Misuse of client funds is a very serious matter and can lead to disbarment. The ethical rules require clear records of each client trust account transaction. Client trust account funds may only be distributed to the client or to a person designated by the client.

It is important that the paralegal be able to recognize the kinds of funds that must be deposited in a client trust account. Paralegals sometimes receive funds from clients and must be able to give appropriate instructions to the law firm bookkeeper. More often, a paralegal will be called on to explain how specific funds will be handled.

There are four types of funds that must be placed in a client trust account:

- Funds belonging to the client, such as an insurance payment.
- Funds belonging to third parties, such as escrow funds related to a real estate transaction.
- Retainers paid by the client. Retainers are payments against which future legal services will be charged. These payments belong to the client until the legal services are performed.
- Settlement proceeds. When a client settles a legal dispute, the settlement check is usually made payable to the client

and the lawyer. Because the proceeds belong partly to the client, the entire settlement check must be deposited in a client trust account.

Docket Control

Docket control is more than noting deadlines on a calendar. It is the process of recording, tracking, and organizing deadlines for several clients and client matters. In many law firms, the responsibility for docket control is given to a paralegal. Effective docket control requires a broad knowledge of court rules, the complexity of legal tasks, and the schedule of the person assigned to perform the task.

Computers manage modern docket control. Electronic docket control can be as simple as recording the events on a computer calendar, or as complicated as making entries in integrated case management software. In either case, it is not enough to know when the deadline is. Docket control also involves planning to meet the deadline. To assist in planning, the paralegal will designate one or more reminder dates, or ticklers, before the deadline. These reminder dates are also recorded and tracked. For example, if a court order establishes a hearing date of March 15, the paralegal may set a reminder date thirty days in advance to allow time to complete necessary research. A fifteen-day reminder might be sufficient to arrange for subpoenas of witnesses and a one-week reminder will allow for a final meeting with the client before the hearing. The experience of the paralegal and the preferences of the supervising attorney govern the amount of lead time given for specific legal tasks.

 Fact

The importance of deadlines in a legal office requires heightened vigilance to avoid mistakes. Where possible, a deadline should be noted by two separate individuals—a paralegal and a secretary or a paralegal and a lawyer—and recorded in two separate places. Regular communication to compare notes of upcoming deadlines is crucial and can be a means of acquiring additional assignments from a busy lawyer.

The paralegal must take care to record every deadline in a legal matter. Some deadlines have severe consequences if they are missed. A missed statute of limitations, for example, will prevent the client from recovering damages. A missed trial date can result in dismissal of a lawsuit. Common deadlines that must be recorded are:

- The statute of limitations for all claims of the client
- Any deadline listed in a court scheduling order
- Appointments or scheduled meeting dates
- Court hearing or trial dates
- Time limits imposed by court rule, such as when the client must respond to a request for documents
- Time limits for performing any act under a contract
- Time limits set forth in any statute requiring the client to do something or after which the client is allowed to do something

In each case, the paralegal must understand the substantive and procedural rules that affect the deadline. Some court rules, for example, specify a deadline that is a specified time after an event. The paralegal must be able to identify the event and accurately perform the necessary calculation to identify the deadline. Once the deadline and appropriate reminders have been identified, the paralegal must relay those dates to the supervising lawyer and the lawyer's secretary.

File and Records Management

When a lawyer handles a legal matter for a client, there will be records. At minimum, there will be correspondence between the lawyer and the client, a fee agreement, and a bill. Complex legal matters can involve several boxes of documents from the client, extensive correspondence, multiple drafts of documents, and research memos. These file materials must be properly filed in a way that allows them to be retrieved when needed. In addition, the confidentiality of these file materials must be protected.

Opening a Client File

When a law firm begins work on a new client matter, a new file is opened. In most law firms, this process involves assigning the new matter a unique numerical designation. The exact numbering system varies from law firm to law firm. Some systems assign the client a number and designate separate legal matters within that number; other systems assign a number to the type of matter (estate planning, family law) and give a unique divider to every client matter within that topic. Less commonly used are systems that combine numerical and alphabetical designations, systems that assign designations by assigned lawyer, and systems that simply assign sequential numbering without regard to other factors.

The numerical designation of client files serves a number of purposes. First, by using a number instead of the client's name, a numerical system minimizes breaches of confidentiality. Second, a numerical system facilitates records filing by allowing client files to be quickly located in a file room. Third, a numerical system allows specific billing and comprehensive checks for conflicts of interest.

Once a numerical file is open, the contents of the file must be organized. The process of subdividing a file is largely a matter of personal preference with the lawyer. I once worked for a lawyer who subdivided his files into "Correspondence" and "Other." Other lawyers prefer more subdivisions. Whatever system is used should be consistent for all client matters of the same type; for example, all personal injury litigation matters should have the same basic subdivisions. In addition, the subdivision system should allow for quick retrieval of documents to reduce the risk of lost or misplaced documents.

Computerized records management can assist with some aspects of records management. Most law firms have some sort of computerized conflict catalog. These systems allow the law firm to check for conflicts of interest by searching an electronic database rather than a paper record. Computers are also used to store electronic document images. This technology allows multiple persons to have access to a document while at the same time preserving the document's integrity. It also minimizes the opportunities for lost or misplaced documents.

Alert

Most lawyers refer to their client files by the name of the client—the "Smith matter," or the "Jones divorce." These lawyers often insist that the file display the name of the client and the type of legal matter for easy reference. A system such as this can cause infractions of confidentiality rules when files are left in places where unauthorized persons can view them. A paralegal should always take care not to display client information to anyone other than the client or another law firm employee.

File Closing Procedures

Nearly every document in a client file belongs to the client. When the file is closed, the client should have the opportunity to retrieve those documents. This is especially true when the client has provided original documents to the law firm.

Once the original client material is removed, it is time to purge the file. This means examining the file for duplicate information. If the file contains four identical copies of a summary judgment motion that is also available in electronic form, it is not necessary to retain any of the hard copies. Purging allows the law firm to save space when storing closed files.

Because the obligation of confidentiality still applies after the legal matter is concluded, closed files should be stored and treated as discretely as open files. A closed file should be destroyed when permitted by the law firm's record retention policy. The length of time that closed files are retained will vary according to the type of matter.

Chapter 5

Ethics and Professional Responsibility

The cornerstone of any legal practice is the client. Without clients, lawyers and paralegals would have nothing to do. One of the most important factors in attracting and keeping clients is the reputation of the legal professional—not just a reputation for quality legal work, but also a reputation for ethical behavior. A paralegal must understand and follow the principles of legal ethics to provide the best legal service value to the client.

How Ethical Rules Affect Paralegal Practice

Ethical behavior in this context means acting in a way that lives up to the standards of behavior in the legal profession. Because the legal profession exists to serve clients, the standards of ethical behavior focus on the obligations of the legal professional to the client. The ethical rules of the legal profession also address the obligations of the legal professional to opposing parties and to the court.

The busy paralegal must know and understand how these ethical rules come into play during an ordinary day. Any situation has the potential to create an ethical problem that must be resolved correctly.

Ethical violations can affect the outcome of the client's case and can result in disclosure of information that is embarrassing or harmful to the client. A paralegal must understand that rules of client confidentiality do not permit a third person to be present for any conversation that addresses important client information.

The paralegal's reputation for ethical behavior is an important asset. It must be diligently protected. The best protection is compliance with the ethical standards of the profession.

 **Question**

What kinds of problems can result from violations of the ethical rules of behavior?
The paralegal who gives a client legal advice is committing unauthorized practice of law. If the advice turns out to be incorrect, the client may decide to sue the paralegal and the supervising attorney. The attorney may face professional discipline. The client may seek another law firm, resulting in a loss of business and referrals.

Regulation of the Legal Profession

Compliance with the ethical standards of the legal profession is not left to chance. All states have mechanisms to oversee the ethical behavior of attorneys. This type of direct regulation consists of a defined set of ethical rules and a means of enforcing those rules. By contrast, no state has a separately defined set of ethical rules or enforcement mechanism governing the ethical behavior of paralegals.

Regulation of Lawyer Ethics

Attending law school and passing the bar exam are two of the requirements for obtaining a license to practice law. Compliance with the rules of ethical behavior is one of the conditions for retaining that license. Each state has a code of ethical behavior for attorneys. While there is no national code of ethics for lawyers, the ethical codes of the individual states tend to follow the ethical behavior standards created by the ABA. Most states follow the newest version of these ethical standards—the Model Rules of Professional Conduct. (A few states still follow the older Model Code of Professional Responsibility.)

All ethical codes control the behavior of attorneys in a number of ways. The restrictions range from the very specific—when a lawyer can receive a gift from a client—to the very general—the attorney's obligation to protect client confidences.

Attorneys who violate the state code of ethical behavior can be punished. All states have enforcement mechanisms that review and evaluate complaints of unethical conduct by attorneys. A client, an opposing party, another lawyer, or a judge can make a complaint of unethical conduct. If, the complaint is found to be justified after an investigation and hearing, the state supreme court may sanction (punish) the lawyer. The type of sanctions depends on the severity of the offense. An attorney may receive a reprimand for a relatively minor offense. Offenses that are more serious may call for a period of probation requiring the lawyer to abide by specific conditions or a period of suspension from the practice of law. The most serious offenses can result in disbarment or the termination of the lawyer's right to practice law.

Because paralegals are not licensed to practice law, the lawyer has an ethical obligation to supervise the work of the paralegal. The duty of supervision includes an element of responsibility—in all states, the lawyer is responsible for ensuring the ethical behavior of supervised paralegals. Under these provisions, a lawyer can be punished if the paralegal violates any of the ethical rules governing the lawyer.

Alert

Both of the major paralegal organizations, the NFPA and the NALA, have established codes of ethics for paralegals. These paralegal ethical codes are similar to the Model Rules of Professional Responsibility. Because of attorney supervision, however, these ethical codes do not set the ethical standard for paralegals. Attorney supervision requires that the paralegal meet the ethical standard required of the lawyer.

Because lawyers are responsible for the behavior of their paralegals, the paralegal is indirectly responsible for compliance with all the ethical rules governing lawyers. The most important ethical rules affecting the paralegal are the rules addressing the unauthorized practice of law, paralegal competence, the confidentiality of client communications, conflicts of interest, and prohibitions on fee splitting.

Unauthorized Practice of Law

Each state has a system of licensing attorneys. These licensing procedures help protect the public from unqualified or incompetent attorneys. It is unlawful for a nonlawyer to practice law; in some states this activity can lead to criminal penalties. Few of these statutes define "the practice of law."

Knowing what conduct constitutes unauthorized practice of law is very important. Because paralegals perform so many legal tasks that were previously performed by lawyers, it is necessary to identify when this conduct might cross the line into unauthorized practice of law.

The ABA defines the practice of law as the exercise of professional judgment on behalf of a client. The essential component of the ABA definition is the exercise of professional judgment on the specific legal problem of a client. Using the standard of the exercise of professional judgment, we can narrow the kinds of activities that constitute the practice of law. There are least four activities that always involve the exercise of professional legal judgment.

Establishing the Attorney-Client Relationship

A paralegal must never suggest to a client that an attorney will or will not represent them. No matter how clear the matter seems to be, no matter how sure the paralegal is of the decision of the attorney, the paralegal is simply not authorized to make this decision. The creation of an attorney-client relationship has many consequences. It imposes duties on both the attorney and the client—duties that are not specifically imposed on the paralegal.

This is not to say that the paralegal is prohibited from communicating the lawyer's decision. It is perfectly proper for a paralegal to write or call a client to tell them that the lawyer has accepted or declined the representation. In fact, facilitating communication between the lawyer and the client is one of the major duties of a paralegal.

Essential

A paralegal must be careful to not make statements that contradict any disclaimer of representation. Vague statements like, "I'm sure we will be able to help," or even, "I look forward to working with you," confuse the prospective client and may create an expectation of representation. Keep your comments confined to gathering information and reinforcing that any decision on representation is the lawyer's responsibility.

Setting Legal Fees

A paralegal must never agree to charge a client a specific fee. Obviously, this is a matter of great importance to the client. Many clients will press the paralegal for information—"How much is this going to cost?" "What do you usually charge?" In each case, the paralegal should refer the client to the lawyer for this information.

Again, it does not matter if the paralegal is experienced or competent. The specific fees charged for legal matters can vary greatly depending on the complexity of the matter, the length of time it takes to address the client's problem, and whether there are unforeseen difficulties. The attorney has an ethical obligation to discuss all fee matters with the client prior to undertaking representation. The paralegal cannot perform this essential duty for the lawyer.

Representing a Party in Court

The general rule is that a paralegal may not represent a client in court. The privilege of appearing on behalf of another person is limited to lawyers because they have specific training in the rules of procedure and evidence that apply in court proceedings. In addition, every court proceeding requires the lawyer to exercise professional judgment on behalf of a client—whether to assert an objection, what questions to ask a witness, or how to respond to a judge's question.

Nevertheless, the bright-line rule that a paralegal cannot represent clients in court is fading. Paralegals may appear on behalf of clients in some federal administrative proceedings. Other courts are opening their doors to paralegals as well—Maryland allows nonlawyers to appear on behalf of tenants threatened with eviction, lay advocates appear on behalf of women in domestic violence proceedings in North Dakota, and other states are experimenting with allowing paralegals to appear in court on behalf of clients in other limited matters.

 Fact

A person who represents herself in court, even if not licensed to practice law, is not guilty of the unauthorized practice of law. Every state allows litigants to appear pro se, or on their own behalf.

Offering Legal Opinions or Advice

Of the four activities that constitute the practice of law, the prohibition against giving legal advice is the clearest. Clients come to lawyers because they need help with a legal problem. They expect that the advice they receive will come from someone with the training and expertise to provide that advice. Legal advice ordinarily deals with the consequences of a course of conduct and affects the client's legal position or rights.

It is the close working relationship between lawyers and paralegals that creates problems in this area. A client who is aware of the relationship between the paralegal and the lawyer may rely on statements by the paralegal just as if they came from the lawyer. The client does not differentiate between a paralegal who is offering her own opinion (improper) and a paralegal who is relaying advice from the attorney to the client (proper). To the client, it is all legal advice.

The paralegal must be vigilant to avoid giving legal advice to clients. The temptation to share your education and expertise becomes greater as your knowledge and competence grow. When a client calls wanting to know the options for dealing with a custodial dispute, it is difficult to simply gather information and tell the client you will discuss the problem with your supervising attorney. Anything more, however, runs the risk of giving legal advice and constitutes the unauthorized practice of law.

E ssential

A paralegal should always clarify her role when dealing with clients or other persons to avoid confusion between the paralegal and the lawyer. This is a good time to reinforce the idea that the paralegal cannot offer legal advice.

The paralegal must also take special care to avoid giving legal advice to persons other than clients. Being in the legal profession is a bit like being a medical doctor—people are constantly asking for an off-the-cuff opinion on their legal problems. Paralegals must resist the temptation to try to assist these persons, even if the request comes from a family member and the paralegal is absolutely certain of the answer. Even advice that seems common sense to you may be given greater weight because it comes from a person with legal training.

Competence

Every client wants his legal team to handle problems quickly, knowledgeably, and efficiently. Clients want lawyers and paralegals who are competent. Lawyers and paralegals have an ethical duty to perform legal services in a competent manner.

What is competence? It is providing legal services with a reasonable degree of legal knowledge and skill. The level of legal knowledge and skill varies from case to case. It depends on the area of the law, the client's goals, and the complexity of the case. A great deal of legal skill and knowledge is required, for example, when representing a client who is purchasing commercial property subject to long-term government financing interests. A lawyer or paralegal who does not have the necessary legal knowledge or skill in that area of the law acts unethically by undertaking to represent this client.

Lawyers and paralegals become competent to handle specific legal matters in a number of ways:

- **Legal education.** A quality legal education provides skills in legal analysis and research. These skills enable the legal professional to identify and acquire the legal knowledge needed for competent representation of a client. Legal analysis and research skills not only allow mastery of an unfamiliar area of the law, they are indispensable when responding to periodic changes in the law.
- **On-the-job training.** There is no better way to become competent at a task than to perform that task. Because legal education cannot possibly address every area of the law or every legal problem, most lawyers and paralegals develop competence through on-the-job training.
- **Association with experienced legal professionals.** Part of the reason lawyers practice in groups is to take advantage of shared expertise. Developing legal knowledge and skills is often easier when you can call on the experience of a senior lawyer or paralegal.
- **Continuing legal education.** In many states, lawyers are required to fulfill a continuing legal education requirement in order to maintain their license to practice law. These lawyers attend seminars conducted by colleagues experienced in the field to increase their legal knowledge and stay abreast of developments in specific areas of the law.

 Fact

A bad outcome is not evidence of incompetence. The duty of competence requires only that the paralegal use reasonable care in applying legal knowledge and skill to the legal problems of the client. Even competent paralegals cannot guarantee a good outcome.

The obligation of competence falls equally on the lawyer and the paralegal. Paralegals must take affirmative steps to maintain the required degree of legal knowledge and skill. The ethical paralegal is continually looking for ways to improve competency. The ethical paralegal also guards against common competency traps:

- **Failure to disclose inexperience when a legal task is assigned.** Many lawyers will assume a paralegal is competent to perform a legal task unless told otherwise. If the paralegal is not competent, the lawyer may be personally responsible for any adverse consequences resulting from poorly performed legal work.
- **Allowing work product to be used without review by the supervising attorney.** A busy attorney working with an experienced paralegal may get into the habit of using the paralegal's work product without reviewing it first. Although it is gratifying to have the confidence of the supervising lawyer, this situation poses serious ethical problems.
- **Failure to keep track of deadlines.** Some deadlines, if missed, can have serious adverse consequences for the client. Virtually all law firms have some sort of reminder ("tickler") system to keep track of deadlines.
- **Documentation errors.** Do not rely on the review by the supervising attorney to discover error in a document you prepared. Carefully review every legal description, document disclosure, and contract clause that passes your desk. Ask questions if you are not sure that a word or phrase is correct.

Confidentiality

Confidentiality is the cornerstone of the attorney-client relationship. Clients come to lawyers for advice that is independent, free of emotion, and thorough. Not all legal problems are simple and straightforward. Many times the client possesses crucial information that is embarrassing, detrimental to achieving the legal goal, or is evidence of a crime. Nevertheless, no lawyer can give complete legal advice to a client without knowing all the facts.

The doctrine of attorney-client confidentiality encourages full and frank discussion of all the facts while protecting the client's sensibilities. The rule of confidentiality says, quite simply, that an attorney may not disclose any information received from a client without that client's prior permission. In some states this doctrine is extended to prohibit disclosure of information about a client received from another source, but which the client would find embarrassing if disclosed.

E ssential

A paralegal must be on constant guard against breaches of confidentiality. It is often tempting to share information with others, especially others that seem to share the same interests as the client. The bright-line rule of no discussions of client matters with third parties is designed to overcome that temptation. When it comes to confidentiality, it is always better to err on the side of caution.

There are exceptions to the rule of confidentiality. Information can be disclosed to third parties if the client consents. Information necessary to the representation may be disclosed—the client cannot insist that the fact that he hired a lawyer be kept confidential when the purpose of the representation is to begin a lawsuit. Other exceptions deal with the client's intent to commit a crime and the collection of legal fees. It is always a good idea to discuss the disclosure of confidential information with the supervising attorney before relying on any of the exceptions.

How Paralegals Can Protect Client Confidentiality

Paralegals work closely with clients and lawyers and are privy to client confidences on a daily basis. Because breaches of confidentiality undermine the trust of the client in the law firm and may have disastrous consequences for the client's case or reputation, the paralegal must guard against common breaches of confidentiality:

- **Inquiries from nonclients about client matters.** This often occurs in matters involving family. For example, a daughter calls your office and asks you to tell her what her father (your client) put in his will. This information is confidential and may not be disclosed without permission.
- **Overheard conversations.** It is common for persons who work together to talk about their work. Speaking with another paralegal in your office about a client matter is not a breach of confidentiality. If that conversation takes place in a common area, such as a hallway, elevator, or restroom, the risk of being overheard is a breach of confidentiality.
- **Use of telephones.** Cellular transmissions are essentially radio waves that can be monitored by anyone with the proper equipment. Some states make an exception for digital transmission plans, but care should still be taken to ensure that both ends of the conversation have digital capability. Also, the use of cellular or speakerphones in public places raises confidentiality issues.
- **Computers.** If the client insists on e-mail communication, the paralegal must adopt practices that minimize the possibility of a breach of communication, such as encryption and careful proofreading of all outgoing e-mails. The computer screen is also a potential breach of confidentiality. If client information appears on the screen, the paralegal should take steps to prevent viewing by unauthorized persons.

Conflicts of Interest

Clients hire lawyers for independent legal advice. They expect, and deserve, the undivided loyalty of their legal team. To ensure that loyalty, lawyers and paralegals are ethically obligated to avoid conflicts of interest between clients.

A conflict of interest arises when the interests of one client are adverse to the interests of another client. This situation can arise between two current clients or between a current client and a former client. A paralegal must avoid both situations.

Conflicts Between Existing Clients

Paralegals often serve a screening function, gathering factual information from new clients before the lawyer accepts representation. These pre-representation conversations can be tricky, especially when the prospective client may want the lawyer to assert a position contrary to the interests of another client.

The paralegal's role in preventing conflicts between existing clients is to gather as much information as possible about the prospective client, the nature of the problem presented, and any other involved parties. Each prospective client must pass a "conflicts check" before the attorney-client relationship is formed. In most firms, the conflict information is maintained in a computer database. The paralegal must take great care to check for possible variations in client names—as, for example, when a client named "Johnson Bros., Inc." is entered in the database as "Johnson Brothers."

Conflicts with Former Clients

The rule against conflicts of interest with former clients is essentially a rule against switching sides in a dispute. A lawyer who has once represented a client cannot, after the representation is ended, represent another client in a matter that is the same or substantially related to the prior matter.

Alert

A paralegal subject to an ethical wall must be proactive in avoiding contact with the conflicting representation. When there is a possibility of a breach in the wall, the paralegal must act by leaving the room, terminating a conversation, or refusing to handle documents. Only active measures can assure the effectiveness of the ethical wall.

The rule against conflicts of interest with former clients is of particular importance for the paralegal who is changing employers. The paralegal is bound by the obligation of confidentiality with respect to all client matters at the former law firm. If the new employer represents clients in matters that are the same or substantially similar to matters the paralegal previously worked on, the conflict of interest rule would disqualify the paralegal from working on the case. Worse, because it is presumed that anyone employed at a law firm is privy to all the client information received by anyone at the law firm, the conflict of interest rule would disqualify the paralegal's new employer from continuing to represent its client.

This harsh result is avoided by prompt identification of these potential conflicts and the erection of an *ethical wall.* A paralegal seeking new employment should compile a list of all matters he worked on at the former law firm. That list should be presented to the new employer, who should perform a conflicts check on each matter. If conflicts appear, the paralegal can be "walled off" from the conflicting representation. An ethical wall requires:

- A written memo to all employees of the new firm explaining that the paralegal is not to perform any legal tasks on the walled-off file.
- Instruction in the memo indicating that no employee may discuss the walled-off file with the paralegal.
- A physical file that should be marked or flagged to identify it as a restricted file. Of course, the paralegal must take steps to avoid contact with the walled-off file.

Fees and Fee Splitting

Paralegals may not share directly in the fees a lawyer collects from a client. All lawyers are prohibited from sharing professional fees with nonlawyers. This prohibition extends to agreements between a lawyer and a nonlawyer to distribute the fee after it is earned.

This ethical rule is grounded in the preservation of the professional independence of the lawyer. When a nonlawyer has an interest in the outcome of a legal representation, the lawyer is no longer able to exercise completely independent judgment on behalf of the client. The limitation on the professional independence of the lawyer is the same whether the nonlawyer is an independent contractor, such as a private investigator, or an employee, such as a paralegal.

Because the rule against fee splitting is related to the representation of the client, it does not apply to a lawyer who wishes to share general law firm profits with a nonlawyer. Year-end bonuses are common in law firms and there is no ethical prohibition against allowing paralegals to share in the overall financial good fortune of the firm. The fee-splitting prohibition only bars the sharing of fees related to specific, identifiable client matters.

The Licensing Debate

One of the hot issues in the paralegal profession is the question of whether paralegals should be licensed. Licensing proposals have been debated in at least ten state legislatures, although none have been enacted as yet. The interest in licensing stems from the growing number of independent paralegals and legal technicians. These practitioners offer limited paralegal services to the public without the supervision of an attorney. There are two main proposals to control these types of practitioners.

General Paralegal Licensing Proposals

General licensing proposals apply to all paralegals. Any paralegal, whether practicing under the supervision of an attorney or not, would be required to meet certain licensing criteria. These criteria generally include a minimum education requirement and expectations of continuing education after licensure. Paralegals would not have to be certified by a parent organization. The limitations on paralegal duties would remain the same, except that some proposals would allow paralegals to appear in court on behalf of clients. No general licensing proposal would allow paralegals to give legal advice.

Limited Paralegal Licensing Proposals

Limited paralegal licensing proposals are directed toward those paralegals who practice without the supervision of an attorney. These proposals allow the freelance or legal technician paralegal to provide paralegals services on routine legal matters. Legal technicians could handle simple divorces, will executions, real estate transactions, and bankruptcy filings without the supervision of a lawyer, and they would also be allowed to give legal advice to clients on these limited matters.

Split of Opinion

The dispute over how to respond to these proposals has divided the paralegal profession. Each major organization has a different set of concerns about paralegal licensing. These positions are an indication of the evolving understanding of the proper role of the paralegal in the American legal system.

- **The American Bar Association.** The ABA opposes the mandatory licensing of paralegals, and it states that the obligation of attorney supervision is sufficient protection for the public. The ABA believes that allowing paralegals to be licensed will create confusion because some members of the public might believe that a licensed paralegal can offer legal advice. In addition, some attorneys predict an increase in the cost of legal services because lawyers will be forced to hire paralegals with more education who demand higher salaries.
- **The National Association of Legal Assistants.** The NALA also opposes the mandatory licensing of paralegals. Although the NALA has an established process for certifying paralegal competence, the organization believes the process should be voluntary. Of primary concern to the NALA are its many members who might not qualify as paralegals under any proposed licensing plan.
- **The National Federation of Paralegal Associations.** The NFPA supports the mandatory licensing of paralegals. The NFPA also has an established procedure for certifying paralegal competence, but it regards this as a supplement to mandatory licensing. The NFPA believes that licensing will increase the access of the poor to legal services by allowing paralegals to handle routine matters without the supervision of an

attorney. The NFPA also believes that the current lack of licensing allows many unqualified persons to practice as paralegals. The NFPA sees licensing as a means of raising the standards of the profession while eliminating unqualified practitioners.

Chapter 6

The American Legal System

Many people base their understanding of the American legal system on what they learned in a high school government or civics class. Others rely on newspaper summaries of legal events. Few think about what the law is or where it comes from. For the paralegal, however, these are daily exercises—using an understanding of the sources and types of law to assist clients with legal problems. This chapter covers the basics of the American legal system.

Unique Sources of American Law

The law pervades American life, but few of us have a clear understanding of what the law is. Simply put, the law is established rules of conduct. Through the law we are able to know what our rights are, what our duties are, and what our privileges are. We use this understanding to regulate and conform our conduct. The law allows us to predict the consequences of our actions and to order our conduct accordingly, when three characteristics are present:

- **Stability.** For the law to be an effective guide to conduct, it must be stable. Frequent changes in the goals and purposes of the law breed uncertainty and make the law ineffective as a guide to conduct.
- **Predictability.** The law allows individuals to predict the consequences of their actions. We expect that similar actions will result in similar consequences.
- **Flexibility.** The law must advance as circumstances change. Our system of law must take into account social, scientific, technological, and economic changes when evaluating the consequences of specific actions.

The American legal system is modeled on the English common-law system of law, which rested primarily on a single set of laws and a single court system. The American legal system is considerably more complicated, involving the interplay between a written constitution, national legislation, administrative rules, and a strong common-law tradition. To make matters worse, each of the four sources of law in the American legal system—constitutional, statutory, administrative, and common law—are found at both the state and federal level. Each of the four sources of law can have a significant effect on how the law guides conduct.

Constitutional Law

The United States is a republic. The powers, limitations, and organization of the government are set forth in a written constitution. The U.S. Constitution is a model for governments around the world and a major source of law in the American legal system.

The Constitution is based on the principle of *federalism*—the division of the duties and responsibilities of government between a national, or federal, government and the governments of each individual state. Following the principle of federalism, the Constitution grants the federal government certain enumerated powers. All other powers not specifically delegated to the federal government are reserved by the states. This allocation of the powers of government is sometimes referred to as "state's rights." The allocation of the powers of government also has a significant effect on the operation of law in the United States.

The Federal Constitution

The language of the U.S. Constitution is generally sweeping and vague. The drafters of the Constitution wanted a document that would allow for inevitable changes in social attitudes toward government and the law and economic changes that might influence the direction of the law. In spite of its broad language, however, the Constitution establishes the fundamental principles on which the American legal system is based.

The Constitution is the supreme law of the land. This means that no other source of law may conflict with its provisions. A federal or state statute that conflicts with the Constitution is invalid and cannot be enforced. A judicial decision that fails to follow the Constitution is not effective. The final interpretation of the meaning of the Constitution rests in the hands of the United States Supreme Court.

Essential

The body of the U.S. Constitution contains no protections of individual rights. That task is left to the Bill of Rights. Similarly, the original Bill of Rights did not protect individuals from infringement of those rights by the states. That protection was created in the Fourteenth Amendment. When we speak of rights "guaranteed by the Constitution," we are speaking of a body of law that is constantly evolving.

The principle of federalism and the supremacy clause of the Constitution affect the development of law in three ways:

- **The exercise of individual rights.** The Bill of Rights guarantees each individual citizen certain rights. Because the rights of freedom of speech and assembly, freedom from unreasonable searches and seizures, the privilege against self-incrimination, and the right to a jury trial are included in the Constitution, they cannot be limited or abrogated by the states. The Constitution also grants individuals the right to due process when a fundamental right is affected and to have the equal protection of the laws. State and local laws may not deprive any citizen of the rights guaranteed by the Bill of Rights.
- **The relationship between the federal government and state governments.** The Constitution grants certain powers to the federal government. In some cases, the powers of the federal government may not be exercised by the states, such as the

power to negotiate treaties with foreign governments. In other cases, the states may exercise a specific power, but only if the federal government has not acted. When there is federal legislation, the states are precluded from enacting any legislation on the subject. On the other hand, where the federal government has not acted, the states are free to choose their own approach.

- **The relationships between states.** To minimize the conflicts created by separate state legal systems, the Constitution requires each state to give "full faith and credit" to the legal decisions of another state. Thus, a litigant who obtains a verdict in one state may collect on the verdict in another state, even if there is a difference in legal theory between the states.

State Constitutions

Each state has its own constitution. Most of them follow the structure of the U.S. Constitution, while reflecting individual variation in the form of state government. For example, all the states but one follow the federal model of a two-house legislature; only Nebraska follows the unicameral legislative model. There are also variations in state judicial systems that are quite significant. Judges are appointed in some states; in others, judges are elected. No state allows its judges to serve for life as in the federal system.

 Fact

A state cannot limit any rights granted to individuals by the U.S. Constitution or federal law, but they are free to expand those rights. States have the power to act in the best interests of their citizens, so long as the rights granted do not conflict with the U.S. Constitution or a federal statute.

Statutory Law

Statutory law is also known as enacted law. It is the law that comes to us from the legislature of our elected representatives. Statutes govern matters ranging from defining certain actions as crimes, to specifying procedures for the sale of real property, to allowing individuals to sue for workplace discrimination, to collecting taxes to support the operations of government. Enacted law is created at the federal, state, and local levels of government.

Federal Statutes

Federal statutes usually address matters of national interest. Sometimes these statutes are exclusive and have no state counterpart. The enforcement and interpretation of these statutes is entirely within the federal system. An example of an exclusive federal statute is the National Labor Relations Act.

Other federal statutes are concurrent with state statutes. The enforcement and interpretation of concurrent statutes can be in federal court or in state court. An example of a concurrent statute is a federal antidiscrimination statute. Many states have their own antidiscrimination statutes. The enforcement and interpretation of the federal statute can be made by a federal court or by a state court that is also hearing matters related to an alleged violation of the state statute.

State Statutes

Each state has its own set of statutes. These statutes govern the activities of the citizens of the state. Statutes reflect the judgment of the state legislature about what legal rules best fit the needs of the citizens of that state. Non-resident persons present in the state are subject to the statutes in that state. Presence in a state is not limited to physical presence—acts such as entering into a contract with a person from another state can subject a non-resident to the laws of that state. Many state statutes are designed to accomplish specific objectives of importance to the citizens of that state. Other state statutes are enacted to resolve specific disputes that arise between citizens of the state.

Because of these differing purposes, state statutes vary from state to state. Different states might have different interests or a different solution to a problem. Thus, the specific statutes of a state are only enforceable within the territorial jurisdiction of the state.

Alert

The differences in state law sometimes lead to "choice of law" questions. These are disputes where it is not clear which state's law should apply. Differences in state law can significantly affect the rights of the parties. Many written contracts between citizens of separate states contain choice of law provisions to avoid just this dispute.

Local Ordinances

City councils or county governing boards establish local ordinances, to cover matters of specific local interest such as zoning issues, licensing requirements for liquor sales, and snow removal regulations. The state government specifically delegates to local government the authority to pass certain ordinances. Other ordinances are enacted to fill gaps in state statutes. In all cases, local ordinances that conflict with state statutes are invalid.

Uniform Laws

The differences between state statutes on a particular subject can make it difficult to anticipate the consequences of a course of action. For example, a business that orders supplies from a manufacturer in another state cannot know whether the damages for breach of that contract are governed by the law of the state of the buyer or the state of the manufacturer. This is especially troublesome when one state allows significantly greater protection for the buyer. Discrepancies in state law are often found in the fields of commercial transactions, enforcement of child support obligations, and probate procedures.

One response to these discrepancies is the creation of uniform laws. *Uniform laws* are the product of discussions among judges, lawyers, and legal scholars who are interested in minimizing the disruptions created by variations in state statutes. Model statutes were generated in specific areas where variations in state statutes create troublesome issues of interpretation.

Essential

Many areas of the law fall exclusively into one category of statutory law or another. Intellectual property issues, such as copyright, trademark, or patent infringement, are controlled exclusively by federal statutes. Probate law, on the other hand, is almost entirely governed by state statutes. Many areas of the law overlap the three sources of statutory law—a real estate transaction is regulated by state law, but can present federal issues of pollution abatement as well as local ordinance issues of zoning or building code compliance.

Uniform laws are not laws at all until a state legislature enacts them as a statute. Of course, each state is free to adopt, reject, or change any portion of a uniform law. Surprisingly, however, the variation between proposed uniform laws and the actual statutes enacted by state legislatures are minor. Legal practitioners are able to advise clients that provisions of the Uniform Commercial Code and the Uniform Probate Code are the same in the states that have adopted them.

Administrative Law

Administrative law is created by administrative agencies of the government through powers granted by the legislature. When the legislature feels the need to control or monitor a particular problem or industry, the solution is often to contact an administrative agency. Because the legislature often lacks the time, staff, and expertise to oversee all of the legislation it enacts, these duties are delegated to an administrative agency.

An administrative agency embodies the powers of all three branches of government. It serves an executive branch function by investigating and enforcing the rules of the agency. Many administrative agencies have the authority to adjudicate disputes over violation of agency rules. Some administrative agencies employ special judges to hear these cases. An administrative agency also has the power to create rules and regulations that further the legislative purpose. The scope of the powers given to an administrative agency is found in a statute known as an *enabling act*. Through the enabling act the legislature defines the purpose of the administrative agency and the limits of its authority.

Administrative agencies appear in all areas of the law. Typical agency regulations are found in the areas of pollution, housing, health, employment discrimination, criminal corrections, and workplace safety. The regulations promulgated by these agencies have the force of law and are treated as statutory enactments. Most states have a compilation of agency regulations separate from the state's enacted statutes. The federal compilation of agency regulations is known as the Code of Federal Regulations (CFR).

Lawyers who work in the area of regulatory compliance often employ paralegals. A lawyer who practices in the area of housing development may have frequent dealings with the federal and state housing agencies. A lawyer representing clients who buy and sell securities must be familiar with the regulations of the Securities and Exchange Commission. Paralegals can be of great assistance in researching and interpreting agency regulations in both these fields.

Common Law

The common law is also called case law. The common law is the name for those legal principles created by judges in the absence of some other source of law. While the term *judge-made law* is currently out of favor, law created by judges is the foundation of the legal tradition in this country.

The common law tradition pre-existed the United States Constitution. In eleventh-century England, the local customs and traditions of each region of the country resulted in disparate rules of law. To facilitate the growth of trade and commerce, William the Conqueror sought to establish uniform rules of law that applied to every part of the country. For the law to be effective in regulating and predicting conduct it needed to be consistent. The need for consistency led judges to adopt two principles that govern the common law to this day—precedent and *stare decisis*.

 Alert

The role of the common law in the American judicial system was established in the case of *Marbury v. Madison*. The decision in that case created the concept of judicial review—the right of the courts to determine whether the actions of the other branches of government were permitted by the Constitution. The concept of judicial review allows the court to examine and interpret statutes and administrative regulations when necessary to resolve a legal dispute.

Precedent

Achieving consistency was not easy for eleventh-century judges. With little statutory authority to advise them, these judges were charged with instilling predictability into the law. The task was made more difficult by the fact that the judges could not anticipate legal disputes, but could only decide disputes based on the facts before them.

Ultimately, these common-law judges settled on the concept of precedent. Simply put, the concept states that the resolution of a current dispute should be guided by a prior decision on a dispute that involved similar or identical facts. Precedent is not personal to the deciding judge; a decision by one judge serves to guide the decisions of all judges within the jurisdiction. Because judicial decisions were no longer subject to differences in regional or judicial outlook, precedent brought stability and predictability to the law.

Today, the concept of precedent underlies all legal analysis. Precedent enables the legal professional to determine the specific legal consequences that will follow from a specific set of facts. The paralegal researching a client's problem looks for cases involving similar facts. This type of case is on point because similar facts allow the prediction of a similar application of the rule of law. These predictions can be used to define the boundaries of a contract or to modify behavior that risks legal consequences.

E ssential

Not all precedent is created equal. The structure of the American legal system allows each state to create and interpret its own laws without limiting the right of other states to do the same. A decision of the supreme court in one state is a mandatory precedent for all the courts in that state. It is merely a *persuasive* precedent for courts in another state—those courts may follow the decision, follow only part of the decision, or choose not to follow the decision at all. Precedent is only mandatory within the limits of the court's jurisdiction.

Stare decisis

Closely related to the concept of precedent is the doctrine of *stare decisis*. The term is an abbreviated version of the Latin *stare decisis et non quitor movere*, which means to "stand by (or adhere to) decisions and not disturb that which is settled." In effect, the doctrine of *stare decisis* admonished judges to follow the concept of precedent in reaching their decisions.

The value of combining *stare decisis* with the concept of precedent is obvious. Similar disputes based on similar facts result in similar outcomes. The rules of law become established principles with the only variations occurring where there are significant factual variations. The law became consistent and predictable.

The doctrine of *stare decisis* is not rigid, however. By requiring judges to reason by analogy to prior cases, *stare decisis* also permits judges to depart from precedent, as circumstances warrant. Changes in social attitudes, economic conditions, or the growth of technology can justify a departure from precedent. These departures are not only allowed, but are required if the law is to remain flexible in responding to legal disputes.

Modern Status of the Common Law

The development of the common law established many of the legal principles we rely on today. English common law evolved because there was no other source of law available, and it developed largely without the benefit of a written constitution or large body of statutory law. Today, the definition of common law relies on this history. The common law is law established by judges in the absence of any other controlling legal authority.

In recent years, both federal and state legislators have attempted to make changes in the law by enacting statutes. The proliferation of legislative enactments has had two effects on the common law.

First, some legislative enactments are designed to incorporate the common law into statute. These statutes codify the common law and become the authority relied on by the courts. Many states have codified the common law in the fields of marriage and criminal law.

 Fact

State or federal statutory law is often referred to as the "code" of that jurisdiction. When legal professionals say that a legislature has "codified" the common law, they mean the principles of the common law have been enacted as statutes.

Second, when the legislature disagrees with the result reached by the common law, it may enact a statute to change that result. These statutes supplant the common law and are called statutes in derogation of the common law. Such statutes may reflect impatience with the pace of change of the common law.

Third, a legislature may enact legislation in an area of the law where there is no common-law principle. Again, these statutes are designed to speed the development of the law or to prevent the common law from expanding in a specific way. Statutes enacted in the absence of common-law principles direct the development of the law and become the controlling legal authority in that arena.

Chapter 7

The American Court System

The array of courts in the American judicial system can be bewildering. There are trial courts and appellate courts at the federal level and at the state level. Each jurisdiction has specialty courts. Each court serves a different function. The opinions of some courts are critical to solving a client's problem; other pronouncements are safely ignored. A well-educated paralegal must know the role of each of these courts and how each can affect the outcome of a client's legal problem.

Unique Structure of the American Court System

Each court in the American court system serves a specific function. The function of the court is defined by the constitutional provision or statute that created the court. Although variations abound, there are two types of courts: trial courts and appellate courts.

Trial Courts

Trial courts are courts that resolve factual disputes. The premise of the common law is that the law develops through the resolution of actual factual disputes presented by persons with opposing interests in the outcome. The trial court is charged with hearing the dispute and arriving at a resolution.

The primary concern of trial court is to determine the facts of the dispute. The determination of facts comes in two steps. First, the parties must present their version of the facts. In the discovery process, the parties exchange information about the case. This information is sifted, analyzed, and organized in ways designed to persuade the trial court to reach a specific result. At trial, the parties present their version of the facts in accordance with the rules of evidence. Both versions of the facts are presented, together with arguments about the credibility or relevance of particular facts.

Second, after all parties present their version of the facts, the trial court must decide which version is the truth. This function of the trial court is the *finder of fact* role. The facts decided by the trial court are used to determine the outcome of the dispute between the parties.

In cases involving a jury, the jury is the finder of fact. In these cases, the jury determines the facts on the basis of instructions from the judge. The instructions also ask the jury to reach a conclusion based on the application of established legal principles to the facts. This conclusion is called a verdict.

 Fact

Since trial courts are the first line of dispute resolution, the work of most lawyers and paralegals is concentrated at this level. Facts and the interpretation of facts are the most important part of a trial court-level practice. Paralegals must become adept at recognizing, developing, and responding to facts that affect the outcome of a legal dispute.

Arriving at a verdict often involves resolving factual discrepancies. A jury may hear evidence from a witness that a driver was exceeding the speed limit at the time of the accident. The driver may present evidence that he was driving within the speed limit. The jury has the responsibility of resolving this factual dispute and determining the probable facts of the accident.

When the parties choose to present their case to a judge sitting without a jury, the judge assumes the role of finder of fact. The judge's role in this type of case is similar to that of a jury, except that the judge does not receive instructions on the treatment of the evidence. In most cases, the judge will prepare written findings of fact. The findings of fact are the equivalent of a jury verdict.

The application of law to fact is the exclusive function of the judge, regardless of who served as finder of fact. The application of law to fact determines the outcome of the dispute. In cases where the parties agree to the facts, they may ask the judge to apply the law to the facts without the need for a finder of fact. These situations allow the trial court to resolve a legal dispute short of trial for matters when the facts are clear.

Appellate Courts

A party who disagrees with a decision of a trial court can appeal. An appeal removes the dispute to another court called an appellate court. An appellate court can be the highest court in the particular legal system or it can be an intermediate appellate court.

Even though appellate courts are superior to trial courts, they do not serve the same function. The main function of the trial court is determining facts; the main function of an appellate court is the selection and application of rules of law to the facts determined by the trial court. Appellate courts do not receive evidence—the presentation of a new witness or document is not allowed. The primary concern of the appellate courts is whether the applicable legal principles were applied correctly to the facts determined by the finder of fact. In general, an appellate court will affirm (agree with) or reverse (disagree with) the trial court's application of law to fact.

Alert

Even though appellate courts do not determine facts, their decisions are based on the facts of the dispute as determined by the trial court. It is often useful to carefully examine the facts of an appellate court opinion and compare them to the facts of the client's case. An appellate opinion involving facts that are identical or substantially similar to the client's facts is "on point."

The decisions of appellate courts are usually in writing. This allows these decisions to be reviewed and critiqued by lawyers, legal scholars, and other courts.

How the System Affects the Case

The American court system actually consists of fifty-one separate court systems. The Constitution established the federal court system. Each state has its own court system. While each system has slightly different rules and procedures, they all follow the basic structure of trial courts and appellate courts. Within this court structure, there are limits on the type of dispute each court can decide.

The authority of a court to decide a dispute is called the *jurisdiction* of the court. A court that lacks jurisdiction cannot decide a legal dispute. The jurisdiction of a court has three components—geographical jurisdiction, personal jurisdiction, and subject matter jurisdiction. The absence of *any one* of these components deprives the court of the authority to decide the legal dispute.

Geographic Jurisdiction

Geographic jurisdiction refers to the authority of the court to act on disputes that occur within a defined geographic area. The specific jurisdiction of the court depends on the type of court.

The courts with the broadest geographic jurisdiction are the highest courts in the court system. These courts have jurisdiction over all matters arising in that court's system. For example, the supreme court of a state has jurisdiction over all legal disputes arising within the territorial borders of the state. The Unites States Supreme Court has geographic jurisdiction over legal disputes arising within the boundaries of the United States.

Lower courts may have limited geographic jurisdiction. Many state court systems establish trial courts that only have authority within a specific county. Some states utilize intermediate courts of appeal that only hear appeals from within a defined district within the state.

Personal Jurisdiction

Even if the dispute arises within the geographic jurisdiction of the court, it still may lack authority to decide the dispute if it has no jurisdiction over the parties. The ability of the court to resolve a dispute in a manner that is binding on the parties is defined by the court's personal jurisdiction over the parties.

Personal jurisdiction can be established in two ways: a party can voluntarily submit to the jurisdiction of the court or the court can acquire involuntary jurisdiction over a party. Voluntary personal jurisdiction is primarily used to describe the jurisdiction over the party who begins the lawsuit. That party, usually called the plaintiff or the petitioner, chooses the court that will decide the legal dispute. Even if the court would not have personal jurisdiction over the plaintiff, the commencement of a lawsuit is an implicit agreement to abide by the decisions of the court.

Essential

The primary factors that must be present before a court may exercise "long-arm" jurisdiction are whether the defendant purposefully sought the protections and benefits of the state's laws and whether the actions of the defendant caused injury within the state. These requirements are present to prevent courts from claiming long-arm jurisdiction over parties that have only casual contact with the state.

Involuntary personal jurisdiction is more complicated. The court must have personal jurisdiction over the person responding to the lawsuit, usually called the defendant or respondent. Involuntary personal jurisdiction over defendants is established by *service of process* on the defendant while the defendant is within the territorial jurisdiction of the court. Service of process is easily accomplished if the defendant is a resident of the jurisdiction or regularly does business in the jurisdiction. Establishing involuntary personal jurisdiction over other persons depends on the ability of the court to extend its authority outside its geographic boundaries by means of long-arm statutes. The Constitution strictly limits the scope and effect of long-arm statutes.

Subject Matter Jurisdiction

All courts have limitations on the kinds of legal disputes they can decide. These limitations are based on the subject matter of the dispute. A court without subject matter jurisdiction cannot decide a legal dispute even if the dispute arose within its geographic jurisdiction and the court had personal jurisdiction of the parties.

The subject matter jurisdiction of the court comes from the authority granted to it under a constitution or by statute. A challenge focuses on any limitations in the court's authority imposed when the court was created. There are five types of subject matter jurisdiction:

- **Original subject matter jurisdiction.** The court is the first one to hear the legal dispute. Courts of original jurisdiction are always courts charged with the responsibility for finding facts. A court of original jurisdiction may have other limits on its subject matter jurisdiction as long as it resolves the legal dispute first. Trial courts are courts of original jurisdiction.

- **General subject matter jurisdiction.** The court can hear any kind of legal dispute, no matter what the subject matter. Courts with general subject matter jurisdiction exist in both state and federal court systems. A court of general subject matter jurisdiction does not have to be a court of original jurisdiction; an appellate court may have general jurisdiction over appeals that arise in its geographic area.

- **Limited subject matter jurisdiction.** The court can only hear particular kinds of disputes. Small claims courts are courts of limited subject matter jurisdiction because they can only hear cases of a certain value.

- **Exclusive subject matter jurisdiction.** Only this court is able to decide a certain type of legal dispute. These courts are sometimes called specialty courts because they are established to devote specific legal expertise to a particular type of dispute. Many states have courts devoted to deciding disputes involving tax, workers' compensation, or housing matters. A court of exclusive jurisdiction can also have original or appellate jurisdiction over the subject matter. When a court has exclusive subject matter jurisdiction, no other court is allowed to decide disputes involving that subject matter.

- **Appellate subject matter jurisdiction.** This allows review of the decision of a court of original jurisdiction. An appellate court may have the authority to hear appeals on any kind of legal dispute (general jurisdiction) or only be allowed to hear appeals in a particular area of the law (limited or exclusive jurisdiction).

The Federal Court System

The federal court system consists of courts of original jurisdiction, intermediate courts of appeal, and the United States Supreme Court. The structure of the federal court system is the model for most state court systems. Like all court systems, the federal court system has a very clear hierarchy.

E ssential

The Constitution specifically reserves certain powers of government to the individual states. Because of this, the federal court system may only hear cases that are specifically described in the Constitution— disputes involving a federal statute or federal constitutional issue, disputes between citizens of separate states, and other specific issues. If the case does not involve one of these issues, the parties must remain in state court.

United States District Courts

The primary courts of original jurisdiction in the federal court system are the U.S. District Courts. Population, workload, and other factors determine the district covered by each court. Every state has at least one district. There are also district covering each of the territories owned by the United States and the District of Columbia. The U.S. District Courts are courts of original, general jurisdiction and have authority to hear disputes involving the application of federal statutes or the Constitution, or cases involving disputes between citizens of different states.

Closely related to the district courts are the federal courts of limited jurisdiction. These courts consider specialty cases relating to veterans' affairs, tax matters, international trade, and certain kinds of federal claims. In addition, the federal court system includes courts that hear disputes within the exclusive jurisdiction of federal administrative agencies.

The United States Circuit Courts of Appeal

The federal court system includes several intermediate appellate courts. These courts are known as the United States Circuit Courts of Appeal. The federal system divides the territorial United States into twelve circuits. Each circuit has a court of appeals that hears appellate matters that arise form the districts within that circuit.

The Circuit Courts of Appeal are courts of general appellate jurisdiction. They review all appeals from the courts of original jurisdiction in their circuit. Most of these appeals come from the district courts, but the Circuit Courts of Appeal are also authorized to hear appeals from some courts of limited, original jurisdiction.

The federal court system also includes a special court of appeal called the United States Court of Appeals for the Federal Circuit. This court has specific authority to hear appeals from most of the specialty courts in the federal court system.

United States Supreme Court

The United States Supreme Court is the highest appellate court in the land. In addition to exercising jurisdiction over appeals from the Circuit Courts of Appeal and the Court of Appeals for the Federal Circuit, the U.S. Supreme Court also has the authority to hear appeals of the final decisions of state supreme courts.

Many people forget that the United States Supreme Court is also a court of original jurisdiction. Article 3 of the United States Constitution grants the Supreme Court original jurisdiction over "all Cases affecting Ambassadors, other public Ministers and Consuls, and those in which a State shall be Party." In addition, the Chief Justice of the Supreme

Court is charged with the responsibility of presiding over trials involving the impeachment of the President. Fortunately, the Supreme Court seldom exercises its powers of original jurisdiction.

 Fact

The U.S. Supreme Court exercises discretion over the cases it will decide. One of the parties must first petition for *certiorari*. This is a request that the Supreme Court hear a case that presents a significant issue, such as the constitutionality of a statute or the infringement of a fundamental right. The justices grant or deny certiorari on the basis of the importance of the issue presented and whether the facts of the case allow the court to address an important issue.

The State Court Systems

State court systems are often similar to the federal model. The particular structure of a state court system is often a matter of historical anomaly, with courts bearing odd-sounding names that belie their actual function. Regardless of the names of these courts, however, the basic functions are the same.

Courts of Limited, Original Jurisdiction

Most states have a two-part structure to their trial courts. At the lower level are courts of limited, original jurisdiction. These courts are established to hear specific types of cases, usually involving limited amounts of money or a specific area of the law. In some states, these courts are called municipal courts or magistrate courts; these courts are also called Justice of the Peace Courts or Courts of Common Pleas. Other states establish special courts to hear disputes in housing, domestic relations, or probate matters.

Courts of General, Original Jurisdiction

All states have trial courts of general, original jurisdiction. In some states, these courts are superior to courts of limited jurisdiction and handle matters involving serious crimes and civil disputes. In other states, there are no courts of limited jurisdiction and the trial courts of general jurisdiction hear all legal disputes. Trial courts of general, original jurisdiction are usually called district courts, circuit courts, or superior courts.

Intermediate Courts of Appeal

Many states have established intermediate courts of appeal to hear appeals from the courts of general, original jurisdiction. In these states, the volume of appeals overwhelmed the state supreme court. The solution was to create an intermediate court of appeals to correct the errors of the trial courts. Intermediate courts of appeal usually have a significant number of judges who sit in panels of three to decide appeals.

Some states extend the concept of specialty courts to the level of the intermediate courts of appeal and establish a specialty intermediate court of appeals. For example, a state might establish a court of appeal for the specific purpose of hearing appeals from a specialty tax court.

State Supreme Courts

All states have a high court, a court that is the last step in the appeal process. This court is commonly called the supreme court of the state and is a court of general, appellate jurisdiction. It is the last step in the state court hierarchy; the only appeal from a state supreme court is to the U.S. Supreme Court. This type of appeal is strictly limited. The only allowable grounds for such an appeal is that the decision of the state supreme court is in conflict with the provisions of the Constitution, or where there is a question of interpretation of a federal statute.

Alternative Dispute Resolution

Alternative dispute resolution (ADR) is the name for a group of options for settling disputes between parties. ADR allows the parties to resolve their differences outside the courtroom, usually with the assistance of a neutral third party. The ADR process has become increasingly popular with litigants for four reasons:

- *Litigation* (the process of resolving a dispute in the court system) can be a lengthy process. Even a simple litigation matter may take over a year to conclude. Matters that are more complicated are often unresolved for two or three years or more. ADR is a streamlined process that shortens the length of litigation.
- Litigation is also expensive. The litigation process tends to foster an attitude of uncovering every possible fact, examining every possible document, and exploring every possible legal theory. This approach is driven, in part, by the fear of being surprised at trial. Because so many fee arrangements are based on the hourly rate, this approach also tends to increase legal fees. ADR encourages early resolution and focuses on reaching agreement rather than marshalling evidence of differences.
- Litigation creates precedent. The fundamental feature of the American legal system is that disputes with similar facts are decided in a similar fashion. In some cases, litigants want to resolve a dispute without creating a precedent to guide the decision of future disputes. ADR is a private agreement between the parties and is not binding in future disputes.
- Most litigated disputes are resolved by voluntary settlement. By some estimates, as many as 95 percent of all civil cases settle before trial. A significant number of these cases settle "on the courthouse steps," or just as trial is about to begin. ADR starts the process of negotiation much earlier and results in fewer last minute settlements.

The parties may choose any ADR procedure they like—days-long arbitration hearings before panels of experts or an informal evaluation of the case by an experienced ADR professional. Although most states allow the court to order ADR, the vast majority of ADR proceedings are voluntary. The parties can choose a procedure that is binding or nonbinding. ADR usually takes place on a schedule that is convenient for the parties. Typical ADR procedures fall into two categories: negotiated settlement ADR procedures or quasi-litigation ADR procedures.

Alert

The timing of the ADR procedure is as important as the form of the procedure. The success of ADR depends on the belief of each party that all the facts were heard. If the progress of the factual development in the case is not significantly advanced, one of the parties may resist settlement in the hopes that additional facts will change the view of the case. For this reason, most ADR procedures are more successful if they take place after the parties have engaged in some fact investigation and development.

Negotiated-settlement ADR Procedures

Negotiated-settlement ADR procedures are based on the premise that the parties want to settle their dispute but may require the assistance of an independent third party in reaching agreement. Most states allow any qualified person selected by the parties to serve as the independent third party. Even in states that register persons trained in ADR procedures, the parties are free to choose any third party they think will help them resolve their case. Negotiated settlement ADR procedures can take several forms.

The early neutral evaluator is usually an experienced practitioner in the field. The early neutral evaluator reviews the facts of the dispute and provides an independent analysis of the legal principles involved. The results of this analysis are communicated to the parties. The evaluator does not become involved in any subsequent negotiations and the results of the analysis are nonbinding. Because early neutral evaluation takes place early in the litigation process, it is sometimes used to prevent parties from becoming entrenched in their positions.

The most common form of negotiated-settlement ADR is mediation. In *mediation*, the parties select an independent third party, not necessarily a lawyer. The parties provide the mediator with information supporting their respective positions, but the mediator is not responsible for deciding the dispute. Instead, the mediator attempts to find common ground between the parties and suggests possible solutions to remaining disagreements. This process is often carried out with the parties in separate rooms, with the mediator engaging in "shuttle diplomacy" to bring the parties to an agreement. While the mediation process itself is not binding, any agreement reached by the parties *is* binding and can be enforced by the court.

Quasi-litigation ADR Procedures

In some cases, the parties may require a more formal approach to resolving a dispute. The disagreement may center on the resolution of a specific factual issue, the application of a principle of law, or some other issue that is not easily negotiated. For these disputes, a quasi-litigation ADR procedure is appropriate.

The most common quasi-litigation ADR procedure is arbitration. *Arbitration* is a litigation substitute—instead of submitting evidence to a judge or jury, the evidence is submitted to an arbitrator. Because the arbitrator is not a judge, the rules of evidence are somewhat relaxed. Nevertheless, arbitration requires the testimony of witnesses and the submission of detailed position papers outlining the facts and legal principles in the case. At the conclusion of the case, the arbitrator will usually take the case under advisement and render a decision within thirty to sixty days.

The use of arbitration varies widely. In some states, arbitration is required for certain kinds of claims. Arbitration is often the preferred means of dispute resolution in contractual matters. Agreements to arbitrate are often seen in insurance policies, construction and development agreements, financial documents, and other contracts where prolonged litigation of a dispute might affect the value of the contract. Collective bargaining agreements typically call for the arbitration of employee grievances. More recently, employers have begun including arbitration clauses in employment agreements. These agreements often specify that the arbitrator be selected from a list maintained by the American Arbitration Association or another independent arbitration administrator.

The Role of Paralegals in ADR

Because one of the goals of ADR is to lower the cost of litigation, the ADR process relies heavily on the use of paralegals. Paralegals can participate in the ADR process in three ways:

- Paralegals act in support of a supervising attorney as in any other matter. The ADR process often finds the paralegal more directly involved in selecting, organizing, and summarizing the factual material that is presented to the independent neutral.
- Paralegals can act as independent neutrals. A paralegal with the proper training and experience can often serve as an effective independent neutral. This is especially true in family law disputes or the early stages of employment disputes.
- Paralegals can appear on behalf of clients in ADR proceedings. Some states and administrative agencies allow a paralegal to appear on behalf of a client in ADR proceedings. Check the local rules before representing a client and always obtain the client's consent.

Chapter 8

Choosing a Legal Specialty

The law is expanding at an unprecedented rate. The effect of this is clear: the day of the general legal practitioner is over. The law is to broad, too complex, and too rapidly changing for anyone to stay abreast of developments in all areas. Legal professionals, including paralegals, must specialize to be able to meet client demands of efficiency and effectiveness

Specialization: The Key to Job Security?

Most lawyers and many paralegals say that they specialize in a particular area of the law. The term, however, is somewhat misleading. A legal specialty is not the same as a medical specialty. A doctor who specializes in cardiac surgery practices only in that area of medicine. A lawyer who "specializes" may actually practice law in several different areas of the law. In fact, it is not uncommon for a legal professional to list two or three specialties.

The situation is similar for paralegals. In its 2002 National Utilization and Compensation Report, the National Association of Legal Assistants reported that the average paralegal respondent claimed to practice in three specialty areas of the law. In all, thirty-six specialty areas of practice were identified.

The same survey sought to determine whether the claimed areas of "specialty" really demanded the majority of a paralegal's time. The report found that significant number of respondents spent less than 20 percent of their time performing tasks in the area of specialization. The only specialty area where respondents reported devoting 80 percent or more of their time to assigned tasks was civil litigation.

Together, these findings suggest that true specialization is extremely rare. A legal professional may concentrate on a certain area of the law, but clients have many kinds of legal problems. The legal professional must be competent and comfortable in several areas of the law. The selection of a specialty does not mean that other areas of the law can be ignored.

 Fact

The term *specialty* is a misnomer when applied to the legal field. Legal professionals may concentrate their practice in one particular area, but they are also free to branch out into other areas of the law. A legal specialty is simply any area of the law that interests the practitioner and comprises a significant portion of the practice.

The good news is that this form of diversified specialization offers significant advantages. Legal work is often cyclical—the demand for legal services in a specific area of the law fluctuates. A paralegal who is competent and comfortable in several areas of the law is valuable in each of these areas. This allows the law firm to continue functioning smoothly and efficiently. If a job change is necessary, the diversified paralegal has more to offer a new employer.

When to Decide

Many beginning paralegals start their education with an idea of what area of the law most interests them. Others are attracted to an area of the law as they study. Still others do not select an area of the law but simply accept one dictated by their first job.

The truth is that you can select a specialty at any time in your career. Picking a specialty is a matter of becoming familiar with the law and procedures in a particular field. You will become familiar with some areas of the law through your education, but there are many specialty fields that are not addressed in the paralegal curriculum.

On-the-job training creates a specialist. Work in an area of the law long enough to decide if you like it. If not, take steps to move to another area, either within your firm or with another firm. Many paralegals hold several positions before they decide on a specialty.

Alert

The decision to pursue a legal specialty is not a lifelong commitment. While you should choose a specialty carefully, legal specialties are relatively easy to change. A change of job or a change of assignments that has you working in a different area of the law is all that is required. As you gain competency with different areas of the law, you may find that you have several specialties.

How to Decide

It is unwise to limit your options until you have had a chance to actually work in a specific area of the law. The statistics on time spent working in a specialty suggests that even specialists must have other interests. If you work in a large law firm, you will be exposed to many areas of the law. Even paralegals who work for a solo practitioner will have varied assignments. Deciding on a specialty involves a combination of several factors—personal preference, opportunity, and legal trends.

Personal Preference

Deciding on a specialty is a matter of personal taste. Your attraction to an area of the law should be more than just getting a job. Some people are attracted to an area of the law because of the intellectual challenge the field offers. Others are seeking a high degree of client contact. Still others are attracted to the attention to detail required in certain positions. There are areas of the law to fit everyone. Select one—or more—that allows you to do what you love.

Opportunity

Sometimes selecting a specialty is simply a matter of opportunity. You may be interested in family law, but the firm you work for already has an experienced family law paralegal. Your work is concentrated in civil litigation, and that becomes your specialty.

Beginning paralegals are often offered opportunities in fields that they never considered as a possible specialty. One friend recommends another for a job, an in-firm assignment is made based on availability, or the supervising lawyer takes on a client matter involving a different area of the law. Any of these events creates an opportunity to explore a different area of the law.

If you are not being exposed to different areas of the law in your current job, develop your own opportunities. Ask for more varied assignments, take continuing legal education courses in varied fields, or volunteer with organizations in a field that interests you. Cross-training in several different areas of the law provides the opportunity to transition smoothly to different specialty areas.

Job Trends

Some specialties are dictated by job trends. Certain areas of the law are developing while others are slowing. Several years ago, many civil litigation paralegals were specializing in tobacco or asbestos litigation. Those were "hot" fields at the time—there was a lot of activity involving many lawyers. Today, there is less demand for paralegals in these specialties.

Some law firms follow job trends. If there is a demand for a certain legal service, the law firm will try to fill it. Paralegals who work for these types of firms may be swept along with the trend into a new specialty area. Other firms do not follow job trends, either because of lack of interest or lack of capacity. These firms do not have clients demanding the latest service, or simply lack the resources to move into a new legal area. Paralegals in these firms will not have the option of exploring a specialty in a developing field of the law.

What Are the Options?

The National Association of Legal Assistants identified thirty-six areas of legal specialization in its 2002 Report. Not all of those are available in every area. For example, specialties in international law or immigration law tend to be concentrated in large metropolitan areas. Generally speaking, the narrower the specialty, the more likely that it is limited to paralegals in large firms in large cities.

The most popular specialties are still civil litigation, wills and probate, real estate, and family law. Those areas of the law are discussed elsewhere. There are, however, several other specialties that deserve mention.

 Fact

Legal specialty areas are often quite broad. This tends to hide the great variety of legal issues included in the specialty. For example, the specialty of civil litigation encompasses all kinds of litigation, including auto accidents, product liability, medical malpractice, construction litigation, employment litigation, commercial disputes, and contract matters. There may be many opportunities for variety even with a specialty.

Employment Law

The term *employment law* covers a wide number of topics and subtopics—collective bargaining agreements, safety in the workplace, employer and employee rights, contract negotiation, wrongful termination, reasonable accommodation, discrimination, and sexual harassment, to name a few.

Contract considerations are becoming more common in the employment arena. Employers who deal with unions have always had contracts that define nearly every aspect of the employment relationship. Nonunion employers sometimes seek the same arrangement with their employees. This process often involves checking to ensure that proposed contract provisions do not conflict with statutory requirements, or drafting personnel policies that help define the employment relationship. In some cases, an employer will negotiate a separate contract with a highly valued employee that requires careful drafting.

Statutes and administrative regulations govern many parts of the employer-employee relationship. The Occupational Safety and Health Administration govern workplace safety; the Fair Labor Standards Act controls wage rates, and the Equal Employment

Opportunity Commission regulates responses to complaints of workplace discrimination. Both employers and employees require assistance resolving disputes in these areas.

Medical and Health Law

The medical and health law field also covers a variety of subspecialties. Law firms, insurance companies, medical providers, and government agencies are all involved in the delivery of health care services. The delivery of services and the charges for those services are heavily regulated. Paralegals provide assistance in assuring compliance with applicable statutes and regulations.

The cost of health care claims is a matter of concern for some insurance companies. These companies often employ paralegals with medical training to review a patient's history and treatment to determine whether the patient is eligible for services. These paralegals also review medical records to assist the insurance companies in controlling claim costs.

When there is a bad result from medical care, the patient may sue the doctor or nurse in a medical malpractice lawsuit. These lawsuits often center on the contents of the medical records and the opinions of expert medical witnesses. Law firms regularly employ legal nurse consultants (paralegals with a nursing background) to assist in evaluating these claims.

Bankruptcy Law

Federal bankruptcy law offers insolvent debtors the opportunity to obtain protection from creditors and relief from debt. The bankruptcy system is a separate court system with separate rules and regulations. These regulations are often highly technical. The bankruptcy process requires the filing of certain forms at certain times and compliance with requirements regarding disclosure of debts and assets.

The field of bankruptcy law offers great opportunities for paralegals. Both debtors and creditors need assistance to protect their interests in a bankruptcy proceeding. Paralegals are often assigned the responsibility of interviewing the client, obtaining the information required by the court to file a petition for bankruptcy or a claim of a creditor, reviewing the information provided by the client, and preparing the appropriate forms for filing with the court. Recent changes in the bankruptcy law have created even more opportunities for paralegal involvement in the bankruptcy process.

Intellectual Property Law

Intellectual property is the product of the creative imagination of the mind. This field of law deals with the protection of a person's interest in the arts and ideas. There are three distinct areas of intellectual property law:

- **Copyright law** protects literary and artistic works from unauthorized use by others.
- **Trademark law** protects business from misappropriation of identifying marks and symbols.
- **Patent law** protects the interests of inventors in receiving the benefit of their work.

Intellectual property rights are somewhat different from other property rights, because misappropriation is so easy. Proof of rights in intellectual property is often difficult. Furthermore, intellectual property rights can survive the death of the owner. Paralegals working in this area are highly specialized and often spend much of their time working on very narrow issues of law and interpretation.

Environmental Law

Both federal and state governments have enacted statutes designed to protect the environment. These statutes protect us from pollution, provide for cleanup of polluted sites, specify protected habitats, and preserve the nation's natural resources. Environmental law, usually practiced before administrative agencies, is divided into compliance and enforcement. Corporations, developers, environmental watchdog groups, local governments, and citizens are all concerned with compliance. Developments must meet environmental requirements; procedures for hazardous waste disposal are specified, and permit applications must be completed. Paralegals are involved in all aspects of compliance for all interested parties.

If there is a breach in compliance, enforcement is required. Paralegals may be involved in reviewing the evidence of noncompliance and in drafting a settlement of the charges. If litigation results, paralegals provide litigation support.

Other Developing Areas

There are many other growing areas of the law. Whether a particular specialty is available in your area depends on the nature of the specialty and the needs of the clients. Most areas of the law develop in response to client demand.

The 2002 Report of the National Association of Legal Assistants shows certain specialties have had the greatest growth in the number of respondents designating the area of law as a specialty—entertainment law, Native American/tribal law, telecommunications law, Social Security law, and collections law.

How Specialty Choice Affects Compensation

The effect of choice of legal specialty on salary is not clear. The reasons for this are varied. First, as noted above, the designation of a legal specialty does not necessarily translate into time spent in that specialty. This makes it difficult to correlate salary with the activities of the specialty. Second, some of the more limited specialties are centered in large, metropolitan law firms. These employers tend to pay higher salaries across the board. Again, it is difficult to attribute higher salaries to the specialty itself.

The available evidence, in the form of salary surveys from the National Federation of Paralegal Associations and the National Association of Legal Assistants, suggests that certain specialties command higher salaries than others. The highest-paying legal specialties, as reported in these surveys, are corporate law, environmental law, real estate, entertainment, and intellectual property law. The lowest-paying fields are family law, probate, criminal law, bankruptcy, and workers' compensation.

As with any salary information, the reported results are generalities. The salaries in your area may vary significantly. It seems to be generally true, however, that specialty fields with high profit margins, high demand for qualified paralegals, and a requirement of some specialized training command the highest salaries.

E ssential

There is no clear relationship between the choice of a legal specialty and the salary paid to the paralegal. In most cases, higher salaries are paid to paralegals with more experience or with substantial additional training in a specialty field. If you are a beginning paralegal without any special training, you can expect an average salary for your area, no matter what "specialty" you choose.

Predicting the Next Hot Specialty Area

It is virtually impossible to predict the next hot specialty area for paralegals. Clients drive the demand for legal services. Changes in the political landscape may cause short-term demand for legal services in a specific area, but these often fade away after a short time.

Nevertheless, there are two areas of the law that seem to have great potential to generate client demand over the next several years. First, it is inescapable that the baby boom generation is getting older. The bulk of the baby boom generation will reach retirement age in a few years. We have already seen some of the effects of that anticipated event: changes to Social Security and Medicare and the growth of assisted living communities. The need for elder law services is likely to increase steadily over the next few years. Those services include estate planning, living wills, health care directives, patient's rights, and guardianships. The increased demand for these services, which paralegals already provide, is expected to result in continued opportunities for the foreseeable future.

Second, the field of computer law is growing. Issues of intellectual property protection, privacy protection, and the impact of electronic communications on contract law and other aspects of business law continue to be raised as business becomes more reliant on this technology. A paralegal with an understanding of the underlying legal specialty and a substantive knowledge of computer software and networking will have a great advantage in this field.

Chapter 9

Criminal Law

Criminal law is often the type of law that comes to mind first, for the general public. The popular view of criminal law is influenced by media coverage of certain trials, popular novels, and a variety of television law and crime shows. While these portrayals contain many inaccuracies, the field of criminal law offers exciting and challenging paralegal opportunities. Read on to see if this might be the area of law for you.

Why Criminal Law?

The field of criminal law presents many opportunities for a paralegal. Public prosecutors, also known as district attorneys, county attorneys, or state's attorneys, employ paralegals. As a part of the prosecution team, paralegals may be responsible for drafting the criminal complaint, organizing the presentation of evidence, keeping crime victims informed of the status of the prosecution, or researching questions of law related to the charges.

As employees of public defenders or private lawyers who practice criminal law, paralegals perform similar tasks on behalf of the accused defendant. A paralegal is responsible for investigating the factual basis for the charges, for reviewing and analyzing the results of the police investigation, and for researching possible defenses available to the defendant.

Paralegals are also employed in organizations that provide ancillary support to the criminal justice system. Many victims' rights organizations employ paralegals to assist in explaining the legal process to victims and provide support and access to victims' services.

The Difference Between Civil and Criminal Law

Criminal law has three fundamental differences from civil law. First, criminal law is primarily statutory law. Second, criminal violations do not require an identifiable victim—the criminal law protects society's interests. Third, the burden of proof in a criminal case is significantly higher than in a civil case. These differences are important to understanding the operation of the criminal justice system.

The Statutory Basis of Criminal Law

Although the *roots* of the criminal law are in the common law, all of today's criminal law is statutory. The definition of what constitutes a crime is established by the legislature. Congress defines federal crimes; state crimes are defined by the state legislatures. The definition of a crime specifies the act that constitutes the crime—all crimes require a prohibited act and a prohibited intent.

The Prohibited Act

The statutory definition of a specific crime includes a description of the prohibited act. The description must be sufficiently specific to allow persons to avoid committing the act. The requirement of specificity contrasts with *tort law*, where an "unreasonable" action can lead to civil liability. The criminal law does not permit such vague terms. Thus, while it may not be unreasonable to drive more than thirty miles per hour through a school zone, it is a violation of the criminal statute.

The requirement of an act is an important part of criminal law. A person cannot be punished for thinking about doing a prohibited act. The commission of a crime requires that the thought be turned to action and that the act be one that harms society.

In most cases, a person must actually do something to commit a criminal act. The requirement of an act of commission is our most common understanding of a crime—a person commits a robbery, commits a theft, or commits a murder. The doing of the prohibited act defined in the statute is the crime.

Some crimes, however, are defined by the failure to act. These acts of omission define the crime as not doing something the law requires you to do. The failure to register for Selective Service or to pay taxes is a criminal act that is committed by not doing something. Crimes of omission are usually the kind of act that furthers a regulatory scheme of the government. There are very few crimes of omission against persons or property.

The Prohibited Intent

The level of intent varies with the crime, but some degree of intent is necessary for a crime to be committed. For example, first degree murder requires a high degree of intent. The defendant must form the intent to kill another human being, but must also have held that intent long enough so that the death is premeditated (sometimes called "malice aforethought"). On the other hand, the intent required to commit the crime of speeding is merely the intent to do the act of driving above the speed limit.

E ssential

The issue of the required mental state is central to several common criminal defenses. For example, a claim of insanity is based on the idea that a person suffering from certain mental illnesses cannot distinguish between right and wrong. These people do not have the required mental state to commit a crime. Similarly, the juvenile justice system treats children differently because criminal acts by children do not indicate the same mental state as criminal actions by adults.

The element of intent helps us determine the degree of punishment that is proper for a particular crime. The defendant's state of mind at the time of the crime is part of the definition of many crimes. Both first-degree murder and manslaughter require the act of taking a life. The difference between the two crimes is the state of mind of the defendant—premeditation is different from a crime of passion or recklessness. The criminal justice system punishes a death due to premeditated murder more severely than one caused by recklessness.

Crimes Are Offenses Against Society

Many crimes have victims. When a burglary, rape, or assault is committed, we are able to identify a specific person who was harmed by the act. There are, however, crimes that do not have an identifiable victim. These "victimless" crimes do not cause harm to a specific person, but are offenses against society as a whole. Prostitution and many drug crimes are described as victimless crimes.

There is no requirement that a specific person be harmed by a criminal act. Acts that are defined as criminal present a danger or harm to society and it is in society's interest to prohibit these acts. In a criminal case, the prosecutor acts for the good of society, not for the benefit of a particular person. For this reason, the state is empowered to enforce the criminal law without the consent of the victim. No crime requires the victim to "press charges." If the state can prove the required elements of the crime from available evidence without the cooperation of the victim, the cooperation of the victim is not needed.

The Burden of Proof

All crimes require the state to prove that the defendant committed the prohibited act and possessed the required state of mind. The proof of these elements must be established "beyond a reasonable doubt." This burden of proof is one of the primary distinguishing differences between the criminal law and civil law. The other is the presumption of innocence. Taken together, the presumption of innocence and the burden of proof beyond a reasonable doubt protect individual citizens from an overreaching government.

The Presumption of Innocence

The presumption of innocence is at the heart of the American criminal justice system. This presumption extends to all elements of the criminal charge. The government has the burden of proving every element of the criminal charge; the defendant need not produce any evidence or prove any fact to prevail at trial.

Proof Beyond a Reasonable Doubt

Proof beyond a reasonable doubt is the highest level of proof required in the law—it is the kind of proof ordinary people rely on in making important decisions. It is required in all criminal cases because criminal cases involve prosecution and punishment by the state. Conviction of a crime can be punished by loss of liberty, but only monetary interests are at risk in a civil case.

Fact

The presumption of innocence is simply a means of requiring the state to prove its case. It does not mean that the defendant is actually innocent. In fact, our criminal justice system does not rely on proof of innocence. A defendant is found guilty when the state has proven its case and not guilty when the state has not proven its case. A verdict of not guilty is not the same as a finding of innocence.

Types of Crimes

The field of criminal law divides crimes into several categories. The category of crime dictates the type of criminal act, the mental state, and the degree of punishment. Three broad categories of crimes are crimes against the person, crimes against property, and white-collar crimes.

The categories of crimes are further divided by the designated punishment for the crime. The categories of punishment are felony, misdemeanor, and petty misdemeanor. Each represents a different category of punishment.

Felonies are the most serious crimes. A *felony* is any crime that is punishable by imprisonment for more than one year. The seriousness of a felony crime is indicated by the possible sentence for the offense. Some felonies are capital crimes—crimes that are punishable by the death penalty. Other felonies are punishable by sentences up to life imprisonment, up to ten years' imprisonment, and up to five years' imprisonment.

Crimes that are punishable by incarceration of one year or less are *misdemeanors*. Misdemeanors are regarded as less serious offenses that do not require time in prison—nearly all misdemeanor sentences are served in a county or local jail. In many states, any crime that is not specifically categorized as a felony is treated as a misdemeanor.

 Fact

Conviction of a felony entails the loss of certain rights, such as the right to vote and may be a permanent bar to certain kinds of employment. Previous felony convictions can be used when considering enhanced sentencing options. The difference between a felony and a misdemeanor is often a critical point in plea bargain negotiations.

Petty misdemeanors are offenses that do not require incarceration. These offenses are usually punishable by a fine. Petty misdemeanors are often administrative offenses, such as failure to acquire a necessary permit. Since petty misdemeanors do not require incarceration, there is no right to a jury trial for these offenses.

Crimes Against Persons

Crimes against the person are the most serious crimes because the offense involves physical harm to another person. Crimes against the person are also called violent crimes for this reason. The great majority of crimes against the person are felonies.

Homicide is an obvious crime against the person. The death of another person, whether caused by recklessness, the heat of the moment, or premeditation, is the ultimate act of violence. The differences between the degrees of homicide—first degree murder, second degree murder, and manslaughter—are differences in the intent of the defendant. The greater the degree of intent, the greater the degree of punishment.

Of course, aggravating circumstances have an effect on the perceived seriousness of the crime as well. A defendant convicted of homicide may face enhanced penalties if the homicide involved illegal drugs or the use of a gun. The federal government may seek the death penalty if the victim of the homicide was a federal law enforcement officer.

Other crimes against the person include robbery, sexual assault, and assault and battery. These crimes typically require that the offense use a degree of force or that the victim be placed in fear of physical harm. Each crime requires a violent act or the threat of a violent act.

Essential

When a defendant is charged with a crime, the charge is presumed to include all of the "lesser" offenses encompassed by the act. A charge of second degree murder requires a specific mental state. If the prosecution cannot prove that mental state, it may be able to prove the mental state needed to establish the crime of manslaughter. The prosecution need not prove the elements of each crime—the lesser offense is included in the greater one.

Crimes Against Property

Crimes against property do not usually involve force or fear of harm. The criminal act is the act of damaging or attempting to gain the property of another. Crimes that damage the property of another include trespass, vandalism, and arson. Crimes that attempt to gain the property of another are burglary, larceny, theft, and forgery.

Crimes that damage the property of another may involve violent acts, but because there is no physical injury to a person, they are not classified with other violent crimes. The intent of these crimes is the damage to property, even if harm to a person occurs. For example, a person who willfully and maliciously burns a building owned by another has committed the crime of arson. If the owner is trapped in the building or is killed trying to extinguish the fire, the defendant may also be guilty of a crime against the person.

Alert

The distinction between crimes of violence and crimes against property can seem artificial. A homicide need not involve physical violence—as in the case of a poisoning. By the same token, a crime against property may be extremely violent, as when a burglar uses force to break into a locked house. The difference lies in the threat of physical harm to the victim, not the physical act that constitutes the offense.

Crimes that attempt to gain the property of another are also distinguished from crimes against the person by the lack of physical harm. A robbery has the purpose of gaining the property of another, but is a crime against the person because it requires placing the victim in fear of physical harm. *Larceny*—the wrongful taking of the property of another—however, does not require physical harm to the victim. In fact, it is possible to commit larceny without the victim's knowledge that the act has taken place. Other crimes against property that do not require any knowledge on the part of the victim include forgery and obtaining goods by false pretenses.

White-collar Crimes

White-collar crimes are a special category of crimes against property. These crimes are usually business-oriented. Most white-collar crimes involve the use of a business position or occupation to commit the crime. Many, but not all, are in furtherance of some business interest. This does not mean that the offender does not receive personal gain, but personal gain is seldom the primary motive for these crimes.

The business scandals of the last few years have made the public well aware of the many varieties of white-collar crime. It includes insider trading as in the Imclone scandal and accounting fraud as in the Enron scandal. It also includes embezzlement, bribery, and wire and mail fraud. White-collar crimes are typically complex and difficult to prove. Convictions in these cases usually rely on a combination of documents and the testimony of participants. Because white-collar crime is not considered a violent crime, offenders are often sentenced to serve time in minimum-security prisons.

Crimes Committed on the Internet

The prevalence of the Internet has created a new category of crime—cybercrime. Cybercrime is simply an ordinary criminal act committed by the use of a computer. The use of the computer seldom changes the nature of the crime, although it does raise issues of detection, preservation of evidence, and enforcement.

The amount of data stored in computers provides increasing opportunities for that information to be stolen or misused. Data manipulation or theft can result in significant financial losses for business. Although advances in computer security systems have made some kinds of computer crime more difficult, business are still subject to potential theft of financial information, copyright or trademark information, or other forms of proprietary information.

A less direct form of cybercrime is the use of the computer to impersonate another person. After using the computer to steal "identity" information, the criminal then poses as the victim to access the financial resources of the victim. The ease of stealing identity information and the plentiful access to financial resources on the Internet has caused the rate of reported identity thefts to skyrocket. Some estimates place the number of identity theft victims at more than 300,000 per year.

More and more law enforcement efforts are directed at the detection and prevention of cybercrime. Cybercrimes are often difficult to detect. Even when the results of the crime are known, prosecuting the offenders requires an intimate knowledge of computers, computer networks, computer security systems, and computer data storage. Many legal professionals find this area of the criminal law offers tremendous opportunities for specialization. In response to this rapidly growing area of crime, state and federal legislatures have enacted statutes specifically directed at controlling cybercrime.

Constitutional and Procedural Protections

The framers of the U.S. Constitution valued the rights of the individual over the rights of government. To protect the individual from the abuse of the power of government, particularly with respect to the government's powers of prosecuting crime, the Constitution contains several provisions that protect the individual. These protections, found in the Bill of Rights, prevent the government from being overzealous in pursuing the punishment of criminals. The protections of the Bill of Rights fall into three categories: protections against improper collection of evidence of a crime; protections against denial of individual rights in the trial of a criminal charge, and protection of individual rights after trial is complete.

Protections Against Improper Collection of Evidence of a Crime

Every individual suspected of committing a crime is entitled to certain protection from government activity in collecting evidence of the crime. First, individuals are protected against unreasonable searches and seizures by the Fourth Amendment. This provision requires the government to make a showing of probable cause before searching the property of or arresting the defendant. The Fourth Amendment prevents law enforcement from "fishing" for evidence based on mere suspicion. A warrant to search the defendant's property must be based on reasonable information that suggests the defendant committed a crime. The information must establish a probability that the warrant is justified.

Individuals also receive protections from the Sixth Amendment, which guarantees the right to counsel at various stages of a criminal proceeding. It is the Sixth Amendment that requires law enforcement to give a *Miranda* warning to every person taken into custody. *Miranda* rights include the right to remain silent and the right to counsel. Although its scope has been challenged over the years, the basic contours of the warning remain. Of course, *Miranda* has limitations—persons not in police custody do not receive the warning and the ruling does not protect persons who do not clearly state the desire to consult with an attorney.

 Fact

Constitutional protections for criminals are sometimes referred to as "technicalities." It is true that the protections of the Constitution can shield the guilty from prosecution, but the same technicalities allow ordinary citizens to be free from unwarranted government intrusion into their affairs. Constitutional technicalities ensure that all crimes are prosecuted for the right reasons and in the right way.

If law enforcement violates the provisions of the Fourth or Sixth Amendments, the evidence they gather is tainted. Evidence obtained in violation of the individual's constitutional rights will be excluded at trial. In addition, any additional evidence that is found as a result of an unconstitutional action by law enforcement, will be excluded as well. This exclusionary rule is a deterrent to misconduct in the investigation of crimes.

Protections Against Denial of Individual Rights in the Trial

The Bill of Rights provides several protections of the rights of individual who are tried on criminal charges. These protections include:

- The Fifth Amendment privilege against self-incrimination.
- The Sixth Amendment guarantees the individual the right to be represented by counsel at trial.
- The Sixth Amendment guarantees the individual the right to a trial by a jury of his peers.
- The Sixth Amendment guarantees the individual the right to confront the witnesses against him and to cross-examine those witnesses to test the believability of their evidence.

- The Sixth Amendment guarantees the individual the right to a speedy trial, thereby preventing the government from holding an individual without trial for an extended period.

Protection of Individual Rights after Trial Is Complete

The U.S. Constitution also protects the individual after the trial is complete. The Fifth Amendment guarantees the individual the right to be free of double jeopardy. This is the right to not be tried twice for the same crime. Double jeopardy does not apply to mistrials or retrials after a conviction is overturned on appeal. When the defendant is found not guilty, however, the government may not retry the defendant on the same charge.

If the defendant is convicted, the Eighth Amendment prevents the government from imposing "cruel and unusual punishment." The parameters of what is "cruel and unusual" can vary. In the 1970s, the Supreme Court felt that capital punishment violated the Eighth Amendment. More recently, the Court used the Eighth Amendment to disallow the execution of minors. Eighth-Amendment violations often figure prominently in lawsuits over prisoners' rights.

Prosecution and Trial

The basic steps in the prosecution and trial of a criminal case are similar in all jurisdictions. The procedural rules at each step in the process may vary, but the process itself follows the same general outline:

1. **Arrest.** The defendant is taken into custody by law enforcement. The arrest of the defendant can be with or without a warrant. The defendant should be advised of the right to counsel at the time of the arrest.

2. **Booking.** The defendant is processed after arrest by being searched, fingerprinted, and photographed to provide a record of the arrest. The defendant is given the opportunity to contact legal counsel.

3. Initial appearance. The prosecution is required to file formal charges against the defendant within a reasonable time after the arrest. The defendant appears before a judge for the recitation of the charges and the entry of an initial plea—usually not guilty. If the defendant remains in custody, the judge must consider an application for bail.

4. Indictment. Once the defendant has made an initial appearance, the charges are refined. The prosecutor may present the evidence collected by law enforcement to a grand jury. If the grand jury finds sufficient cause to proceed, it issues an indictment. The indictment must contain the specific charges that the prosecution will attempt to prove at trial.

5. Information. In some jurisdictions, the prosecution may choose the alternative of presenting the basic outline of the criminal case to a judge in a preliminary hearing. The defendant has the right to participate in the hearing and may offer evidence. Few defendants do so, however, because the amount of evidence necessary to certify a criminal case for trial is minimal. Once the judge decides that there is probable cause to proceed to trial, a charging document called *an information* is prepared. The information serves the same function as an indictment.

6. Arraignment. After the charging document is prepared, the defendant is again brought before a judge to hear those charges. A plea of not guilty is customarily entered, any demands for speedy trial are made, and the case is scheduled for trial.

7. Guilty plea. If the prosecution and the defendant can reach an agreement on a criminal charge and an offense that satisfies both sides, the defendant may plead guilty. Plea bargains are used to dispose of the majority of the criminal cases in the American judicial system. Plea bargains can be the result of a number of factors such as evidentiary problems, exchange of information, or a desire to limit the punishment.

8. **Trial.** If the parties are unable to reach a plea bargain, the case proceeds to trial. If the defendant is found guilty, the judge will ask for a presentencing report. The presentencing report provides information to assist the judge in deciding on a sentence. At sentencing, the judge may impose any sentence allowed by law.

The Paralegal's Role in a Criminal Case

The landscape of the criminal law is constantly changing. New laws are enacted, new enforcement initiatives are pursued, and new court opinions restricting or expanding the law are issued regularly. A criminal law paralegal must stay abreast of these trends to provide effective service to criminal clients.

The primary role of the criminal law paralegal is evidentiary. All the facts of the case must be reviewed, verified, and compared to other facts. The smallest fact can create reasonable doubt. Paralegals are often assigned tasks relating to interviews of witnesses, reading investigative reports, preparing motions, preparing exhibits, and assisting with the management of witnesses and exhibits at trial. Because this area of the law evokes strong emotions, a criminal law paralegal must be able to place the goals of the criminal justice system above personal opinions about the crime or the defendant. Above all, a criminal law paralegal must be objective.

Chapter 10

Torts and Product Liability

Tort law, also called personal injury law, is one of the most visible areas of the law. Personal injury lawyers advertise on late night television, newspapers report on the latest big verdict, and politicians rail against runaway juries and excessive attorneys' fees. Nearly everyone has an opinion about the need for tort reform. Despite this, tort and personal injury law remains a growing and exciting field with many paralegal opportunities.

What Is Tort Law?

Before beginning to study an area of the law, it is helpful to set the parameters of the field. What is tort law and how does it differ from other areas of the law? The answers to these questions are mainly phrased by identifying what tort law is not.

Tort law is not criminal law. Criminal law deals with the relationship of the individual to society. It defines the behavior that society expects from its citizens and imposes punishment for failing to meet those standards.

Tort law is not contract law. Contract law governs dealings between individuals, but, for the most part, the individuals are able to define the conduct they expect from each other. Contracting parties voluntarily assume obligations; in tort law, the conduct expectations are implied.

Tort law is different in that it sets forth our expectations for our behavior toward individuals that we do not even know. Tort law protects us against invasion of our personal interests. A person suffering a tort is entitled to be "made whole," or to be compensated for all losses caused by the breach of duty. Tort law includes injuries that are intentional, injuries that are negligent, and injuries caused by the products we use every day.

Fact

The definition of a tort is "a breach of a legal duty that causes harm to another, but is not a breach of contract or a crime." This broad definition allows tort law to address diverse topics and provides excellent opportunities for specialization within the field.

Intentional Torts

Tort law classifies conduct-causing harm by the actor's awareness of the risk of harm. Conduct accompanied by a high degree of awareness of the risk of harm is classified as intentional. Intentional torts occur when the actor knows or is substantially certain that the conduct will result in harm.

The "intent" required to commit an intentional tort is not the same as criminal intent. The law of intentional torts does not demand proof of intent to cause specific harm, nor does it require proof of motive. A bad state of mind is not required. It is quite possible to commit an intentional tort in the absence of a bad motive or a desire to harm.

Intentional torts are concerned with the actor's state of mind, but only with respect to the act itself. Only a purposeful act or an act that presents a substantial certainty of harm is necessary.

Intentional Torts Against the Person

Intentional torts against the person are the most common kind of intentional tort. These torts can stand alone, but they are frequently included as a part of some other claim. For example, a plaintiff claiming wrongful termination from employment might also make a claim of defamation if the stated reason for the termination is false. A plaintiff claiming medical malpractice against a surgeon for removing an appendix without consent can assert a claim of battery as well. The primary intentional torts against the person are described below.

Assault

An assault is an act that causes another to be in fear of immediate harmful or offensive contact. The victim must be aware of the intentional act, the threatened contact must be immediate, and the contact must be harmful or offensive. A child who throws a rock at a passing car commits an intentional act, but not an assault if the driver is not aware of the child's actions. A shouting match where one party threatens physical violence in the future is not an assault because the threat is not immediate. When an assault occurs, the victim is entitled to compensation even if there is no physical damage.

Battery

Battery is the harmful or offensive touching of another without that person's consent. Although this tort is often confused with assault, as in assault and battery, they are separate and distinct torts. Assault requires the knowledge of the victim; battery does not. When a defendant attempts to punch the plaintiff and misses, there is an assault, but no battery. Similarly, when the defendant sneaks up behind the plaintiff and hits him over the head, there is a battery, but no assault.

Battery does not require bodily touching. A person can commit battery by throwing a rock, striking another with an automobile, or removing a chair as a person is about to sit. It is not necessary that a battery victim be harmed—mere offensive touching is sufficient.

False Imprisonment

False imprisonment is the confinement or restraint of another without lawful justification. False imprisonment occurs when the defendant places boundaries on the ability of the victim to move freely. Boundaries on the movement of the victim can be in the form of physical barriers, the present exercise of physical force, present threats of physical harm, the exercise of claimed legal authority, or a refusal to release. The victim must have no reasonable means of escape from confinement. Claims of false imprisonment are often asserted against merchants who detain suspected shoplifters. Most states recognize a "shopkeeper's privilege" that shields merchants who act with probable cause from claims of false imprisonment.

Intentional Infliction of Emotional Distress

Intentional infliction of emotional distress is conduct that is extreme and outrageous and intended to cause severe emotional distress. Conduct that is merely hurtful does not qualify; intentional infliction of emotional distress is not designed to address every kind of emotional injury. A rejection of a marriage proposal may cause severe emotional distress, but it is not extreme and outrageous. Falsely informing a mother that her child has been killed is extreme, outrageous, and intended to cause severe emotional distress. Because it is so difficult to prove that conduct is extreme and outrageous, intentional infliction of emotional distress claims are rarely successful.

Defamation

Defamation is an untrue factual statement about the plaintiff that is published to a third party. Publication in this context simply means "made available"—it is sufficient if the third person saw or heard the untrue statement. Statements to the plaintiff that are not published to third persons, even if false, are not actionable. Statements of opinion cannot be a basis for a defamation claim because they cannot be proven false. If a factual statement is proven true, there is no defamation.

E ssential

Other intentional torts against persons include invasion of privacy, fraud and misrepresentation, and intentional interference with contract or business relations. These intentional torts generally involve a deliberate infringement on the known rights of another. Claims based on these theories often fail because of the difficulty of proving the necessary knowledge.

The law of defamation is extremely complicated, especially when the false statement concerns a public official, such as a politician. Because such statements are protected by the First Amendment, the plaintiff must prove both falsity and "actual malice" (a knowing or reckless disregard of the truth) to establish defamation. A similar standard applies to statements about public figures (athletes, television personalities, etc.).

Intentional Torts Against Property

The law protects property ownership interests against intentional interference. In fact, the first recognized torts involved intentional acts directed to property. Today, the law recognizes three intentional torts against property: trespass to land, trespass to personal property, and conversion.

Trespass to Land

Trespass to land is just what the name implies. It is an intentional invasion of an interest in real property (land) without the permission of the owner. The trespass can be by physical presence on the land or by the placing of some object on the land. Remedies for trespass include payment for any damages caused and removal from the land.

 Alert

Whether a person is classified as a trespasser or as a person who enters property with permission can have a significant effect on the duty the landowner owes to that person. A higher duty of care is owed to those who come onto the land with permission. For trespassers, the only obligation is to warn them of hazards on the property that they would not discover for themselves.

Trespass to Personal Property

Trespass to personal property is identical to trespass to land, except that it does not involve real property. Personal property is any form of property that is not real estate or inextricably tied to real estate. Any harm to the personal property of another or interference with ownership rights is a trespass. Taking property without permission is a trespass; retaining borrowed property for an unreasonable period is a trespass, and damaging property is a trespass.

Conversion

Closely related to trespass to personal property is the intentional tort of conversion. *Conversion* is depriving another person of their property with the intent to convert it to your own use. Most conversion involves a theft, but it is possible to convert property by retaining possession beyond the scope of the permission. A person who shoplifts a CD commits the criminal act of theft and the civil tort of conversion. A person who borrows a CD with the permission of the owner and then sells it has committed conversion, but not theft.

Negligence Torts

In contrast to intentional torts, which require intent to act, negligence torts do not require any intent. In fact, negligence torts do not require any action—negligence torts include acts of omission as well as acts of commission. Negligence torts are often called "unintentional torts."

Each negligence tort has four elements. The actor must owe a *duty of care* (see the following section) to the person injured; the actor must have breached (failed to meet) the duty of care; the breach of the duty of care must have caused the injury; the injured person must have suffered damages. The facts that support each of these elements varied from case to case, but each element is present in every negligence case.

Existence of a Duty of Care

We all owe a duty of care to others—to act in a way so that our conduct does not present an unreasonable risk of harm to others. The law also imposes a duty to act with appropriate care for one's own safety.

The duty of reasonable care is a two-sided duty. It encompasses the duty to act to prevent harm as well as the duty to *not* act if a risk of harm is present. This distinction is often referred to as the difference between acts of commission and acts of omission. When you chop down a tree without taking precautions to assure that the tree does not fall on your neighbor's house, you are negligent by commission—the action of chopping the tree is unreasonable. If you are involved in an accident because your brakes failed and the brakes failed because you did not have them serviced properly, you are negligent by omission—the failure to service the brakes is the unreasonable behavior.

We do not owe a duty of reasonable care to everyone in the entire world. No duty is owed when the risk of harm is not foreseeable.

Breach of the Duty of Care

Reasonable conduct does not violate the duty of care. Determining whether conduct violates the duty of care is a two-part process. First, we must decide what care is reasonable under the circumstances to set a standard of measurement. Second, the actual conduct must be compared to the standard of reasonable care.

The Standard of Care

Deciding whether the duty of reasonable care is breached starts with determining how a reasonable person would act under the circumstances. This duty of care is called the *"reasonable man"* standard because it measures each person's conduct against the hypothetical reasonable man. The reasonable man is prudent in all his activities—he crosses the street at the intersection and on the light, reads every contract before signing, obeys every manufacturer's warning, and never exceeds the safe speed for the road conditions. The reasonable man is always aware of his surroundings and considers all foreseeable risks before acting.

Many negligence tort lawsuits focus on the standard of care. The defendant may concede the existence of a duty and even the injuries suffered by the plaintiff, but still claim the standard of care was not violated. For example, if someone falls on a homeowner's steps, the only argument might be whether the standard of care required the homeowner to perform more maintenance than he did.

Evaluating the Conduct

After the standard of care is established, it is time to evaluate the conduct of the defendant. If the conduct of the defendant shows reasonable care, the defendant has not committed a negligence tort. If the conduct is below the standard of care, the defendant will be responsible for any injuries caused by his actions. As noted, the evaluation of whether the conduct violated the standard of care is often subsumed in the determination of what the standard of care is.

Alert

Causation

A critical element in any negligence tort is causation. There must be a link between the violation of the standard of care and the injury. The law of torts requires that the unreasonable conduct be both the factual cause of the injury and the legal cause of the injury.

In most cases, factual cause is easy to establish. The plaintiff is involved in an auto accident and begins to have neck pain immediately thereafter. There is no prior history of neck pain and the plaintiff's symptoms are consistent with the type of injuries known to occur in auto accidents. The auto accident is the *cause in fact* of the plaintiff's injuries.

In other cases, cause in fact is hotly disputed. In one case, the plaintiff was the passenger in a car that was rear-ended by the defendant. Shortly after the accident, the plaintiff began having shoulder pain. Surgery was performed and the plaintiff's pain went away. She sued the defendant driver, claiming her shoulder was injured in the accident. At trial, the defendant presented evidence that it was physically impossible for the car accident to cause the plaintiff's shoulder condition. The jury found that the car accident was not, in fact, the cause of the shoulder surgery.

In addition to being the cause in fact, the unreasonable act must also be a legal cause of the injury. This requirement, known as *proximate cause*, states that the unreasonable act must be a substantial factor in bringing about the injury. Proximate cause becomes very important when the relationship between the unreasonable act and the injury is remote, calling into question the foreseeability of the injury. Proximate cause is also important when there are many causes of an injury—as when a negligently set campfire combines with a lightning strike to burn a barn.

 Fact

Persons interested in tort reform often decry the proliferation of "junk science." In most cases, this term refers to experts willing to testify to a causal link between the defendant's conduct and an injury that is not a well-accepted scientific fact. Proponents of tort reform call for the legislature to place parameters on allowable types of causation testimony. In fact, however, legal causation is not the same as scientific causation and the limits suggested by tort reformers could operate to exclude many valid claims for damages.

Damages

The final element of every negligence tort is damages. The unreasonable action must result in some injury to the plaintiff. The injury must be one that the law recognizes as compensable. The law allows plaintiffs to be compensated for physical injuries, mental and emotional injures, and monetary injuries as long as those injuries are actually suffered.

Recoverable damages fall into several categories. *Compensatory damages* are those amounts that will reimburse the plaintiff for actual losses. Out-of-pocket compensatory damages are medical expenses, repair costs, and lost wages. If the plaintiff will incur out-of-pocket expenses in the future, these amounts are also available as compensatory damages.

Compensatory damages also include damages for non-out-of-pocket losses. These damages, also called noneconomic damages or pain and suffering damages, are more subjective. They include items like pain, mental anguish, damage to reputation, and loss of companionship. Noneconomic damages often lack an objective dollar value.

Another major category of damages is *punitive damages*. These damages do not compensate the defendant for any injury. Instead, an award of punitive damages is designed to punish the defendant. When the defendant has engaged in a course of conduct that is beyond unreasonable to the point of recklessly disregarding the safety of others, the court may award punitive damages as a warning to deter similar conduct in the future. Most states have very strict requirements for when punitive damages can be awarded. In addition, the United States Supreme Court has also placed certain restrictions on how the amount of punitive damages is computed.

Torts Committed on the Internet

The Internet has changed the way people communicate and conduct day-to-day transactions. It is undeniable that the Internet offers unprecedented speed and flexibility in our dealings with one another. It is also undeniable that the Internet offers the opportunity for mischief.

Many torts that can be committed in person can be committed over the Internet. If I can defame a person in a letter to the newspaper editor, I can also defame that person in an online blog. Intentional infliction of emotional distress is possible over the Internet. In fact, the torts that are called "cybertorts" are merely new ways of committing old torts.

Most of what we call cybertorts are torts that do not involve a physical presence or some type of bodily injury. This is not to say that it is impossible to commit these torts over the Internet. Even trespass to land is possible—access to a neighbor's wireless network might be considered a sufficient invasion for this tort.

The more difficult problem with cybertorts is the involvement of Internet service providers (ISPs). Every Internet communication flows through an ISP, raising the question of what duty an ISP owes to prevent its services from being used for tortuous, or even criminal, purposes. The courts have not yet made much progress on this front, but you can be sure that litigation over the role of the Internet in torts ranging from identity theft to privacy of medical records to ISP responsibility for blog postings is not far off.

Strict Liability

The law of torts is the law of avoidable harm. There are certain activities, however, that carry a risk of harm no matter what precautions are taken. Persons who engage in these activities are held to the highest standard of care that tort law allows—strict liability. The concept of strict liability is that the person who created the risk of harm is responsible for the consequences of that risk. The law does not care if persons engaging in these activities acted intentionally or with reasonable care. Strict liability is liability without regard to fault. Strict liability applies to abnormally dangerous activities, such as keeping wild animals, and a specific kind of circumstance known as *res ipsa loquitor*, which will be described following. Abnormally dangerous activities are those where the risk of harm is high and cannot be eliminated, even with the use of reasonable care. Examples include the use of dynamite or the damming of a stream. If either activity causes harm, the actor will be responsible for damages.

 **Alert**

The keeping of wild animals is similar to the concept of abnormally dangerous activity. The risk that a wild animal will escape and cause harm cannot be eliminated. Since the risk of harm from a wild animal is so great, especially with children, the keeper of the animal is strictly liable for any consequences.

The doctrine of *res ipsa loquitor* is commonly misunderstood. Latin for "the thing speaks for itself," it simply means that some events do not occur without fault. While the *res ipsa* doctrine has been applied to many events, the most common are the presence of foreign objects in sealed food containers. Ordinary care requires that foreign objects like glass and animal matter be kept out of these products. The presence of a foreign object "speaks for itself"—someone must have been negligent. If *res ipsa* applies, the defendant is strictly liable for the harm caused.

Product Liability

Product liability developed as an extension of the law of contracts. Contract law provides that the seller of goods makes certain promises about the quality of the goods. These promises are called warranties. If the product fails to live up to the warranties, the buyer has a remedy against the seller.

The law of warranty works well to protect the buyer of goods. If the product is defective, the buyer can recover for any losses under the contract. This approach presents two problems, however. First, if the defective product was resold, as in a manufacturer to distributor to consumer transaction, the consumer had no right to recover from the manufacturer if the product was not as promised. This impediment is called the requirement of *privity of contract.* Second, if the product caused actual physical injury, even a party in privity of contract with the manufacturer is not allowed to recover for those injuries. This is because contract law only addresses the benefit of the bargain and not damages outside the original agreement between the parties. The development of product liability law addresses both of these issues and allows persons injured by manufactured goods to recover from the manufacturer under theories of negligence, breach of warranty, and strict liability.

Product liability claims based on negligence arise in one of three ways. The manufacturer of the product may fail to use ordinary care in designing the product. This results in a design defect claim that the product could have been made safe by a change in the design. Another negligence claim is the manufacturing defect claim. This claim stems from a safe product design that is improperly manufactured. These claims usually center on quality assurance methods and the selection of component materials. Finally, the manufacturer can be negligent in failing to warn of the hazards involved in the use of the product. The presence of warning labels on a product is an effort to forestall a failure to warn claim.

These same claims can arise as strict liability claims. The premise of a strict liability claim in the product liability area is that the product was unreasonably dangerous when it left the hands of the manufacturer. The dangerous aspect of the product can be the result of a design defect, a manufacturing defect, or a failure to warn of a known hazard in the use of the product. Strict liability claims are a favorite of plaintiffs because they impose liability without regard to fault.

E ssential

The first product liability tort cases were limited by concepts of contract law like privity of contract and limitation of damages. Even today, the law of product liability draws heavily on contract law when addressing claims of disclaimer or limitation of damages. A paralegal working in the product liability field should be familiar with contract law concepts, especially the application of Article 2 of the Uniform Commercial Code.

Product liability claimants can also assert breach of warranty claims. These claims are variations of the contractual claims based on the promises about the quality of the product. Every manufacturer warrants that the product is of merchantable quality. Merchantable quality is not perfect quality, but acceptable quality in the industry. Where the manufacturer or seller has reason to know of the specific use the consumer has in mind for the product, the seller may also warrant that the product is fit for that intended use. A seller who knows that the buyer intends to use an aluminum ladder for use near power lines may be responsible if the ladder causes injury during that use and the seller did not caution the buyer.

The Paralegal's Role in a Tort Case

The proposition that all legal matters are based on facts is especially true in the tort and personal injury field. It is here that the paralegal serves an invaluable function: the gathering, organizing, and summarizing of facts relating to tort claims. Recall, for example, the case of the woman who recovered damages from McDonald's because she was burned by the coffee they served. A paralegal was surely deeply involved in developing these facts:

- The medical evidence about the nature of the burns and the physical restrictions caused by those burns—probably obtained through examination of the medical records and discussions with expert physicians
- The cost of all the medical treatment received by the woman—probably obtained through the examination of medical bills and comparison with the opinions of the physicians about the necessity of the treatment
- Evidence about the procedures used by McDonald's in preparing its coffee, including the considerations in selecting the coffee temperature of 180-190 degrees Fahrenheit—obtained through records from McDonalds, discovery responses, and summarizing statements and depositions from McDonald's employees
- Evidence concerning the relative temperatures of coffee sold by other restaurants in the area (10–30 degrees cooler) and coffee from a home coffee-brewer (40–50 degrees cooler)—obtained from talking to witnesses, examining product information, investigating reports to federal and state agencies, and consulting with experts in the field
- Examination of the financial records of McDonald's to produce evidence of profit margins, cost savings, and coffee sales that would allow the jury to determine an appropriate amount of punitive damages

The involvement of a paralegal in a case such as this is critical. It is likely that the work of one or more paralegals contributed substantially to the verdict of $160,000 in compensatory damages and $2.7 million in punitive damages (later reduced to $480,000 by the trial judge). These paralegals may have also contributed to changes in the way in which coffee is sold in this country.

Chapter 11

Family Law

Family law is a field where the use of paralegals has expanded dramatically. Clients going through divorce feel a need to be connected with their lawyer. Too many busy lawyers were unavailable for their clients who found the divorce process foreign and intimidating. The use of paralegals has helped change those perceptions. Today, most family lawyers rely heavily on their paralegals and consider them an integral part of their legal practice.

Why Family Law?

Not so long ago, the legal practitioners in this field were called divorce lawyers or matrimonial lawyers. This area of the law focused on the marital relationship and little else. Most domestic cases were limited to dividing the marital property, setting spousal maintenance and child support, and deciding custody.

Our view of this area of the law has changed dramatically in the last three or four decades. Now a family law practitioner must be knowledgeable about antenuptial agreements, adoption, shifting responsibility for child support, the best interests of the child, visitation rights of grandparents, the tax consequences of dividing pension rights, and a plethora of state and local statutes governing payment of child support and parental kidnapping, just to name a few. It is little wonder that practitioners in this area now call themselves "family" lawyers.

Marriage

There is a tendency to think of the marital relationship as a private relationship between two individuals. In reality, the state (society) has considerable interest in the marital relationship. Marriage is an essential social unit. It is the primary means of transmitting social values and culture. Perhaps most important from a historical perspective, marriage is a means of transferring wealth.

Because of these strong interests in the marital relationship, society has always regulated the rights, obligations, and entitlement to benefits of those involved in the marital relationship. These regulations govern the entrance into the marital relationship and the exit from that relationship. In the United States, there are two main legal traditions that affect our view of the marital relationship: the common-law tradition and the community property tradition.

The Common-law Tradition

Our concept of marriage stems from the historical development of the Anglo-Saxon common-law tradition. That tradition followed the doctrine of marital unity, which developed to deal with the question of control over property. While single women had certain property rights, the marital relationship subsumed those rights:

- A married woman had no right to own personal property. The husband had absolute right to control any property owned or acquired by the wife at any time in the marital relationship.
- A married woman could not dispose of real property without the consent of the husband.
- A married woman could not enter into a contract.
- A married woman lost testamentary capacity (the ability to make a will), and any wills that preexisted the marriage were automatically revoked at the time of the marriage.
- A married woman was entitled to support from her husband. A married woman could not incur debt; any debts were the responsibility of the husband, including debts incurred before the marriage.

The common-law tradition views marriage in economic terms. Marriage was viewed as a contract—the woman exchanged her property and promise of service to the husband in return for the husband's obligation of support.

The Community-property Tradition

The community-property tradition comes to us from Spain and France. It does not include a merger of identity. Instead, the community property states treated the marriage as a partnership. Unfortunately, the partnership was not one of equals:

- The community-property tradition allowed a woman who possessed property before the marriage to retain title to that property. The husband exercised the right of control over the property, but could not dispose of the property without the consent of the wife.
- Property acquired during the marriage was communal property—both the husband and wife acquired ownership interest in the property. As with other property, the husband retained the right of control over the property.

The community-property tradition also addressed the marital relationship in economic terms. Although the married woman possessed more rights in these states, the balance of the economic power in the marital relationship tilted heavily toward the husband.

Changes in the Economic View of Marriage

In the 1830s, the idea that marriage had a firm economic foundation began to show some cracks. Several states enacted statutes known as Married Woman's Property Acts. Popular in common-law states, these acts allowed married women to hold title to personal property. The right of management and control remained in the hands of the husband.

The most significant changes in our attitudes toward marriage occurred in the 1960s. States began to enact legislation that recognized the rights of married women:

- Women were no longer required to assume the husband's surname after marriage.
- Married women were not required to follow the husband to his choice of domicile.

- Married women gained the right to dispose of their own property without the consent of the husband.
- In 1967, the United States Supreme Court held that marriage is a right guaranteed by the U.S. Constitution, stating that marriage is "fundamental to our very existence and survival."

The shifting attitude toward marriage eroded the idea that contractual obligations were the primary purpose of marriage. Parties to a marriage began to define their own rights and obligations because of their own needs and desires. As the relative economic positions of married couples equalized, the pressure to ease the restrictions on entry and exit from the marital relationship increased. This pressure resulted in no-fault divorce, increased use of antenuptial agreements, an expansion of child support obligations, and a rethinking of custody rights.

Types of Marriage Relationships

Most states divide the marriage relationship into three categories: valid, void (prohibited), and voidable. Other types of marital relationships include common-law marriage and cohabitation relationships.

Valid Marriages

A valid marriage is one that is formed in accordance with the requirements of the statutes that create the marital relationship. Most states impose age and competency requirements.

E ssential

The consequences of which relationship constitutes a valid marriage extends far beyond the mere marital relationship. Whether a marriage is valid can have specific consequences for the availability of employment benefits, tax deductions, property ownership, child custody, rights of inheritance, and the right to make health decisions for a loved one. Many legal practitioners in this field specialize in the preparation of legal documents to assure alternative couples of the "rights" marital couples take for granted.

A majority of states and the federal government state that a marriage must be between a man and a woman. If the parties to the marriage relationship meet these "entrance" requirements, the state allows them to form the marriage contract. Every state has ceremonial requirements for marriage. These include specifications as to who can perform the marriage ceremony and the number of witnesses.

Void Marriages

When the law says that a marriage is void, it means that the marriage never existed. Sometimes legal writers refer to these marriages as void *ab initio* (from the beginning). Void marriages include marriages between persons of the same sex (where prohibited), marriages entered into before the divorce of a prior marriage becomes final, and marriages between persons related to one another in a certain degree of closeness.

Void marriages do not require any decree to dissolve the relationship. If the parties have been living as if they were married, however, a legal proceeding may be necessary to divide property. For example, the parties may need to resolve disputes over title to real property or personal assets.

Voidable Marriages

Voidable marriages are those that have some defect in the essential elements of a valid marriage. Unlike void marriages, however, the defect can be remedied. Voidable marriages include marriages between persons who lack capacity, marriages where the consent to marry is obtained by force or fraud.

Common-law Marriage

Common-law marriage is also called "informal" marriage. This refers to the manner of the creation of the marriage, not the rights conferred on the parties. A common-law marriage can only be created in a state that recognizes it as a valid marriage. In states that recognize common-law marriage, certain conditions must be satisfied. The parties (not of the same sex) must agree to be married, the parties must live together as husband and wife after the agreement, and the parties must represent to others that they are married.

The significant problem created by common-law marriages is how they are treated when the parties move to a state that does not recognize them. Some states refuse enforcement of a common-law marriage from another state. This difference in policy may have a significant effect on the rights of the parties in the event of death or divorce.

 Fact

The institution of marriage is regulated by the individual states. Marriages in one state, however, might violate the public policy of another state. The U.S. Supreme Court has not decided whether the Full Faith and Credit Clause of the Constitution allows individual states to refuse to recognize valid marriages from another state. This uncertainty affects gay marriages, common law marriages, or any marriage where there is a difference in the public policy of the individual states.

Cohabitation Relationships

A cohabitation relationship is not a marriage at all. It is a relationship where one person lives with another in the good faith belief that they are married. Such a person is called a *putative* (assumed) spouse. The status of putative spouse exists until the person obtains knowledge of the fact that no marriage exists. A putative spouse has the rights of a real spouse, including the right of maintenance. This is the basis for claims of palimony when an unmarried couple splits up.

Termination of a Marriage

Knowledge of how a marriage is formed is essential to understanding how a marriage is dissolved. There are two ways for the parties to extricate themselves from the marriage contract: annulment and divorce. Both are legal proceedings and both require an order of the court.

Annulment

An action for annulment is not, strictly speaking, an action for divorce of marriage. When the court order is issued, it will not dissolve an existing marriage. Rather, an order for annulment is a declaration that the marriage never existed.

E ssential

It is a popular misconception that an annulment may not be granted if the marriage has been consummated. In reality, most statutes allow an annulment if the parties do not live together as husband and wife *after* the grounds for the annulment are discovered.

A marriage does not exist if the marriage contract is never formed. Like void marriages, marriages subject to annulment have a defect that can prevent the formation of the marriage contract. Unlike void marriages, the impediment to marriage can be removed. The party seeking the annulment must usually allege that the other party lacked the mental capacity to enter into the marriage contract, lacked the physical capacity to consummate the marriage, or was underage.

Divorce

All fifty states allow no-fault divorce. Under a no-fault divorce, none of the traditional grounds for divorce (adultery, desertion, cruelty, or abuse) apply. There are no defenses to a no-fault divorce. The court is obligated to grant a divorce if it is demonstrated that the parties have irreconcilable differences, have lived separate and apart for a specific period of time, or that the parties are incompatible.

One of the parties must petition for divorce. The petition typically includes the names and addresses of the parties and their children, information about the date and place of the marriage, and the reasons for the divorce. As in other types of litigation, the petition must be served on the other spouse. If an answer to the petition is not filed, the divorce will be automatically granted.

While the divorce petition is pending, the court has the authority to make temporary orders on the issues in the petition. A temporary order can set custody and visitation schedules, payment of maintenance and child support, and other matters. The temporary order is usually in force until a final decree is entered.

Few divorce proceedings go to trial. Both courts and legal practitioners encourage parties to settle through mediation or negotiation. If a settlement is reached, a written agreement is prepared and presented to the court. If there is no settlement, a trial will decide issues of property distribution, child custody, child support, and spousal maintenance.

Child Custody

The issue of child custody is often one of the most difficult issues in a divorce. Child custody is not merely the right to live with the child on a day-to-day basis. It can also include the right to make decisions about the upbringing of a child. Child custody decisions traditionally favored the mother, but that has changed dramatically.

Most states now have child custody statutes that require the court to consider the "best interests of the child." These statutes require the court to consider several factors when making a child custody decision, including:

- The wishes of the child's parent or parents as to custody
- The reasonable preference of the child, if the court deems the child to be of sufficient age to express preference
- The intimacy of the relationship between each parent and the child
- The child's adjustment to home, school, and community
- The length of time the child has lived in a stable, satisfactory environment, and the desirability of maintaining continuity
- The child's cultural background

These statutes divide custody into physical custody and legal custody. *Physical custody* refers to the right to live with the child. The parents may alternate physical custody if the court finds that is in the best interests of the child.

Legal custody is the right to make decisions about the child's upbringing and medical care. Traditionally, legal custody and physical custody go hand in hand. In recent years, however, courts prefer to grant joint custody. Under this arrangement, one parent is awarded physical custody of the child, but the parents share legal custody. Under joint custody, the parent share responsibility for major decisions about the child.

The parent who does not have physical custody is allowed visitation rights. Detailed visitation arrangements are often included in the settlement agreement or included in the court's decree. The timing and conditions of visitation can be some of the most difficult issues to resolve. Many courts refer recalcitrant parents to family mediation to resolve these issues. The court may order supervised visitation if it finds that visitation will endanger the safety of the child. Visitation rights are not contingent on payment of child support.

Child Support

The parent who has physical custody of the child is entitled to assistance with the expenses of raising that child. While financial support was traditionally seen as the father's responsibility, all states now allow the court to require either parent to make child support payments to the custodial parent.

 Alert

More and more states are moving to an income-based model for determining child support. This model takes the entire support the child should expect and divides it among the parents in proportion to their income. The income-based model assures that the parent with the larger income bears a greater share of the support obligation than the parent with a smaller income.

The amount of child support is determined by official guidelines. These guidelines designate a percentage of income as child support based on the number of children being supported and the income of the person paying support. Deviations from the child support guidelines are infrequent and may only be made for good cause. An example of good cause is a child with a medical condition who requires additional support. Because nonpayment of child support is a social problem, many state statutes allow the court to order the employer of the non-custodial parent to automatically withhold the child support obligation.

Alimony/Spousal Maintenance

The obligation to support a spouse can survive the termination of the marriage. A continuing obligation to support a former spouse is called alimony or spousal maintenance. At one time, an award of alimony was a common provision in a divorce decree. The number of alimony awards has decreased as the number of two-earner families has increased.

Alimony is intended to allow the former spouse sufficient time to achieve self-support. When the evidence shows that self-support is unlikely, the court may order permanent maintenance. Such awards are usually reserved for former spouses who are unable to work outside the home.

When the former spouse is able to become self-supporting through further education or training, the court may order temporary alimony. Temporary alimony is rehabilitative in nature. It is designed to allow the former spouse to achieve independence. These awards automatically expire after a specified time.

Distribution of Marital Property

When a marriage is dissolved, the only matter that must be decided, other than the dissolution of the marriage, is the distribution of property. Marriage involves the entanglement of many different property interests. Much of the dissolution proceeding is devoted to deciding how to disentangle those competing property interests.

The power to distribute property in a dissolution proceeding is limited to the distribution of the property of the marriage. Marital property is property acquired by the parties during the marriage. Nonmarital property (not subject to disposition by the court in a dissolution proceeding) includes property owned by either party prior to the marriage or acquired by gift or inheritance.

The states follow two main approaches to the distribution of marital property. The community-property system is followed in ten states. The remainder of the states follow the common-law system of equitable distribution.

 ## Question

If state statutes distinguish between marital and nonmarital property, what is the purpose of a prenuptial agreement?
In most states, the parties are allowed to define "nonmarital property" by a written contract (the prenuptial agreement). The definition of the parties need not be the same as the definition in the statute as long as it is not unconscionable. A prenuptial agreement is often used when the statutory definition of nonmarital property does not meet the needs of the parties.

Common-law Distribution

The common-law distribution of marriage historically assumed that the woman lost all legal identity in the marriage and that all marital property belonged to the husband. Beginning in the 1960s, courts began to turn to an equitable distribution model. This model was a part of the no-fault divorce movement—its primary feature is that marital property accumulates through the efforts of both parties.

Marital property is divided in a way that considers the fairness of the distribution—in terms of the length of the marriage, the earnings of the parties, the physical health and capabilities of the parties, and the respective contributions of each spouse to developing the marital estate.

Community-property Distribution

From the Spanish and French civil law traditions, the community-property distribution model assumes that both parties act for the benefit of the marriage. The contribution of each party is counted whether it is financial or not, and each party is entitled to share in the gains of the marriage.

The presumption of the community-property distribution model is that all marital property is owned in co-ownership without regard to financial contribution. Each party is entitled to half of the marital estate. Because this rule can also result in inequities, most courts began to move away from a strict application of community-property distribution to a more equitable distribution model, based on principles of unfairness.

 Alert

Most people understand the concept of community property in the context of a division of marital property after a divorce. In fact, the concept of community property significantly affects other areas of the law, including the law of ownership and disposition of real property and the law of wills, trusts, and probate. A working knowledge of the legal principles behind family law is useful for a paralegal practicing in either of these legal specialties.

Paternity

Litigation to establish the paternity of children is on the rise. Some recent statistics suggest that more than one-third of all children were born to single women. Once called illegitimate children, these children pose unique legal problems.

Establishment of Paternity

All states have statutes detailing the conditions for establishing the paternity of children. The statutes often designate a presumed father if the woman is married at the time of the birth. This presumption becomes unassailable if the husband acknowledges paternity.

In other cases, paternity can be established by voluntary or involuntary paternity testing. DNA testing is nearly conclusive on the issue of paternity. When the litigants can afford the cost of testing, the test results usually resolve the dispute. If the litigants cannot afford the test, statutes allow the litigants to establish paternity by other means.

Fact

The prevalent use of DNA evidence has alleviated some paternity problems and caused others. Questions of the paternity of adopted children, children born as a result of in vitro fertilization, and children born to surrogate mothers, continue to plague the courts. Many of these cases challenge our traditional views of what it means to be a mother or a father.

Right of Support

A common use of paternity proceedings is to establish the right of support. When the child's mother is receiving financial or medical assistance from the state, a local child collection office may commence paternity proceedings to recover child support contributions from the father. In some states, the putative (suspected) father is entitled to court-appointed counsel in resisting the efforts of the state.

The Role of the Family Law Paralegal

The family law paralegal is involved in every aspect of a family law practice. Paralegals participate in initial client interviews and conduct multiple subsequent interviews with the client. A paralegal may be assigned the responsibility for preparing the petition for divorce and subsequent motions for temporary relief. As the parties engage in settlement negotiations, the paralegal can be involved in drafting discovery requests, collecting and analyzing financial information, and working with valuation experts. At the conclusion of the matter, the paralegal may draft appropriate court orders and arrange for the transfer of assets in accordance with the final decree.

Specific assignments will depend on the individual lawyer and client. The family law paralegal must be prepared to assume significant responsibilities in the family law practice.

Chapter 12

Wills, Trusts, and Probate

A large part of the American legal system is based on the private ownership of property. In medieval times, the death of the owner of property was a signal for any interested person to assert a claim of ownership, however tenuous. This system often degenerated into contests of physical superiority and was eventually replaced with our modern system of wills and probate. This field of the law seeks to ensure that the disposition of property after death is orderly and in accordance with the wishes of the testator.

Probate and Nonprobate Property

An understanding of the wills, trusts, and probate specialty begins with an understanding of property rights. The disposition of property after death is the primary concern of this field of the law. There are two types of property interests: real and personal. The disposition of the decedent's property interests depends on the nature of the ownership interest in the property.

Types of Property

Real property is property that is fixed, immovable, and permanent. It commonly refers to land, but also includes structures (buildings) on the land. Real-property ownership rights are not limited to the surface of the land. The owner of real property owns the area below the ground, as in the case of mineral rights. The owner of real property also owns the space above the ground, as in the case of rights of air space.

Personal property is movable property, or everything that is not real property. Personal property can be tangible or intangible.

- *Tangible property* has a physical existence. Sometimes we determine ownership of personal property by a document of title, as in the case of a car or boat. More often, mere possession is the only evidence of ownership, as in the case of a watch, a computer, or a washing machine.
- *Intangible personal property* does not have physical existence. Sometimes the property has no value in itself but simply represents the right to receive something of value. We usually use documents to establish these kinds of property rights. Common examples of intangible personal property include bank accounts, stocks, bonds, annuities, pension plans, accounts receivable, ownership interests in partnerships, and legal claims against others.

 Fact

All kinds of property—real and personal, tangible and intangible—must be distributed after the death of the owner. The fundamental concept of inheritance law is that all property owned by the decedent must be passed to a subsequent owner. If the decedent does not express intentions about the disposition of property, the law will operate to determine ownership.

Types of Ownership Interests

Knowing what kind of property the client owns—real property, tangible personal property, or intangible personal property—is only part of the will equation. The legal practitioner also needs to know the nature of the client's interest in the property.

Classification of the client's interest in the property as a probate asset or a nonprobate asset affects the disposition of the property after death.

Whether an asset is classified as probate or nonprobate depends on the nature of the decedent's ownership interest. Probate assets include property owned as separate property and property owned as community property. Examples of nonprobate property include property owned in joint tenancy, life estates, and designation interests.

Essential

> A *nonprobate asset* is an ownership interest in property that can automatically pass to another person on the client's death. There is no requirement of a court order transferring the ownership interest. A *probate asset* is an ownership interest that does not automatically pass to another person on the client's death. The transfer of ownership interest requires a court order.

Ownership as Separate Property

When one person possesses the entire ownership interest, he owns the property as separate property. The owner has the right to possess, to occupy, to control, and to manage the property. Because no other person possesses any ownership interest in the property, the disposition of the property requires probate.

A *tenancy in common* is a form of ownership as separate property. This may seem strange, since a tenancy in common requires multiple owners. The logic lies in the nature of the ownership interests. Each of the tenants in common owns an undivided share of the property equal to their ownership interest. This does not mean that we carve the property into pieces. It means that the owner of each undivided share possesses the entire ownership interest in that share. The share is not divided with any other owners. Each tenant in common has a complete right of occupancy but shares the right of management and control with the other tenants in common.

An undivided share is not the same as an equal share. Tenants in common can own undivided shares in any ratio imaginable. Whatever the ratio, the shares are undivided when no other person has an interest in that share.

Community Property

Community property is a form of property ownership. The community property system applies only to property acquired during a marriage. Other forms of ownership are available to unmarried property owners. In general, community property is a probate asset because the community-property system does not provide for rights of survivorship. Some states, however, allow the equivalent of joint tenancy for community property and treat community property as a nonprobate asset.

Joint Tenancy

The form of property ownership known as *joint tenancy* is actually joint tenancy with rights of survivorship, sometimes called JTWROS. Joint tenancy allows multiple owners to have an interest in the property. Each of the owners has a shared right of occupancy, management, and control of the property. Unlike a tenancy in common, JTWROS does not separate the ownership interests. A joint tenancy is created by documents showing the interest. A deed to the real property identifies the ownership as joint tenancy, as will the documents showing ownership of a bank account, mutual fund, or other kind of personal property. The right of survivorship provision of joint tenancy classifies this form of property ownership as nonprobate. When one joint tenant dies, that person's interest automatically transfers to the remaining joint tenants.

Life Estates/Remainder Interests

A life estate is a commonly used estate-planning tool. It divides the ownership interest between the present interest (the life estate) and the future interest (the remainder). Although the life estate can take many forms, the form most frequently encountered is, "To A for life, then to B." Life estates are nonprobate assets. Because the ownership interest transfers automatically after death, there is no need for a court order. The life estate can be an effective estate-planning tool if the estate is small and the real property is the only asset. To avoid disputes, there should also be a small number of heirs. There are tax advantages to using life estates in some circumstances.

Designation Assets

There are certain kinds of property where the client has no possessory interest at all, but only the right to a future benefit. If the benefit is vested (guaranteed), the client also has the right to designate a beneficiary. Common types of designation assets include life insurance policies, qualified benefit plans, IRAs, 401ks, and similar financial devices.

The designation of the beneficiary determines whether the designation asset is a probate or nonprobate asset. The client who specifies her spouse as beneficiary creates a nonprobate asset. If the spouse predeceases the client, however, probate issues arise. Often the secondary beneficiary is the client's estate. Most designation assets are probated if there is no identifiable, living beneficiary.

The Law of Succession

When a decedent does not provide for distribution of probate property by will, it is up to the state to create a property distribution scheme. In most states, intestacy statutes accomplish this—they are the legislature's plan for distributing your property after death.

The term *intestacy* means "without a will." In a very broad sense, a person who dies without a will is intestate. The distribution of the intestate's property depends on the type of ownership. Property held as joint tenants with right of survivorship passes to the joint tenant. Property owned by the intestate alone passes according to the intestacy statutes. Nonprobate assets are transferred according to the type of ownership; probate assets are transferred according to the intestacy statutes. The intestacy statutes govern the distribution of any probate asset that is not effectively disposed of by a will.

The intestacy statutes have another function. Assume the testator prepares a will disposing of certain pieces of property and bequeathing "the rest, remainder, and residue of my estate to my heirs at law." Who are the heirs of the testator? What if the testator leaves his entire estate to his son, but his son predeceases him? How can the court distribute the estate? In both cases, the court can turn to the intestacy statutes. These statutes define who is an heir and provide a clear path of distribution where a designated recipient is no longer alive to receive the gift.

The Uniform Probate Code establishes hierarchy for the distribution of a decedent's property. The hierarchy of distribution is:

1. Nonprobate dispositions of property control whether there is a valid will or not, subject to certain rights of the spouse of the decedent
2. Dispositions of probate property made under a valid will
3. Intestate succession of all other property

A Special Priority Issue: The "Augmented Estate"

Ordinarily, the nonprobate forms of ownership control the distribution of property after death. Some forms of property, however, are considered a part of the probate estate for purposes of determining the extent of spousal rights in the decedent's estate. This grouping of property is known as the *augmented estate*. The augmented estate consists of the probate property of the decedent and certain nonprobate assets defined by the statute.

E ssential

The augmented estate does not supercede the nonprobate distribution of assets—it simply includes the value of certain assets in the calculation of the elective share percentage of the intestate estate. By making the total value of the estate larger, the elective share (usually defined as a percentage of the probate estate) also becomes larger. Thus, the augmented estate prevents one spouse from disinheriting the other by placing all significant assets in non-probate forms of ownership.

The augmented estate is a mechanism for assuring that a fair share of the estate is transferred to the decedent's spouse.

The Uniform Probate Code allows a spouse dissatisfied with the distribution chosen by the decedent to override that distribution. The spouse may substitute an "elective share" of the estate for the distribution chosen by the decedent. The elective share is based on a percentage of the augmented estate, the length of the marriage, and other factors.

The calculation of the precise amount of the elective share is very complex and requires a detailed examination of the property owned by the decedent and the forms of ownership utilized. Often, the task of identifying the property subject to the augmented estate calculations is delegated to the probate paralegal.

Distribution of Intestate Property

Intestacy statutes provide for distribution of property according to the nearness of the relationship to the decedent. Property is distributed to those persons in direct relationship to the decedent by *right of representation.* The right of representation allows the distribution of property among multiple descendants, often of different generations. The allocation of property by right of representation is made by one of three methods:

- If the descendants are *issue* of the decedent (direct lineal descendants), the estate is divided into equal shares at the first generation below the decedent, regardless of whether there is any person alive in that generation.
- After direct lineal descendants of the decedent, the next in line for distribution are the decedent's parents. If they have predeceased the decedent, the right of representation divides the estate into equal shares at the first generation where there are one or more living descendants.
- Where the intestate distribution scheme progresses to the decedent's grandparents, the right of representation varies slightly. Instead of distributing equally at the point where a living descendant is discovered, the entire estate is distributed among the first level containing living descendants.

Problems with Intestate Succession

There are a number of problems with intestacy succession. Aside from the complex distribution schemes caused by augmented estates, exempt property, and rights of representation, the intestacy statutes do not reflect the wishes of the decedent.

The intestacy statutes have no conscience. They do not care where the property came from or if it has sentimental or other value to persons not in the scheme of distribution. The intestacy statutes divide everything equally without regard to any special need of the heirs. No deferred payments are allowed—the child of six receives his share immediately, just as a child of twenty-six. Finally, the intestacy statutes make no provision for special bequests.

Wills

Will preparation focuses on property ownership and its distribution after the death of the owner. The owner of property has the right to control the disposition of property during life; that right extends to directing the disposition of property after death. The property a person owns at the time of death is known as the decedent's estate. Most adults own some property, even those who think they have no need for a will. This is because the kinds of property subject to disposition on death include items most people overlook when cataloging their assets.

When we think of the kinds of property subject to disposition on death, we ordinarily think of real estate interests, tangible personal property (cars, jewelry, furniture, etc.), and cash and cash equivalents (bank accounts, certificates of deposit, money market accounts, and treasury notes). To be sure, after death, transfers commonly include items like these. They are not, however, the only items of property that are distributed on death.

The decedent may control a variety of less well-known property interests. The right to control the payment of life insurance proceeds is a property interest. An investor may hold interests in marketable and nonmarketable securities. The owner of a business should consider the disposition of items such as partnership interests, accounts and notes receivable, and liabilities. An employee receiving certain fringe benefits can determine the disposition of an interest in an employer-funded qualified benefit plan (including the designation of a beneficiary), in a nonqualified deferred compensation plan maintained by the employer, or in death benefit plans maintained by the employer.

Reasons for Preparing a Will

A will is the most flexible of the methods of distribution of property after death. All wills are written, contain a declaration of intent concerning the disposition of property, and provide that the declaration is effective only on death. Wills are written so we will know the intent of the testator (the person giving the directions in the will) after death. Wills make it unnecessary to rely on the memory of someone who might have an interest in the disposition of the property. Because a will is an expression of the testator's intent, a will is ambulatory. That is, a will is an expression of intent that can change. The testator's intent is final only on death.

Wills have several advantages over other methods of transferring ownership interests after death.

- Wills are flexible and allow the unequal distribution of assets.
- A will allows the testator to clearly express intentions about the disposition of assets.
- A will allows the testator to separately consider the needs of beneficiaries, including special circumstances such as deferring payments to minors or the creation of special purpose trusts.
- A will allows the testator to address some sort of situation the legislature did not consider, such as disposition of a unique asset or the requirements of a unique personal situation.
- A will allows the testator to control the choice of persons who will administer the estate, who will distribute the assets for an incapacitated beneficiary, or who will be responsible for the moral and ethical education of the testator's children.

Not everyone who owns property can prepare a will. Every state has statutes that regulate the preparation of wills. In general, these statutes require that the testator have legal capacity and testamentary capacity, that the will be in writing, and that the will be signed and witnessed. Additionally, these statutes specify how the courts interpret a testator's ambiguous expressions of intent.

Letters of Instruction

Letters of instruction are not part of a will. They are usually a separate document detailing the testator's wishes about any number of items; they can address funeral arrangements, organ donation, and other matters. In this sense, letters of instruction are useful and valuable. Every testator should prepare letters of instruction and discuss them with loved ones, spiritual advisors, and others.

E ssential

Letters of instruction should not be used to express instructions about the disposition of property that are inconsistent with the provisions of the will. It is improper, for example, to prepare a will calling for equal distribution of property and attach letters of instruction naming alternate beneficiaries and specifying a different distribution plan. Where letters of instruction are in conflict with the express provisions of a properly drafted will, the probate court may ignore them.

Every testator should understand, however, that there is no way to enforce these letters of instruction after death. Testators who use letters of instruction to dispose of property create problems for the legal professional. As a paralegal, you may be asked to spend time with a client who insists on discussing the letters of instruction. Even though letters of instruction are not enforceable, you should refrain from giving legal advice. Suppose the client wants to leave instructions for the disposition of a family heirloom in the letters of instruction—directing a family member to hold a specific ring until a granddaughter reaches age eighteen. Although the client knows that this wish is unenforceable in this form, a paralegal should not give legal advice about the effect of this instruction. Be aware of the limits of the letters of instruction and make the supervising attorney aware of the client's intent.

Trusts

A trust is a mechanism that allows a person to enjoy the benefits of owning property without being the actual owner of the property. Trusts are often used as estate-planning devices to minimize taxes, to protect property from creditors, or to control the purpose of a gift. Typical recipients of trusts are family members and charitable organizations.

The Basic Structure of a Trust

The creation of a trust involves a severance of two aspects of title to property. While we ordinarily think of ownership as having a single identity, the law recognizes at least two attributes of ownership: the legal title to the property and the beneficial title to the property. The *legal title* is what we mean when we speak of title—it encompasses the right of possession and disposition of the property. The *beneficial title* is the right to the benefits from the use of the property. A person who owns a house might choose to rent it to a college student in return for monthly rental payments. The right to rent the property is the legal title to the property; the right to receive rent is the beneficial title to the property. If the owner chooses to live in the home, he is exercising both legal and beneficial title rights.

A trust divides the legal and beneficial title and places them in the hands of separate persons. The person who owns the property (the *settlor* or grantor), conveys the property to a trustee with the instruction that the trustee use the property for the benefit of the beneficiary of the trust. The trustee holds the legal title to the property—the power to possess and dispose of the property—but that title can only be exercised on behalf of the beneficiary. In the usual case, the settlor specifies the duties of the trustee in making distributions to the beneficiary.

The trust property can be any kind of property. Trusts have been created to manage real property or money. A trust can manage investments or the disposition of personal property. In some cases, trusts are created to manage business interests.

Inter vivos trusts

A trust created while the settlor is still alive is known as a living, or *inter vivos*, trust. Living trusts are created by a trust document signed by the settlor. The trust document is usually accompanied by another document that transfers ownership of the trust property to the trustee; this document can be a deed, a bill of sale, or any other document that transfers title. The trust document must specify the purpose of the trust, the duration of the trust, and include an enumeration of the trustee's duties.

A living trust can be revocable or irrevocable. A revocable trust can be dissolved by the action of the settlor. This power of revocation has specific tax consequences and makes the revocable trust less attractive as an estate-planning tool. It does, however, have other uses.

The settlor cannot dissolve an irrevocable trust. The transfer of the property is final—the trust will last as long as the trust purpose exists. There are specific tax- and estate-planning advantages to an irrevocable living trust and it is a quite commonly used device.

The trustee owes a duty to the beneficiary to properly manage the trust property and to provide periodic reports. Paralegals are often involved in gathering and summarizing the trust records for such reports. In addition, the trust may buy or sell property if permitted by the trust document. A paralegal can be extremely useful in preparing the necessary documents for this kind of transaction.

Testamentary Trusts

A trust created in a will is a testamentary trust. The property owned by the decedent passes to a trustee and is administered for a named beneficiary. These kinds of trusts can be used to establish charitable foundations, to minimize the taxable consequences of probate, or to prevent an irresponsible beneficiary from wasting the inheritance. Most testamentary trusts expire after a certain period. Only charitable trusts are allowed to exist in perpetuity.

Probate

Probate is the process of obtaining an order of the court distributing any assets of the decedent that are not distributed as nonprobate assets. The probate process involves several steps, all of which may be handled in whole or in part by a probate paralegal.

First, the probate process must be commenced. This usually involves identifying the beneficiaries under the will and providing them with notice. A personal representative must be appointed. Creditors of the decedent must be identified.

Second, the property of the decedent must be identified. This is called *marshaling the estate.* Property is located, assigned a value, and prepared for distribution. This is a sometimes easy process— your teal blue Nash Rambler to your favorite nephew—and sometimes difficult. The more orderly the decedent, the more orderly the marshaling of assets. Some decedents, however, fail to share the location of assets with loved ones. Considerable detective work is involved in locating a lost bank account or verifying the disposition of an antique table that some relative thinks is missing.

 Alert

The probate paralegal should insist, to the extent possible, on being the central repository for all receipts, checks, bills, and other income and expenditures of the estate. This relieves the personal representative of the burden of monitoring the day-to-day administration of the estate and provides a central location for all the documents necessary to support a final accounting of the activities of the estate.

Third, the marshaling of assets must include an identification of liabilities as well. The estate must pay the expenses of the decedent's last illness and any unpaid taxes. Property that is subject to mortgages or liens must be identified and steps taken to preserve these assets.

Fourth, after the estate is marshaled, the property must be distributed. If the decedent left a will, it will probably describe who receives what. Problems can arise, however, when specific gifts refer to property that has not been located, property that is subject to a lien, or property that lacks sufficient value to satisfy a monetary bequest. If distribution is allowed, the paralegal will arrange for transfer of the asset and documentation of that transfer.

Fifth, the estate must respond to claims from creditors and other interested persons. Claims against the estate diminish the assets available for final distribution.

Finally, the estate must be closed. Closing an estate requires the permission of the court. Permission is granted based on a final accounting showing the proposed payment to creditors, the proposed distribution of any remaining assets, and the filing of tax returns.

The Role of the Wills, Trusts, and Probate Paralegal

Wills, trusts, and probate are fields of law where the paralegal can have more contact with the client than the lawyer does. These fields involve the collection of information and identification of assets. Strict attention to detail is a must, as is an ability to deal with clients and family members at a most stressful time. Many paralegals who do not like the hurly-burly of a busy litigation or family law practice find their niche in these areas of the law.

Chapter 13

Real Property

Nearly every person in this country has contact with the law of real property. Home ownership is the single biggest legal transaction in the lives of most Americans. Other people rent property and are affected by the rights and responsibilities of landlords and tenants. The law of real property also extends to other areas of the law, and even paralegals working in other areas encounter real-property issues. A basic understanding of real-property principles is essential for all practicing paralegals.

Why Real-property Law?

The use of paralegals in an active real-property legal practice is almost essential. Even the simplest real-property transactions require attention to detail. A paralegal can be involved in every stage of a real-property transaction, from the preparation of the purchase agreement to recording title documents after the closing. A real-property transaction demands accuracy—from the legal description of the property to the allocation of property tax payments, and from the examination to protect against defects in the chain of title to the payment of escrowed funds held by a third party to ensure the performance of some contractual obligation.

The necessary attention to detail also requires a broad knowledge of applicable statutes and regulatory provisions. A single real-property transaction can require consideration of financing issues, pollution control and cleanup laws, zoning issues, and antidiscrimination laws. The impact of these laws can be significant. For example, many pollution cleanup laws require the current owner to bear the brunt of the cost of cleanup. A client who purchases a building that formerly housed a gas station may face thousands of dollars in cleanup costs if the risk of pollution from an underground storage tank is not adequately addressed in the transaction documents.

Each of these aspects of a real-property practice calls out for the use of paralegals. A properly trained paralegal can verify the property description and compare that description against previously recorded instruments when verifying title to the property. A paralegal who understands real-property concepts can review a real estate transaction closing statement and compare the charges reflected on the closing statement with the requirements of the contract to purchase the real estate. Paralegals often perform legal research to identify applicable statutes and regulations that might interfere with the client's use of the property. Real-property paralegals offer the lawyer the advantages of expertise, flexibility, and cost-savings.

Types of Rights

The concept of "real property" refers to land and all things attached to the land. Items that are not land, but are attached or "affixed" to the land are called "fixtures. Common fixtures include buildings, foundations, wells, and the like. Things that are permanently attached to these items are also considered fixtures, so that the permanent plumbing and electrical wiring in a house are considered fixtures. Easily removable items are not considered fixtures.

 Alert

The distinction between fixtures and nonfixtures is often important in residential real estate transactions. If the buyer wants the seller to leave behind a window treatment or an ornamental lighting fixture, it is better to include these items as additional personal property in the purchase agreement than to assume they are included in the sale as fixtures to the property. When in doubt, items that are included or excluded from the sale should be specifically described.

Real-property ownership is actually several different rights. These rights, or incidents of ownership, include the rights of *possession, use, exclusion, benefit,* and *disposition* of the real property. The right of possession is the right to have, hold, and keep the property. The right of use allows the owner to put the property to any desired use. The right of exclusion permits the property owner to prevent others from entering the property. The right of benefit from the property entitles the owner to any profits generated from the use of the property. The right of disposition allows the owner to transfer an interest in the property to others.

Not every form of real-property ownership involves all these rights. The law recognizes several type of ownership of real property based on which real-property rights the owner possesses. The major types of real-property ownership are ownership in fee simple, life estates, concurrent ownership interests, and future interests.

Fee Simple Ownership

Fee simple ownership is the highest form of real-property ownership. The owner of a fee simple interest in real property can exercise all of the incidents of ownership, subject to the regulatory powers of the local, state, and federal governments. An owner of real property in fee simple may develop the land for a strip mall or allow the land to remain in its natural state. The owner of a fee simple interest in land may give or sell a part of the ownership interest to another. The right of possession may be transferred to a renter in exchange for monthly payments. The right to use the property may be transferred by means of an easement that allows a neighbor to use a portion of the land as a driveway. The property can be encumbered, or subjected to the interest of another, if the owner chooses to use the property to secure a mortgage. The owner of a fee simple interest can dispose of the property on death by transferring ownership interest to an heir, devisee, or trustee.

Life Estates

A life estate is an ownership interest that lasts only as long as a designated person is alive. The designated person need not be the owner of the property. An interest in land can be transferred "to Joe for his life." This type of life estate conveys a property interest to Joe that ends when Joe dies. If, however, the transfer is "to Joe for the life of Jim," Jim has no interest in the property. He is simply the "measuring life." The property interest acquired by Joe does not end when Joe dies if his death occurs before the death of Jim. Joe's heirs have a continuing interest in the property that does not terminate until Jim dies.

Even though a life estate is a limited interest in land, the owner may exercise many of the incidents of ownership. A life estate can be transferred or encumbered, or the property can be rented for the length of the life estate. These interests are not as valuable as the interests granted by a person with fee simple interests, but they do have some value. The life estate is sometimes used as a means of avoiding probate—the parent sells the property to an heir, but retains a life estate interest. When the seller dies, the life estate ends and the full ownership interest in the property transfers to the heir.

 Question

Can I use a life estate to prevent the government from taking my house to pay for my medical care?
The answer to this complicated question depends primarily on the nature and timing of the transfer. A transfer for fair market value is less suspect than a gift and the transfer must be made well in advance of the need for medical assistance. In addition, remember that a life estate has some value that may prevent eligibility to some programs.

Concurrent Ownership Interests

A concurrent ownership interest exists when more than one person has an ownership interest in the property. Concurrent owners share the ownership rights in the property. In most cases, the exercise of any of the incidents of ownership requires the consent of all concurrent owners. The primary forms of concurrent ownership are joint tenancy and tenancy in common. The distinction between these forms of concurrent ownership is discussed in Chapter 12.

Future Interests

Future interests in real property are created when the transfer of ownership is conditional or for a limited amount of time. The property interest that arises after the condition or the expiration of time is called the *future interest*. Any person can own a future interest in real property, even the original owner. If the owner of property transfers ownership "to Joe for life," the ownership of the property will return to the original owner when Joe dies. This future interest is known as a *reversionary interest* because ownership reverts to the original owner. If the property is transferred "to Joe for life and then to Carol," there is no interest that returns to the original owner. Joe owns the life estate and Carol owns the rest of the ownership interest in the property. Carol's interest is a remainder interest because it is what remains after Joe's interest.

Future interests are transferable. A person with a future interest cannot interfere with the rights of current ownership. The owner of a future interest does, however, have the right to prevent the owner of a current interest from damaging the land or doing anything that unreasonably affects the future value of the land.

The Residential Real-property Transaction

The residential real-property transaction is the bread and butter of most real-property lawyers. Legal professionals are involved in defining the terms of the transaction, assuring that any contractual conditions are satisfied, examining the title to the property to ensure that the proper ownership interests are transferred, and overseeing the closing. Paralegals are involved in each of these critical stages of a residential real-property transaction.

The Formation of the Sale Agreement

A residential real-property transaction begins with the formation of a contract. The standard elements of contract formation—agreement, consideration, capacity, and legality—apply to a residential real-property sale. In addition, because the contract involves the transfer of an interest in land, the terms of the contract must be in writing.

The residential real-property transaction begins with an offer from the buyer. An offer is more than just a statement of the amount of money the buyer will pay for the property. The offer should also include a description of the property and any conditions that might affect the buyer's willingness to complete the transaction. Common conditions are the ability of the buyer to obtain acceptable financing, the ability of the buyer to sell other property within a specified time, or a requirement that the property pass an independent home inspection.

The buyer usually tenders an earnest money payment. This is the equivalent of a down payment on the buyer's payment obligations under the contract. If the seller accepts the offer, the earnest money serves as security for damages if the buyer breaches the contract.

The Purchase Agreement

The buyer's offer is usually recorded in a purchase agreement. All of the conditions and exceptions proposed by the buyer are listed on the purchase agreement together with the purchase price and a description of the property. In most states, the purchase agreement is on a preprinted form that contains many other provisions. These provisions are often warranties of the purchaser required by statute, or items of standard practice reduced to writing and converted to contractual obligations. For example, a common provision of a preprinted purchase agreement is the requirement that the seller produce evidence of ownership for examination by the buyer.

Title Examination

All residential real-property purchases involve the transfer of title to real property. The title to real property is the evidence of ownership of the property being sold. The document that reflects the transfer of ownership (the deed) is filed with the county office responsible for maintaining the records of real-property transactions, usually called the county recorder. These records are used to verify that the current seller actually possesses a transferable ownership interest. The inspection of these records is known as a *title examination*.

Although title examinations once took place in the county recorder's office, another method of title examination is used today. Today a title examination consists of examining an abstract of the transaction documents recorded with the county recorder. The abstract is prepared by a registered abstractor, who examined the transfer documents related to a specific parcel of property, and provides a summary of the document. Abstracts may be very short if there have been few owners of the property or very long if several people have owned the property.

The examination of the abstract is intended to determine whether there is some reason why that seller cannot transfer a complete interest in the real property. The inability of the seller to provide a complete interest is called a defect in the title. Common defects in the title to real property are failure to remove a lien on the property, unrecorded transfer documents, or a misspelled name on a deed. These errors are easily corrected. Other defects, such as a difference in the property description from one deed to another, are more complicated and often cannot be corrected without great expense.

Alert

Title insurance is not a substitute for a title examination in all cases. Title insurance is designed to ensure that the seller provides marketable title. In many cases, however, there are title problems that do not make the title unmarketable. A prior transfer of mineral interests, for example, would not necessarily make the title unmarketable, but may be significant to the transaction. Lack of access to a parcel of land does not make the title unmarketable, even if the property is unusable.

Because there is no guarantee that a title examination will uncover all defects in title, the buyer of the real property often purchases insurance to protect against a title challenge. Title insurance is issued based on the title examination performed by the buyer's lawyer. The lawyer issues a *title opinion* reporting on the quality of the title disclosed in the title examination. The title insurance company relies on the title opinion and issues an insurance policy agreeing to protect the buyer's interest in a defect-free title.

The Closing

Once the parties have satisfied all of the condition of the real- property purchase agreement, they are ready to complete the transaction.

The final meeting between the buyer and seller is called the closing. The parties come to the closing prepared to sign the documents required to transfer the title to the property and to pay the balance of the purchase price. Because closings require a detailed understanding of the specific documents that must be exchanged and the payment of various expenses and costs, closings are often administered by paralegals.

A residential real-property closing is the formal performance of the obligations of the purchase agreement. Once the parties are satisfied that all the conditions of the purchase agreement are met and that the seller is able to convey good title, the parties can meet and exchange the documents that will complete the transaction.

The first item addressed at the closing is the *closing statement*. This document, usually prepared on a form available from the U.S. Department of Housing and Urban Development (HUD), list all the costs associated with the sale of the property. Closing costs usually include the charges from an appraiser or money paid to a lender. Also included on the HUD form are statements of unpaid taxes and a prorating of utility costs.

Several documents are exchanged at an ordinary closing. The buyer must sign loan documents and a mortgage note suitable for registering the lender's interest in the property. The seller must confirm certain disclosures and sign a deed that transfers ownership to the buyer. A check for the purchase price, less the seller's closing costs and any money owed to a previous lender, is issued to the seller. Many of these documents must be filed with the county recorder's office and this responsibility usually falls to the paralegal.

The Commercial Real-property Transaction

A commercial real-property transaction has the same essential features as a residential real-property transaction. That is, there is a purchase agreement, a title examination, and a closing. The main differences between residential and commercial real-property transactions lie in the title issues and the financing provisions.

Title Issues

Commercial property is subject to a variety of uses. The title examination may involve questions of whether the local authority will permit an intended use of the property. When the approval of local zoning board is required, the parties can make the grant of approval a condition of closing. Similarly, if the proposed development of the property requires approval of an environmental agency or a pollution control agency, the lack of approval may result in the abandonment of the contract.

Issues of title are of more importance in commercial transactions. The commercial property owner must be aware of easements or other restrictions on use that might affect the intended use of the property. When the property has been improved by the prior owner, the question of workman's or artisan's liens on the property must be resolved.

Financing Issues

The development of commercial property often involves sophisticated financing arrangements. Mortgage lenders often impose additional provisions on commercial transactions designed to protect their interests. For example, the mortgage lender may seek protection from losses that might arise from storage of hazardous substances. Many commercial mortgage notes include provisions allowing the lender to require early repayment if the borrower breaches the agreement with the lender. Because homestead property is often exempt from claims of creditors, most lenders require the borrower to waive any claim that the commercial property is protected as homestead property.

 Fact

The complexity of a real estate transaction means that there are a variety of openings for paralegals in the real-property field. Title companies, mortgage companies and banks, title insurance companies, and corporate legal departments all employ paralegals. Each job specializes in a different aspect of the real estate transaction.

Leases

An owner of real property has the right to the benefits from the use of the property. This incident of ownership can be exercised by leasing the property to others in return for payment of rents. In a lease, the owner surrenders the right of possession to a lessee for a specific period of time. Most states require that a lease for a period greater than one year be in writing.

Most leases allow the owner to enter the leased property to make repairs. The lessee, or tenant, assumes certain other responsibilities. In addition to the obligations stated in the lease, all states require the owner to assume other responsibilities, such as providing a livable space and making prompt repairs. State statutes also control the owner's ability to terminate the lease and evict the tenant. Reviewing, interpreting, and enforcing lease obligations is a large part of a paralegal's job when working for a lawyer employed by a local Legal Aid society or a lawyer who represents property owners.

Commercial leases are often more complicated than ordinary residential property leases. These leases might include provisions requiring the lessee to maintain insurance, describing the responsibility for alterations to the property, and governing the ability of the tenant to transfer the interest under the lease by means of a sublease. Paralegals frequently draft or review these provisions for clients concerned about the limitations created in a lease.

The Role of the Real-property Paralegal

In smaller law offices, real-property transactions are likely to be a significant part of the practice. Paralegals also hold positions in corporate legal departments where complex real property transactions are the norm. Other paralegal positions that involve the law of real estate include working for a bank mortgage department or a title company. In each of these positions, the paralegal might be called on to interview a client involved in a real-property transaction, assist in specifying the conditions to be included in a purchase agreement, secure abstracts and examine title, or attend a closing. Many of these tasks are performed with minimal supervision by the supervising lawyer, but are nonetheless critical to a successful real-property transaction.

Contracts and Commercial Transactions

We tend to think of contracts as multipage documents, thickly laced with legal terminology, and containing the dreaded "fine print." While this is true of some contracts, most contracts are simple and ordinary. In fact, simple and ordinary contracts permeate our lives and drive our economy. Nearly every field of law requires an understanding of contracts.

Why Contract Law?

Contract law touches every part of our lives. We enter into written contracts to buy a house or a car. We form contracts of employment, often without any writing. A contract is formed when we purchase a new television or order dinner. Each type of contract imposes different obligations on the parties and provides different benefits. If the contract is broken, the parties may suffer harm.

Paralegals are often involved in contract disputes. From a dispute over a repair bill to a major commercial transaction, lawyers rely on paralegals to assist them in protecting the contractual interests of the client. To be effective, a paralegal must understand the basic principles that apply in this area of the law.

The Formation of a Contract

Every contract involves an exchange of promises. One party agrees to do or not do something in return for the agreement of the other party to do or not do something. When a contract is formed, these promises become legally enforceable obligations. The existence of a contract allows each party to enforce the obligations of the other party.

Not all exchanges of promises are enforceable. We make promises all the time—a promise to meet someone for dinner, or to take out the garbage—that do not create enforceable contracts. A legally enforceable contract must satisfy four requirements. There must be an agreement between the parties, there must be an exchange of consideration, the parties must have the legal capacity to enter into a contract, and the contract must have a legal purpose. If one of these requirements is missing, no contract is formed.

Agreement

The agreement required to form a contract is sometimes called the "meeting of the minds." This means that the parties to the contract must agree on the same thing at the same time. To determine whether the parties have agreed about the same subject matter at the same time, the law divides agreement into offer and acceptance. Both must be present in order to satisfy the requirement of an agreement.

Offer

An offer is a promise of future behavior. An offer can be a promise to do something, as in an offer to pay someone to paint a house. An offer can also be a promise to *not* do something, as when a litigant agrees not to sue in return for a settlement. An offer need not be in any specific form, but it must be intentional, definite, and communicated.

Only intentional offers satisfy the requirement of an agreement. The offer itself must indicate intent to be bound by its terms. A statement that appears to be an offer may not be intentional if it is obviously a joke, or made in anger or excitement. Unintentional offers are usually identified by a great disparity in the terms of the promise. For example, a person who is late for work because her car will not start might exclaim, "For two cents, I'd sell this piece of junk." The offer is not intentional because of the clear disparity in value. Similarly, a friend who makes the admiring comment, "I'd pay a million bucks for a house like that," does not intend to make an offer to buy the house. As a rule, an offer that sounds too good to be true will not satisfy the requirement that the offer be intentional.

To ensure that the parties agree about the same thing, the law requires an offer to be definite. This is also expressed as a requirement that the offer be reasonably certain. This requirement allows the court to determine the terms of the contract and to decide on the remedy for failure to live up to the terms of the contract. An offer to pay you $2,000 to paint a house is a definite offer—the court can tell whether the house is painted and whether the $2,000 was paid. On the other hand, an offer to pay some money if you paint the house is considered indefinite, since the court has no way to tell what amount of money the parties agreed on for the painting of the house. Indefinite offers cannot be the basis of an enforceable contract.

An offer must be communicated to the person entitled to accept the offer. An offer can be communicated in a variety of ways—orally, in writing, by e-mail, or in any other reasonable manner. An offer must be made to a specific person even if that person cannot be identified at the time the offer is made. For example, when I post an offer to pay a reward for a lost object, I promise to pay the reward to whoever returns the object.

Essential

An offer does not last forever. In legal terms, an offer can be terminated for a number of reasons. Acceptance terminates an offer by creating an enforceable contract. For example, an advertisement to sell a car for $1,500 to the first person to accept is terminated when the first person accepts. The second person may not accept the offer even if the terms are agreeable because the offer no longer exists.

An offer can be terminated by rejection of the offer. If the person who receives the offer is not willing to agree to the terms of the offer, the offer is rejected. A rejected offer cannot be revived by a later acceptance; to be considered further, the offer must be revived by the person who originally made the offer.

If the person receiving the offer responds in a way that changes the terms of the offer, the original offer is rejected and the new terms become a counteroffer. For example, if the offer is to sell a car for $1,500 in cash and the person accepting the offer writes a check, the proposed acceptance changes the terms of the offer. The original offer is rejected. Unless the new terms are accepted, no contract is formed.

An offer can be terminated by lapse of time. There is no requirement that an offer remain open indefinitely. Most offers are no longer available for acceptance after a reasonable amount of time has elapsed. What constitutes a reasonable amount of time varies with the nature of the offer. An offer to buy harvested fruit may expire after a few days. An offer to purchase a business may remain open for weeks or months.

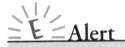

Alert

The requirement of an exact match between the offer and the acceptance is known as the *"mirror image rule."* This rule applies to all parts of the offer. For example, if someone offers to sell you her car for $5000 in cash, your offer of $4800 is not an acceptance because it violates the mirror image rule. It is also a violation of the mirror image rule for you to write a check in acceptance of the offer, because the offer specified cash.

Finally, an offer may be withdrawn. The person making the offer has absolute control over the offer and, in most cases, has the ability to withdraw the offer at any time. This is true even if the offer states that it will remain open for a specific amount of time. Since there is no acceptance that converts the promise to keep the offer open into a legally enforceable obligation, it can be withdrawn. An exception is an option contract, where the parties actually enter into a contract to keep an offer open for a specified time.

Acceptance

The person who receives the offer may create a legally enforceable contract by accepting the offer. The expression of acceptance must be unequivocal. It cannot change the terms of the offer in any way. To satisfy the meeting of the minds requirement, the acceptance must be the "mirror image" of the offer.

An acceptance that changes the terms of the offer is not an acceptance at all—it is a counteroffer. Because a counteroffer changes the terms of the original offer, it is really an offer to form a contract on the new terms.

Like an offer, the acceptance of the offer must be communicated to the person making the offer. Historically, many disputes over contract formation concerned the method and timeliness of acceptance of an offer. Communication of acceptance must be made in a reasonable manner and within a reasonable amount of time.

What is a reasonable manner of communicating acceptance depends on the offer. If the offer specifies a means of acceptance, the acceptance must be communicated in that fashion. Thus, if the offer requires that acceptance be made by singing telegram, the only means of acceptance is by singing telegram. On the other hand, if the offer does not specify, acceptance can be communicated by telegram, by facsimile, by e-mail, or by letter.

One problem created by the requirement of reasonable communication of acceptance is the issue of when acceptance is made. Obviously, acceptance is communicated when it is actually received, but what if the selected means of communication is not instantaneous? When communication by letter was much more common than it is today, the courts created the "mailbox rule": acceptance of an offer was effective at the time of mailing, rather than at the time of actual receipt. This rule has not been extended to other forms of communication.

Consideration

The enforceability of the exchange of promises in a contract comes from the requirement of *consideration*. Both parties to a contract must provide consideration. The consideration provided must have value. Value can be determined by the price of what is exchanged as in the exchange of money for property. A legal right to be able to do something or not do something also has value, however. Thus, an agreement to stop smoking in exchange for an item of sentimental value satisfies the consideration requirement.

Value is only one part of the consideration requirement. In order for consideration to support a legally enforceable contract, it must be bargained for. That is, the offer and acceptance must both be premised on the exchange of the consideration. An agreement to sell a car for $1,500 contemplates the exchange of money for specific property. If the seller also includes a pair of fuzzy dice not mentioned in the offer and acceptance, the exchange of the dice cannot be the consideration supporting the contract.

Essential

> Many supposed contracts fail for lack of consideration. The law of contracts requires consideration from both parties to the contract. The consideration must have legal value, not just value to the parties. An agreement to stop smoking cigarettes has legal value because the activity is legal; an agreement to stop smoking marijuana has no legal value because the activity is prohibited.

Sufficiency and Adequacy of Consideration

The value of consideration is largely in the eye of the beholder. Because the forms of consideration vary so widely, the courts distinguish between consideration that is legally sufficient and consideration that is simply inadequate. All consideration must be legally sufficient, but not all consideration must be adequate.

Legally sufficient consideration has two aspects. It must be *legally detrimental* to the person promising the consideration or it must be *legally beneficial* to the person receiving the consideration. There is no requirement that consideration be both detrimental and beneficial. For example, when a grandfather offers to pay for college if his grandson agrees not to drink alcohol until he is twenty-five, the promise not to drink alcohol is a detriment to the grandson because it is something he is legally entitled to do. The promise does not, however, directly benefit the grandfather. If the same agreement called for the grandson to promise not to smoke marijuana, that promise cannot be legally sufficient consideration because it is not a detriment to promise not to do something that is illegal.

Sometimes legally sufficient consideration is both detrimental and beneficial. A promise to pay money for property is detrimental to the person who must pay and beneficial to the person who receives the money. Most commercial transactions have this characteristic.

The law permits the parties to a contract to make a bad bargain. Parties are not allowed to sue because they agreed to pay too much for something or because they did not realize the value of what they were selling. This rule is based on the assumption that the promises in a contract have the value the parties assign to them. As long as those promises are legally sufficient consideration, the courts are reluctant to second-guess the parties.

Past Consideration

All contractual promises are promises about the future. Since consideration is a necessary part of any promise, the consideration must also take place in the future. An agreement to care for your grandmother in return for her promise to give you her house involves promises of future behavior. When your grandmother promises to give you her house because you have cared for her in the past, however, only one of the promises is in the future. The care you provided your grandmother in the past is not legally sufficient consideration because there is no current detriment associated with past acts. Similarly, the performance of existing obligations cannot serve as consideration.

Capacity

The exchange of promises supporting a legally enforceable contract must take place between persons capable of making those promises. The capacity of the parties to form a contract is the third requirement of a valid contract. In most cases, capacity is not an issue. It can be a very serious issue, however, when one of the contracting parties is a minor, under the influence of drugs or alcohol, or suffering from a mental disability.

The question of capacity is the question of whether the person is able to understand the nature of the obligations required in the contract. Minors are presumed not to understand the nature of contractual obligations and a contract with a minor is generally unenforceable. This is true even if the other party was not aware they were making a contract with a minor.

Similarly, a person under the influence of alcohol or drugs may not appreciate the consequences of a proposed contract. It is not necessary that the contracting party induce the intoxication or even be aware of it. The lack of appreciation of the consequences prevents a "meeting of the minds."

The conditions of minority and intoxication are both temporary. A minor will eventually become an adult and an intoxicated person will eventually become sober. For this reason, contracts with these persons are not automatically void. Rather, they are *voidable*. This means that the person making the contract has a choice about whether to live up to the contractual obligations or not once the issue of capacity is removed. The contract can be disaffirmed (treated as if it never existed), or the contract can be ratified (treated as if the party possessed the capacity to form the original contract).

 Fact

The idea of voidable contracts stems from the fact that lack of capacity may be a temporary condition. Infancy, intoxication, and some types of mental incapacity are not permanent. If every other requirement of contract formation is present, the law allows the incapacitated party to retain the benefit of the bargain if it seems like a good idea after the incapacity is removed. The party who was not under any incapacity is not given the same choice to avoid the consequences of their actions.

Two issues occur when a party to a contract suffers from a mental disability. If the mental disability prevents the person from appreciating the consequences of the agreement, there is no contract because of the disability. This type of contract is voidable; if the mental disability is cured, the party may ratify the contract. If the court has adjudged the person mentally incompetent, however, the issue is more than the existence of a disability. A finding of incompetence permanently removes the contractual capacity of that person. The contract can never be enforceable, and is void for all purposes.

Legality

The enforceable obligations of a contract must be legal. If the obligation is prohibited by a state or federal statute or by public policy, no contract can be formed. Contracts to commit murder, to sell a body organ, or to refuse to employ women, all involve violations of the law. Such contracts are void and unenforceable.

Some statutes define which persons can enter into specific types of contracts. Most states limit the persons who can perform certain occupations through licensing statutes. Lawyers, physicians, and dentists must be licensed to practice their professions, for example. A person not licensed to practice the occupation cannot enter into a contract to provide those professional services. A contract to provide legal services made by a person who is not a lawyer is illegal and not enforceable.

The Enforceability of a Contract

Even contracts that satisfy all the requirements of a valid contract can be unenforceable. Contracts should have the attributes of agreement and exchange of consideration; they must be made between competent parties, and have a legal purpose. Nevertheless, there are circumstances surrounding the formation of the contract that make it unenforceable—among them, mutual mistake of fact, fraud, duress, or undue influence, and the absence of a written document.

Mutual Mistake of Fact

The doctrine of mutual mistake of fact focuses on the requirement that the parties agree about the same thing at the same time. A mistake of fact relates to the subject matter of the contract. The mistake must be mutual (shared by both parties).

Mistakes of value do not affect the enforceability of a contract. Objects ordinarily fluctuate in value. The risk that an object will increase or decrease in value is placed on the parties, and the courts will not consider such disputes. A painting purchased at a garage sale may prove to be Picasso—the change in the value of the painting does not make the contract unenforceable.

Mistakes of fact are verifiable and concern the subject matter of the contract. The description of an object is verifiable—I can tell whether the car I am buying is red or blue. Only mistakes of fact can make a contract unenforceable. It is not a mistake of fact to sell a painting that turns out to be a Picasso because the subject of the contract is the painting, not who painted it.

 **Question**

If the purchaser of a painting at a garage sale knows the painting is a Picasso, is it fraud to fail to disclose this information to the seller?
It is not fraud—the law of contracts does not require either party to disclose everything they know about the subject matter of the contract, except in limited circumstances.

A mistake by only one party is not enough to make a contract unenforceable—each party to a contract has the obligation to verify important facts. If both parties make the same mistake, the contract is unenforceable. If the purchaser of the garage sale painting knows the painting is a Picasso, but the seller does not, there is a unilateral mistake of fact

Fraud

A contract is unenforceable if one party has misrepresented facts about the subject matter of the contract. When the misrepresentation is made with the intention of deceiving the other party about the subject matter of the contract and that party relies on the misrepresentation, the agreement is not a meeting of the minds. Some types of fraudulent misrepresentation are prohibited by statute; others require the complaining party to show falsity, materiality, reliance, and damages.

Duress and Undue Influence

Another issue of meeting of the minds is the question of whether the agreement is the result of duress or undue influence. Both must occur at the time the contract is formed and both address the voluntariness of the agreement.

Duress involves the use of physical threats or intimidation to secure an agreement to enter into a contract. Undue influence is the improper use of position or authority over a person to secure agreement. A person claiming duress or undue influence must show that the pressure prevented the exercise of free will. The lack of actual assent prevents the formation of a legally enforceable contract.

Absence of a Written Document

Certain types of contracts must be in writing to be enforceable. These contracts are ones where enforceability depends on an accurate record of the agreement. Because disputes often arise concerning specific kinds of contracts and because recollections based on self-interest seldom assist in resolving these disputes, most states require five kinds of contracts to be in writing to be enforceable:

- Contracts for the sale of land or fixtures attached to the land
- Contracts where the performance of one or both parties cannot be completed within one year of the time the contract is formed
- Contracts that obligate a party to perform a duty owed by another or to pay a debt owed by another
- Contracts made in consideration of marriage
- Contracts for the sale of goods priced at $500 or more

Under these statutes, an otherwise valid contract may be unenforceable if there is no written evidence of the agreement.

Contracts for the Sale of Goods

All states have special rules governing contracts for the sale of goods. These special rules are found in statutes based on the Uniform Commercial Code (UCC), a model set of statutes created by judges, lawyers, and academics in an effort to standardize the law governing transaction involving the sale of goods. Specifically, Article 2 of the UCC addresses the sale of goods.

It is important to note that the Uniform Commercial Code does not replace the common law of contracts. In fact, it is designed as a supplement to the common law. This approach allows Article 2 to encourage a commercial transaction rather than hinder it. For example, when a merchant orders materials from a supplier, a number of contract terms must be considered: price, delivery, method of shipment, and payment. Under the common law, the failure to address each of these items could result in a finding that no contract existed. Article 2, on the other hand, presumes that the parties wished to make a contract. Instead of searching for technical reasons to void the contract, this article helps the parties by providing gap fillers—terms that apply in the absence of any express agreement by the parties.

Essential

Article 2 is designed to facilitate commerce. The provisions of this article only apply if the parties have not included a specific provision in their agreement. The drafters of Article 2 recognized that the ordinary pace of commerce was not conducive to extensive negotiations on every aspect of a contract for the sale of goods. Article 2 eases this burden because it imposes consistency on the interpretation of contracts with omitted terms.

This approach to contracts for the sale of goods offers great flexibility. The parties can reach an agreement on specific provisions that is different from Article 2 or they can simply let this article control. A forgotten term does not endanger the entire transaction; the parties can look to Article 2 for the missing provisions. In practice, this article governs most commercial transactions.

Warranties

The seller of goods makes certain promises about the goods in every commercial transaction. These promises about the goods are called warranties—guarantees that the goods will live up to certain expectations. Article 2 recognizes three types of warranties—warranties of title, implied warranties, and express warranties.

Warranties of Title

Warranties of title are fundamental to every sales transaction. This warranty stipulates that the seller of the goods has the right to sell the goods. The warranty of title assures the buyer that the seller has legitimate ownership rights in the goods. If the warranty is breached, the seller is responsible for any damages suffered by the buyer.

Implied Warranties

Article 2 recognizes two implied warranties. One, the implied warranty of merchantability, arises in every transaction for the sale of goods. This warranty provides that the goods are "reasonably fit" for the "ordinary purpose" of that kind of goods. This warranty assures the buyer that the goods will meet reasonable expectations of performance.

The implied warranty of fitness for a particular purpose arises when the seller knows that the buyer will use the goods in a specific way. For example, if a consumer is staining a wooden deck and asks the merchant to recommend an appropriate paint, the merchant warrants (promises) that the recommended stain is appropriate for that purpose. If it is not, the merchant will be liable for any damages that result. The implied warranty of fitness can arise any time the merchant is aware of the proposed use of the goods and knows that the goods are not appropriate for that use.

Article 2 permits a seller of goods to disclaim or refuse to acknowledge the implied warranties. Generally, such disclaimers must be made at the time of the sale, must be in writing, and must be unambiguous. The disclaimer does not have to use any specific language—the sale of goods "as is" is sufficient to disclaim all implied warranties.

Article 2 allows the seller to avoid, or disclaim, the effect of most warranties. The drafters of this article believed that any disclaimer must be clear and unambiguous. An Article 2 disclaimer must be communicated at the time of sale and it must refer to the specific warranty that is disclaimed.

Express Warranties

A seller may choose to make express warranties about the goods being sold. An express warranty is a statement of fact about the goods being sold. A common express warranty is that the goods will be free of defects for a specified time. In this kind of express warranty, the seller not only chooses the time, but also controls the available remedy. These express warranties often provide for repair or replacement of the goods, at the seller's option.

Another kind of express warranty can arise when the seller specifically describes the goods or uses a model or sample to sell the goods. When the seller uses a specific description of the goods, there is an express warranty that the goods meet the description. Descriptions of goods are found in advertisements and promotional materials. A model or sample is an express warranty that the goods actually delivered to the consumer will be substantially similar to the model or sample.

Performance of Contract Obligations

A contract imposes obligations on each party to satisfy the conditions of the contract. The duty to fulfill these obligations is called the duty of performance. Generally, the duty of performance is the duty to fulfill each of the conditions of the contract. The failure to fulfill the conditions of the contract is a breach of the contract. When one party breaches a contract, the other party (also known as the nonbreaching party) may be entitled to remedies.

A party usually must perform the duties listed in a contract exactly as they are listed. The performance of these duties is the benefit that the other party bargained for—to provide less than full performance would deprive the other party of the full benefit of the bargain. Nevertheless, the failure to perform all of the obligations of the contract exactly as listed will not prevent the enforcement of the contract. A party who, in good faith, performs the obligations of the contract in a way that provides the other party the essential benefits of the contract, has substantially performed the obligations of the contract. Because the performance is substantial, the contract can be enforced, but because the performance is not exact, the other party may be entitled to damages resulting from the inadequate performance.

Fact

Substantial performance is not always inadequate performance. The term *substantial performance* simply refers to performance that is not exactly the performance called for by the contract. Thus, when a retailer enters into a contract to purchase a dozen four-speed blenders and the supplier ships six-speed blenders, the supplier has substantially performed the contract obligations, but the retailer has not suffered any damages.

Circumstances sometimes prevent a party from performing the obligations of the contract. Weather, natural disasters, wars, or changes in the law can affect the ability of a party to perform contractual obligations. When performance is impossible because of circumstances beyond the control of the parties, the performance is excused under the doctrine of impossibility of performance.

Remedies for Failing to Perform Contract Obligations

The failure to perform the obligations of the contract entitles the nonbreaching party to seek remedies for the breach of contract. Contractual remedies are allowed because the nonbreaching party will not receive the benefit of the bargain.

Damages

The most common form of remedy is damages. Damages are the amount of money necessary to compensate the nonbreaching party for the loss of the bargain. Compensatory damages are awarded for the losses actually sustained because of the breach of contract. If the nonbreaching party must replace defective goods from another source at a higher price, the costs of replacement are compensatory damages.

If the breach of contract results in expenses to the nonbreaching party, the award can include these incidental expenses as well. For example, a contract that calls for the seller to pay the cost of shipping the goods is breached when the seller fails to deliver the goods. The costs of replacing the goods are compensatory damages; if the buyer must pay shipping costs for the new goods, these are incidental damages.

Consequential damages may be awarded when the nonbreaching party suffers damages because of the breach, but it is not directly related to the performance of the contract itself. These are damages that stem from the breach, as when the failure to deliver goods causes the buyer to be unable to fulfill other contractual obligations.

Specific Performance

Specific performance is an order that the breaching party fulfill its obligations under the contract. It is reserved for those cases where other remedies are insufficient. The object of the contract must be unique and not easily replaced, such as a custom-made product or an artistic performance. Specific performance is a commonly requested remedy in disputes involving the sale of real estate.

Other Remedies

Sometimes, the best remedy for a breach of contract is to place the parties in the positions they held before the contract was formed. This involves relieving each of the parties of their obligations under the contract. This remedy is called recission. *Recission* of a contract means that neither party is obligated to perform the obligations of the contract.

If one of the parties has partially performed the obligations of the contract, fairness requires compensation for that part performance. If goods have been shipped, they must be returned or paid for. If money has been paid, it must be repaid. This form of remedy is called *restitution*.

Occasionally the parties will agree that the contract does not actually express the agreement of the parties. Since the parties do not require actual performance of the contractual obligations, the terms of the contract must be changed to accurately reflect the agreement of the parties. The remedy of *reformation* allows the court to alter the contract to impose the true obligations contemplated by the parties.

The Role of the Paralegal in a Contract Case

Contract law spans many specialty areas of law. A paralegal must have a working knowledge of contract law to be effective in the fields of real estate law, family law, corporate law, and many other fields. Paralegals are often called on to review contracts to determine the rights and duties of a client under an existing contract. They may be asked to interview a client or witnesses to ascertain the amount and type of damages resulting from a breach of contract. Antenuptial agreements, real estate purchase agreements, and stock buy-sell agreements are all forms of contract. Litigation over product liability claims requires knowledge of the warranty provisions of Article 2 of the UCC. A paralegal is not truly well educated without a command of the basic principles of contract law.

Chapter 15

Business Organizations

The term business organizations tends to conjure visions of large corporations with multiple locations and hundreds of employees. In fact, the law of business organizations addresses every form of business, from a freelance paralegal with no employees to a multinational business conglomerate. Because the needs and objectives of the business determine which form of business organization is appropriate, all paralegals must be aware of the basic structure of business organizations and the advantages and disadvantages of each.

Why Business Organization Law?

The law of business organizations is more than understanding basic business structure, however. Related legal issues include business regulation issues, required licenses and permits, and filing requirements. Paralegals are often charged with the responsibility for overseeing these aspects of business operation. These activities are premised on a sound grasp of the differences in business organizations.

A business organization is simply the form in which a company chooses to do business. The form of the business affects the exercise of the business owner's rights and privileges as well as defining the business owner's responsibility for debts and obligations. There are three main forms of business organization: sole proprietorships, partnerships, and corporations. The newest form of business organization—the limited liability entity—is simply a variation of the three basic forms of business organization.

Sole Proprietorships

The sole proprietorship is the simplest form of business organization—so simple it seldom requires any forms or agreements. The sole proprietorship is the business organization of choice for most small businesses with few employees. A sole proprietor can, however, operate any kind of business from a hair salon to a home-remodeling business, or from a home-based business to a large, multilocation, multiemployee housing-rental business.

Formation of Sole Proprietorships

Simply beginning to do business forms a sole proprietorship. No government licenses are required unless the business is engaged in an activity regulated by the government, such as selling liquor. In most states, the most onerous requirement for forming a sole proprietorship is the necessity of filing a certificate of assumed name. This filing is necessary if the name of the business does not include the name of the proprietor.

Advantages of a Sole Proprietorship

The simplicity of the sole proprietorship is attractive to many beginning businesses. A lawyer who opens a law practice often begins as a sole proprietorship. The owner of a sole proprietorship is entitled to all the profits of the business. In addition, the owner is free to make any decision concerning the operation of the business, such as the nature of the business, the location of the business, and the type of business. This exclusive control gives the sole proprietor great flexibility in the operation of the business.

 **Alert**

Sole proprietors often work from a home office. The paralegal should be alert to possible liability issues arising from this arrangement, such as when the client plans to receive customers or clients at a home office. Many home insurance policies exclude claims arising from the business activities of the insured. Injuries to business visitors may not be covered by such a policy. The client may need additional insurance for these activities.

Another advantage of a sole proprietorship has to do with the taxation of profits. Because the sole proprietor is an individual, the profits from the business are taxed at the individual rate of income, rather than at the corporate rate, which is often higher. In addition, the sole proprietor may deduct any losses suffered by the business from ordinary income from any source.

Disadvantages of Sole Proprietorships

One of the primary disadvantages of a sole proprietorship is that the owner of the business is personally responsible for the debts and obligations of the business. There is no distinction between the personal assets of the business owner and the assets of the business. If the business encounters financial difficulty, the creditors of the business may seize the personal property of the business owner to satisfy the debt.

This personal responsibility can pose impediments to the expansion of the sole proprietorship. Because all the assets of the sole proprietor are the assets of the business, it can be difficult for the sole proprietor to obtain financing. The sole proprietor is limited to loans, because a capital investor cannot acquire an interest in a sole proprietorship without changing the form of the business organization.

A sole proprietorship does not survive the death of the business owner, and if the business owner wishes to sell or transfer the ownership interest, a new business organization must be created.

Partnerships

A partnership is a business operated by two or more persons. The partners form an agreement to contribute to the operation of the business. The contribution may be in the form of labor, skill, or money. The profits and losses of the business are shared equally among the partners.

Each state has statutes governing the operation of partnerships in that state. These statutes are based on the Uniform Partnership Act (UPA), which has been adopted by all states. The provisions of the UPA will control the operation of the partnership unless the partners agree otherwise.

Partnerships are unique among the business organizations in that a partnership is considered a separate legal entity for some purposes, but not for others. A partnership is a separate legal entity that may sue, be sued, and operate under a name different from that of the partners. The income from the operation of the partnership, however, is not attributable to the partnership entity. Rather, this income is "passed through" to the individual partners for federal income tax purposes.

Formation of Partnerships

The crucial element of a partnership is the agreement to share in the risks and rewards of operating a business. This agreement is a contract, and the common law of contracts requires certain partnership agreement be in writing to be enforceable. For example, partnerships intended to last more than one year or partnerships formed to buy and sell real estate must be in writing to satisfy the statute of frauds. The partners create a written partnership agreement.

Advantages and Disadvantages of Partnerships

The primary advantage of a partnership over a sole proprietorship is the ability to share the responsibility of operating the business. Partners can use the business organization to leverage their investment in the business and to secure investors and financing.

Unfortunately, a partnership does not protect the partners from personal liability. Most financial arrangements require each partner to acknowledge individual responsibility for the obligations of the partnership. This responsibility extends beyond the assets of the partnership to the personal assets of the partner.

 Fact

Partners have specific legal obligations to each other. Each partner owes every other partner a *fiduciary duty*. This means that the actions of each partner in the conduct of the business must be for the benefit of the other partners. A partner who acts solely for his own benefit is not acting in good faith and breaches his fiduciary duty.

Worse, each of the partners is responsible for the obligations of the other partners. This means that a partner who sexually harasses an employee exposes all the members of the partnership to liability for any damages award against that partner. This concept is called *joint and several liability*. The concept of joint and several liability applies even if the partners did not know of, participate in, or authorize the action that created the claim.

E ssential

Joint and several liability makes all partners responsible for the actions of one partner. An injured third party may sue the responsible partner, any of the other partners, or all of the partners because the partners are jointly responsible. Each partner is separately responsible for any verdict because the liability is several, or the individual responsibility of each partner.

Another disadvantage of a partnership is the requirement of equal control. Each partner has an equal say in the operation of the business. In most instances, decisions regarding the partnership can be made by majority vote. Decisions that alter the basic structure of the business, such as a change in the terms of the partnership agreement, require unanimous consent.

Termination of Partnerships

The parties who form a partnership also have the power to terminate the partnership. A partnership can be terminated due to the expiration of the duration of the partnership as specified in the partnership agreement, the withdrawal of one of the partners from the partnership, the death of one of the partners, or when one of the partners becomes unable to perform the duties of the partnership.

As with any contract, the parties may specify the duration of the agreement. A partnership automatically expires when the specified time frame passed. Such a clause also prohibits the partners from exiting the partnership prior to the specified date. A partner who wishes to withdraw early can be required to pay the other partners any losses caused by the early withdrawal.

If allowed by the partnership agreement, any partner may withdraw from a partnership at any time. When withdrawal is not prohibited by the agreement, the withdrawing partner is not responsible for resulting losses.

The death of a partner automatically terminates the partnership. The remaining partners may choose to carry on the business operations of the partnership. If this occurs, a new partnership is formed. The financial insolvency of a partner or any supervening illegality has a similar effect—a new partnership can be formed without the affected partner.

A partnership is terminated if a partner is declared mentally incompetent or is otherwise unable to perform partnership responsibilities. These situations usually involve a judicial declaration of incapacity and a finding that the incapacity is permanent. As with other involuntary terminations of a partnership, the remaining partners can form a new partnership.

The termination of a partnership triggers a "winding-up" period. A terminated partnership continues to exist for a reasonable period to allow the partners to conclude the business of the partnership. The only partnership activities permitted during the winding-up period are the collection and distribution of assets.

Limited Partnerships

The partnerships described to this point are known as general partnerships because each partner shares equally in the risks and rewards of the business. Another form of partnership is the limited partnership. A limited partnership requires an additional type of partner—the limited partner—in addition to one or more general partners. A limited partner has no right to participate in any of the management decisions made by the general partners. In return, the liability of a limited partner is restricted to the amount of capital contributed to the partnership. Limited partnerships are popular forms of investment, because the gain or loss from the business is treated as individual income for federal tax purposes.

A limited partnership requires a written agreement. The agreement must define the purpose of the partnership and identify the specific role of each type of partner. A certificate of partnership must be filed with the secretary of state to create a limited partnership.

Corporations

A corporation is a business organization designed to provide greater protection to its participants than either a sole proprietorship or a partnership. A corporation is a separate legal entity. It can sue and be sued, it can own and sell property, and it is treated as a "person" for most purposes in the law. The owners of a corporation are called shareholders. A corporation may have a single shareholder or many thousands of shareholders. A board of directors, who may or may not be shareholders, conducts the business of the corporation. The officers of the corporation conduct the day-to-day operation of the business of the corporation.

Formation of a Corporation

The laws governing corporations vary from state to state. In each state, filing certain documents with the appropriate state office forms a corporation. Articles of incorporation must be filed in all states. The *articles of incorporation* define the corporation and must list the business purpose of the corporation, the names of the persons forming the corporation (sometimes called the promoters), the number of shares of stock the corporation may issue, the name of the business, and the registered address of the corporation. If the articles of incorporation meet the requirements of the state statute, the state office will issue a *certificate of incorporation*.

Once the certificate of incorporation is issued, the promoters must meet to conduct the initial meeting of the corporation. At this meeting, the promoters elect directors and officers, adopt bylaws that govern the operation of the corporation, and issue stock. The promoters may also approve resolutions allowing the directors and officers to obtain financing for the business, to purchase property, or to conduct other necessary activities.

There are several different kinds of corporations. The type name of corporation indicates its purpose. A *private corporation* is one where the purchase of stock is by invitation only. Private corporations usually have a small number of stockholders and the majority stockholder serves as an officer and director. A *publicly held corporation* is one whose stock is traded on one of the major stock exchanges. A *professional corporation* is one where the only stockholders are persons with professional licenses, such as attorneys, architects, or physicians. A corporation can also be formed as a for-profit corporation expected to generate monetary return for its stockholders or a not-for-profit corporation with no such expectations.

 Fact

The name of a corporation must be reserved, usually with the secretary of state in the state of incorporation. In many states, the selection process is conducted over the Internet. A paralegal attempting to reserve a corporate name should have several alternatives in mind because corporate names are assigned on a first come, first served basis.

Advantages of Corporations

Corporations have several advantages over other forms of business organizations. First, because the corporation is a separate entity, it can attract investors to raise capital. The return on investment might be through issuance of stock to the investor or by an agreement allocating a portion of the corporate profits to the investor. The directors and officers are allowed to enter into such agreements on behalf of the corporation.

The corporate form of business organization offers protection from personal liability for its investors. Directors, officers, and stockholders cannot be held personally responsible for the debts and responsibilities incurred by the corporations. This limited liability encourages investment in the corporation because investors are not required to monitor the activities of the business to protect their personal assets.

Termination of a Corporation

A corporation is said to have a perpetual existence. That is, as long as the corporation has investors and remains financially viable, it can continue doing business forever. The loss of any single director, officer, or stockholder does not require the termination of the corporation.

A corporation may be terminated when the business purpose of the corporation no longer exists or when the corporation is no longer financially viable. A corporation can also be terminated if it fails to comply with the reporting and licensing requirements of the state. In any case, a corporate termination is similar to the termination of a partnership. The corporation must formally dissolve, or cease existence. This step can be taken voluntarily or involuntarily. Once the corporate existence is extinguished, the corporate assets must be gathered and sold. The proceeds of this liquidation process are distributed to satisfy the claims of creditors or to pay stockholders.

Limited Liability Entities

All paralegals should be aware of an additional form of business organization—the limited liability entity. These business organizations are very similar to other forms of business organizations. Limited liability entities are popular because they offer tax advantages and protection from personal liability not offered by the other forms of business organization. Most states now recognize limited liability partnerships and limited liability companies as alternative forms of business organization.

Limited Liability Partnerships

The major advantage of a traditional partnership is the ability to pass through income from the business to the partners so that it is taxed at the lower individual tax rate. This advantage is offset by the nearly unlimited *personal* liability of the general partners. The limited liability partnership allows the advantages of a partnership while limiting the disadvantages.

A limited liability partnership is intended mainly for professionals, who ordinarily do business in partnership arrangements. The limited liability form of partnership allows even the general partners to restrict their responsibility for the acts of the partnership to the amount of their capital investment. In effect, a limited liability partnership allows the partners to take advantage of the taxation allowed by a partnership, but avoids extensive personal liability.

Limited Liability Companies

The limited liability company addresses the primary disadvantage of the corporate form of business organization—taxes. In the corporate form of business organization, the profit of the business is taxed at a corporate rate that is usually higher than the individual tax rate. Once the profits are distributed to the stockholders, they are taxed again, this time at the individual tax rate. This double taxation is the price of limited liability.

The limited liability corporation form of business organization allows the business to "pass through" profits to the business investors, who are called members. The members retain the limited liability aspect of the corporate form of business organization, but avoid double taxation.

The Role of the Business Organizations Paralegal

Paralegals are involved in every aspect of business organizations. A paralegal might interview a new client to obtain information about the best form of business organization for that client. Paralegals are often assigned the responsibility of drafting partnership agreements or articles of incorporation and assuring the proper filing of these documents after approval by the supervising lawyer. As the business operates, a paralegal might be called on to draft changes in the business structure or to review proposed activities of management. Many businesses must comply with governmental regulations governing reporting, licensing, and payment of fees. Assuring compliance with these requirements is often delegated to paralegals. In the case of the termination of a business, the paralegal might be asked to determine the requirements for dissolution and to oversee the liquidation and distribution of assets.

Chapter 16

Investigation

Most discussions of legal investigations place investigation in the context of civil litigation, and especially personal injury litigation. While it is true that civil lawsuits account for the majority of investigations conducted by paralegals, knowledge of sound investigation principles is useful in other specialties as well. Legal professionals practicing in the areas of real estate, probate, debt collection, or family law may be called on to perform a legal investigation at any time.

Why Assign a Paralegal?

Accurate and reliable facts are the foundation of all legal advice. Tracking down the facts relating to a client's legal problem takes time, imagination, and perseverance. The pursuit of these facts often falls to paralegals. Fact investigation by paralegals is more efficient and cost-effective than the same investigation by a lawyer.

The pursuit of facts can lead in many different directions. A witness who is unable to talk on the phone may be located many miles from a legal office, requiring a personal visit for an interview. An important document may be located in storage somewhere in several boxes of irrelevant material. A newly discovered fact may call other facts into question and require a review and reassessment of those facts. The important task of following these paths is ideally suited to the paralegal.

Defining the Goals of the Investigation

It is not enough for the paralegal to simply begin gathering information. To conduct an effective and useful investigation, the paralegal must first establish the goals of the investigation. The goals of the investigation allow the paralegal to design an investigation plan to sort, filter, and evaluate the information received in an investigation. Only that information that is relevant to the client's legal problem is useful.

Establishing the Goals of the Investigation

The broad goal of an investigation is often contained in the assignment itself. The paralegal is told to conduct an investigation into possible intestate heirs in a probate case, to examine financial records for evidence of financial mismanagement in a minority shareholder suit, or to find other instances of product failure in a product liability case. These broad goals of an assignment help establish the parameters of the investigation, but they do not provide much focus to the investigation.

To focus the investigation requires an understanding of the context of the investigation. This requires a thorough review of the file materials and the legal result the client seeks. When setting the goals of the investigation, the paralegal should answer three questions:

1. Why is this information important to the client's case?
2. How will this information be used to advance the client's case?
3. How does this information fit with other information about the client's case?

Knowing these three goals allows the paralegal to develop an efficient and effective investigation plan.

Developing the Investigation Plan

Designing an effective and efficient investigation plan begins with preparing a series of questions that must be answered to achieve the goals of the investigation. A complete set of questions can be prepared by conducting a thorough analysis of the factual information known at the time of the assignment.

First, prepare a list of the elements of the claim, issue, or topic to be investigated. These elements can be located in a complaint, an applicable statute, a form book, or an office checklist. The elements are the minimum amount of information necessary to achieve the goal of the investigation.

Second, review the file to determine the known facts. Many of these facts will fit the elements; some will not. Some facts may even contradict the elements. Make a note of all facts and where they fit.

Third, determine if there is any question about the reliability of any of the known facts. No matter how evident, the reliability of facts should not be taken at face value. If there is a way to verify the reliability of the known facts, that step should be included in the investigation.

Fourth, based on the list of the elements and the known facts, compile a list of facts that you do not know. These facts should be related to an element of the case. Unknown facts that are not related to an element of the case are usually not relevant. At the very least, they are not the primary focus of the investigation.

Essential

A competent investigation requires knowledge of the law of the client's case and the rules of evidence. Never begin an investigation without a thorough understanding of these parts of the investigation.

Fifth, beside each unknown fact make a note of where that information might be found. Do not limit yourself to the most likely place the information will be found, but list as many possible sources of the information as you can think of. Possible sources of information include government agencies, business records, trade associations, and other public sources, as well as witnesses specific to the case.

Finally, determine the best way to obtain the needed facts. There are many choices. Formal discovery procedures may be required if the information is in the hands of the opponent; informal procedures may be appropriate if the information is public or in the hands of an independent witness. The best way of obtaining the information may not be the most convenient way. The approach to investigation must be cost-effective while assuring the reliability of the information.

Fact

The available sources of information vary with the type of case and the type of investigation. If you are stumped about where to locate a particular fact, ask. The supervising attorney, the client, or another paralegal in the office may have a useful suggestion. Do not be afraid to use the experiences of others to plan an effective investigation.

Types of Investigation

Once you have a clear view of the goals of the investigation and an investigation plan, the process of investigation begins. If the best means of obtaining information is through formal discovery, the timing and type of discovery methods used should be discussed with the supervising attorney. If you are pursuing an informal investigation, you may investigate in any one of four ways: through correspondence, by telephone, by computer, or in person. Some investigations require all four methods.

Investigation Through Correspondence

When the purpose of the investigation is to obtain documents, a request by correspondence is often the most efficient means of obtaining documents. In a personal injury case, the plaintiff might supply authorizations for review of medical records. The paralegal might simply send the authorization to the provider with a letter requesting copies of the records by return mail. This method of investigation works well if the documents can be described with particularity and the paralegal knows exactly what documents are available.

A pitfall of using the correspondence method of obtaining information is that the responses tend to be limited to precisely the document asked for.

E Alert

Using correspondence is not the same as using a subpoena. Responses to correspondence are voluntary and the recipient is under no obligation to provide all possible information that meets your description. While a general, all-encompassing description of documents may be useful in a subpoena, more precise descriptions are required in a request by correspondence.

Investigation by Telephone

Telephone investigation can be used to interview a witness from a remote location, to verify the existence of documents, or to locate other investigative resources. Clerks and records managers are often very helpful when contacted by telephone to discuss the identity, location, and accessibility of documentary evidence. These conversations often identify other sources of information—names of witnesses, knowledge of information handling procedures, etc.

A disadvantage to investigation by telephone is that there is no record of the investigation. The paralegal's notes of the conversation are of limited utility if the other party does not acknowledge the conversation. When interviewing a witness it is often useful to write a letter confirming the matters discussed in the telephone call. If the information is important, the paralegal should give thought to arranging a more formal contact with the witness. In all cases, the information obtained in the telephone call should be reduced to writing as soon as possible. The memo of the telephone conversation should include the date and time of the conversation, the subject matter of the conversation, the person contacted, their contact information, and a complete summary of what was said. If possible, the summary should be organized according to the elements of the case.

Investigation by Computer

A large amount of information for investigations is available online. Data compilations are available from sources as diverse as the U.S.

Department of Labor or the National Weather Service. Businesses are required to make online filings with the Securities and Exchange Commission. Many courts now allow online access to public information filed with the court, including birth and marriage records, real estate filings, and court pleadings. Proprietary databases such as Westlaw and Lexis provide gateways to "people finders" as well as access to numerous newspaper archives. If the information is publicly available, it is likely that it is available online.

Documents do not lose evidentiary value just because they are available online. The paralegal should be aware of the requirement for authenticating an online document, however. Much of the required information is not available on a printout or download and the paralegal must take care to record the necessary information before leaving the online site.

Investigation in Person

Investigation may involve an in-person interview or a review of records. An examination of records in person might be needed when the paralegal is not sure what documents are available, or when the documents are voluminous and it is not expected that all the documents will be needed. In-person document reviews are also necessary when the paralegal expects the documents to be difficult to follow or to read.

If the in-person investigation involves the interview of a witness, the paralegal should prepare for the interview in the manner described in Chapter 17. Special consideration should be given to the timing of the interview in the context of the investigation. If the witness can only be interviewed once, the paralegal may wish to wait until more information is available.

Investigation Resources

The investigation resources available to the thorough paralegal are practically limitless. The law firm will usually have a list of commonly used resources. The client may offer other potential resources. Expert witnesses are often aware of specialized information not available to the public. The paralegal should rely on all these resources. In addition, the paralegal should compile a personal list of available investigation resources. This list should include sources of information that the paralegal will use in a current investigation or that might be useful in a future investigation. The list of investigation resources maintained by the paralegal should include names and telephone numbers for persons who are regularly contacted in the course of an investigation, such as court clerks, medical records librarians, and motor vehicle records clerks.

 Fact

There are many lists of available resources. Most jurisdictions have a list of court and government personnel and a description of their responsibilities. Trade association Web sites have links to other sites with additional information. Legal publications often include articles on how to locate specific facts. Each of these resources should be marked or copied for easy retrieval.

There are investigative resources as well. A police report may contain a reference to photographs; the statement of an eyewitness might refer to an uninterviewed witness; surveillance of the scene could lead to specific questions for witnesses or parties. The paralegal must use some imagination to determine where useful information can be located.

Important Investigative Qualities

Investigation is not a science. A paralegal can use checklists and techniques to maximize the chances of conducting a complete investigation, but those checklists and techniques do not guarantee success. A successful investigation requires creativity, adaptability, and persistence.

Creativity

The pursuit of facts is not a rote exercise. Facts are found in unlikely places and the investigative paralegal must be willing to pursue the facts wherever they may be found. Reliance on standard techniques is the sign of a poor investigation. The paralegal must be open to possibilities of the investigation. All leads should be pursued. This will likely lead to some dead ends, but many of those can be eliminated with experience. The important factor is to not overlook a possible fact simply because it is unorthodox.

Adaptability

No two investigations are the same. What worked for the last investigation may not work for this investigation. The investigative paralegal must be able to adjust to the circumstances of the case to obtain the desired result. A contact who is usually cooperative may be uncooperative for some reason. An investigative paralegal who is adaptable can alter the investigative approach and still obtain the desired result.

Persistence

Facts do not come to investigators. In some cases, the necessary facts are obvious, but in other cases, more "digging" is required. Investigations can encounter many difficulties. Witnesses are uncooperative, documents are lost or destroyed, or the information may not fit with the goal of the investigation. These problems must not stop the investigative paralegal. The paralegal should not stop until all the possibilities have been exhausted.

Communicating Your Results

At various points in the investigation, the paralegal should report on the results. Although the investigation is on behalf of a client, the paralegal should resist the urge to couch the investigative report in terms favorable to the client. The investigative report should be accurate and complete. It should contain all the necessary information to resolve questions of verifiability or authenticity. The investigative report should address the subject of the investigation clearly and succinctly.

Alert

Any written report of an investigation done at the request of the supervising attorney is protected from disclosure to the opposing parties. In addition, the information you obtain in the course of an investigation is confidential information related to the representation of a client. The results of your investigation are protected by the ethical duty of confidentiality and should not be discussed outside the law firm.

A good investigative report addresses four questions. The answers to these questions determine whether the investigative paralegal has reached the goal of the investigation:

- What facts do I know as a result of this investigation?
- What gaps still exist in my knowledge of the facts?
- What additional investigation is called for and why?
- What is the effect of this information on the client's case?

Chapter 17

Interviewing

One of the most important aspects of being a paralegal is an ability to interview. Interviewing clients and witnesses is the primary means of obtaining information about a legal matter. While documents and physical exhibits may tell part of the story, the context is supplied by human observations and recollections. Paralegals are invaluable partners in the development of this kind of information.

Why Assign a Paralegal?

The process of developing the facts of a legal matter is a painstaking process. It requires persistence, patience, attention to detail, and legal analysis. The law responds to facts—the facts tell us what legal principles apply and how those legal principles apply. It is necessary to know as many facts about a particular legal matter as possible in order to provide the most complete legal analysis.

The central importance of facts places a premium on fact gathering. Paralegals are excellent fact gatherers. A properly trained paralegal can identify legally relevant facts and determine what follow-up facts are needed. In addition, paralegals understand how to arrange facts in relation to applicable legal theories and report those facts in a precise and comprehensive fashion. Many lawyers take advantage of these capabilities by using paralegals to perform nearly all fact-gathering interviews.

Fact-gathering interviews differ from initial client interviews. A fact-gathering interview assumes that the client's legal problem has been identified and that there is a need for additional facts to complete the analysis of that legal problem. Fact-gathering interviews are usually more focused than initial client interviews.

Types of Interviews

There are two sources of facts about a legal matter: the client and persons other than the client. In most cases, the primary source of facts in a legal matter is the client. Factual information about a client's case is obtained in an initial client interview. When additional information is required, a subsequent, fact-gathering interview may be conducted.

When the case requires information from someone other than the client, the paralegal may conduct a fact-gathering interview. There are two main types of fact-gathering interviews. In some cases, you may need to interview someone other than the client—a witness to an accident, the recipient of a contract offer, or a family member with knowledge about a custody dispute. These witnesses are known as lay witnesses. In most cases, lay witnesses may not state opinions; they may only report facts.

Other cases involve witnesses with specific expertise in a particular field. Expert witnesses are allowed to offer opinions based on specific facts. They may have opinions about the value of a piece of property, the business interruption damages suffered after a fire, or the effects of exposure to a certain chemical. Interviews with expert witnesses usually involve a combination of facts and opinions.

The Initial Client Interview

The initial client interview is the easiest and yet the most difficult interview to conduct. It is easy because the client wants to talk to you and knows that you are ready to help with whatever legal problem is involved. It is difficult because clients often think the paralegal needs to know everything they know and provide too much information or the wrong kind of information. The client interview is also an important part of establishing or maintaining a good client relationship.

The supervising lawyer usually conducts the initial client interview; only the most experienced paralegals are able to conduct an effective initial client interview. The initial client interview is where the lawyer obtains information about the legal problem of the client. The lawyer uses this information to evaluate the courses of action open to the client and to decide whether to agree to represent the client. A paralegal attending an initial client interview is often asked to take notes, make copies of documents, and provide the client with any materials the law firm usually distributes to new clients.

Although the paralegal does not have an active role in the initial client interview, attendance at the initial interview allows the paralegal to observe the questioning by the lawyer. This provides information about what facts the lawyer thinks are important and can be useful in guiding subsequent fact-gathering interviews. In addition, clients usually provide background information at the initial interview. This background information can be a valuable tool in planning a later investigation.

The Fact-gathering Interview

The fact-gathering interview is simply the first discussion with the lay witness, or expert. A fact-gathering interview is the first time you are obtaining information about the case from this person. This interview might be your first contact with the facts of the legal matter. A fact-gathering interview might also be conducted after you have acquired significant information about the legal matter, as when you interview an expert witness for the first time.

There is no set format for a fact-gathering interview. Your specific approach to a fact-gathering interview will depend on a variety of things, including whom you are interviewing, your knowledge of the legal matter, and your own personal preferences. Every interviewer has a unique method of conducting an effective fact-gathering interview. Your preparation for the interview should include consideration of these factors.

The questions asked in a fact-gathering interview have two basic characteristics. First, the questions encourage the interviewee to state the facts without regard to the legal effect of those facts. Second, the questions should revolve around an orderly structure based on the legal effect of those facts. While these characteristics might seem to be at odds, they really are not.

Essential

There is a tendency to assume the witness has the same knowledge base and perspective you have. Resist this temptation; ask the witness to explain things even if you think you know the answer, and do not assume that the witness is aware of a fact. Above all, do not worry if the witness states facts at odds with your understanding. There will be plenty of time to address discrepancies later in the case.

Eliciting Facts Without Regard for their Legal Effect

A great majority of your fact-gathering interviews will be of persons with no legal training. These persons possess facts, but do not have the knowledge or training to determine the legal consequences of those facts. It is your job to gather all the facts from this person. This is accomplished by a combination of questions—some open-ended and some closed-ended.

An open-ended question is a question that encourages the interviewee to provide facts. Open-ended questions are unstructured and do not suggest that the questioner is interested in any facts. For example, you may be asked to conduct a fact-gathering interview of a witness to a car accident. You may start the interview with the question, "What did you see?" This is an open-ended question because it does not suggest any significance to anything the interviewee chooses to report.

One disadvantage of an open-ended question is obvious: the interviewee may provide inadequate or irrelevant information. The person may say, "I saw the one car hit the other car," or "I saw a deer run across the road." The first answer is relevant but not specific. The second answer does not appear to be relevant.

Another disadvantage is that responses to open-ended questions tend to combine facts with conclusions or commentary. A client who is asked to describe the circumstances of her firing might say, "They fired me because I am gay." This statement is a conclusion masquerading as a fact. The interviewer really wants to know why the client reached that conclusion.

Alert

Everyday conversations offer a number of options to practice interviewing using open- and closed-ended questions—when asking a child about a school day, when discussing plans for the weekend with a coworker, or when receiving an oral assignment from a supervising lawyer. Use interviewing techniques to obtain the most information possible in each of these situations.

Fortunately, these typical responses to open-ended questions are not fatal to the fact-gathering process. In fact, they actually provide natural bridges to narrower questions that allow the interviewer to develop the facts more completely. For example, in the case of the person who says, "I saw the one car hit the other car," the interviewer might ask, "Did the blue car hit the green car?" Further follow-up questions might include asking where in the roadway the car was struck, which parts of the cars made contact, and what observations were made about the damages to the vehicles.

This type of question is called a closed-end question. Closed-end questions do not allow a meandering response. They focus on facts and allow the interviewer to exert more control over the direction of the interview.

Most initial interviews follow this pattern. The interviewer asks a series of open-ended questions that provide an overview of the facts. The interviewer then asks closed-ended questions that fill the gaps in the previous answers. This move from general to specific is the hallmark of an effective fact-gathering interview. If the interviewer only asks open-ended questions, the responses may be of little value. On the other hand, an interviewer who asks only closed-ended questions may omit critical areas of questioning.

Questioning Within an Orderly Structure

A good interviewer always has an outcome in mind before beginning an interview. This does not mean that the interviewer decides what the response to the question will be. It does mean that the interviewer decides what questions need to be answered. In other words, the interviewer should have a clear idea of what information is needed. In the legal field, the required information is legally relevant facts.

The search for legally relevant facts does not mean that you must exhaustively research every issue before beginning a fact-gathering interview. In most cases, this is not feasible because of time constraints or because you do not know enough about the matter to perform the research. Even if you don't know the specifics of the legal issue, however, you can still make sure the interview has an orderly structure based on the legal effect of the facts.

Each fact-gathering interview has a broad legal purpose. You interview the client to determine if there are sufficient facts to support a claim of defamation. You interview a witness to see if that witness will support your client's version that the other driver ran the red light. You speak to an expert because the cause of the fire determines whether there is insurance coverage. In each case, there is a broad legal context; there are words and concepts that have *legal meaning*.

The orderly structure of the fact-gathering interview is defined by this legal meaning. When a client complains of defamation, your legal training should help you frame the structure of the interview. What was said? To whom was it said? Where was the statement made? When was it made? Was the statement false? This kind of legal analysis must be second nature to the effective interviewer. In addition to gathering the facts, the interviewer must think about what the facts mean in the context of the legal matter at hand.

Assessing Credibility

The facts elicited from the witness should be credible. Credibility in the legal context is often a matter of evidence. The rules of evidence allow the credibility of a witness to be challenged on the grounds of prior criminal convictions or showing a reputation for untruthfulness. The paralegal should carefully explore these issues with the witness.

Of course, a credible witness is also a believable witness. The paralegal must constantly weigh the information from the witness against the known information in the file. If the facts given by the witness are not consistent with the known facts, it is necessary to examine the facts more closely.

 **Alert**

Never give a witness the impression that you do not believe him. You may question a witness closely about the facts. You may ask the witness to repeat an explanation or version of events. Always ask these questions respectfully and without any indication that you believe or disbelieve the witnesses' statements. A witness who thinks you doubt his veracity is very dangerous to the client's case. He may hold back crucial information or he may simply change his story at an inconvenient time.

Assessing the Witness' Knowledge of the Facts

Closely related to credibility is the question of whether the witness actually knows the facts. Many witnesses think they know something they do not. A classic example is the supposed eyewitness to a crime who turns out to need glasses. Witnesses who are distracted or predisposed to a particular conclusion may not possess adequate knowledge of the facts. These deficiencies must be discovered in the interview. Careful questioning of a witness should explore what the witness knows and how the witness knows it.

Defining the Goals of the Interview

All interviews have goals. The fact-gathering interview may only elicit general facts. Legal analysis and application of law to facts will come later. A follow-up interview, on the other hand, may be devoted solely to the application of law to facts. Determining the goal of the interview is a critical component of conducting an effective interview.

The first step in defining the goal of any interview is to carefully review the assignment. If the assignment is to "interview Mrs. Smith and get the necessary information so we can start her divorce," you will approach the interview in a different way than if the assignment is to "get the necessary information from Mrs. Smith so we can prepare her will." The former is much more definite and focused; the latter is open and undefined.

Whether the assignment is focused or open, the interview has a goal. Each assignment describes the desired end. Each assignment provides the legal context so the paralegal can approach the interview with an overall structure in mind.

Some assignments lack a clear statement of goal, as when the supervising attorney says, "Go talk to John Jones and find out what he knows about the client's accident." If you receive this kind of an assignment, you should request additional information. Who is John Jones? Why do we think he knows anything about the accident? Do we think he will help the client or hurt the client? What is the critical information we think John Jones has? The answers to these questions will help define the goal of the initial interview with John Jones.

The task of defining the goals of an interview is often daunting to a new paralegal. Inexperience leads to a fear of forgetting a crucial area of questioning. A possible solution is for the paralegal to use a checklist.

A checklist is an outline of the major issues in a particular area of the law.

Some law firms maintain checklists for recurring issues such as initial interviews of clients or specific issues requiring detailed information. Checklists are also available from several commercial sources. In either case, a checklist is designed as an aid to a full and complete interview process.

A checklist is only a guide. It would be a mistake for a paralegal to assume that obtaining responses to questions on a checklist constitutes an effective interview. A checklist is, by its very nature, generic. It may include questions that are irrelevant to the specific issue at hand and may omit other important information. The paralegal must be flexible and alert when using a checklist.

E ssential

Conversations with witnesses rarely follow a prescribed format. If you try to force a witness to provide facts in the order called for in a checklist, you will quickly frustrate the witness and cut off the natural flow of information. A good interviewer knows when to abandon the checklist in the interest of obtaining as much information as possible.

Always remember that all legal problems depend on facts. When in doubt, opt for gathering more facts rather than less.

Preparing for the Interview

Whether the interview is a fact-gathering interview or a follow-up interview, good preparation is the key to a successful outcome. Preparation is more than just defining the goals of the interview. Good preparation also involves considerations of knowledge of the information in the file, the physical setting of the interview, the appearance of the interviewer, and the tone of the interview.

Knowledge of the File

Be sure to know the file before conducting an interview. Unless you are conducting an initial client interview, it is likely that there is information in the file. There may be correspondence with a witness, a statement on a police report, or a document signed by the witness. Be familiar with this information—no one likes to answer repetitive questions.

The Physical Setting

Where you conduct an interview is almost as important as how the interview is conducted. We have been speaking about interviews as if they were all conducted in a lawyer's office. In fact, a busy paralegal must be prepared to conduct interviews at the client's place of business, in the client's home, on the street, in a courthouse hallway, or at the local diner. An interview takes place whenever the paralegal talks to someone who possesses knowledge about a legal matter.

No matter where the interview takes place, you should pay attention to certain things. First, minimize interruptions. This is more easily accomplished in your own office—close your door, send phone calls to voice mail, put your computer to sleep, and clear the space of any material not related to the matter at hand. Whether the interviewee is a client or a witness, their time is important. Do not allow distractions to intrude on the interview process if you can help it.

Minimizing interruptions is more difficult in other physical settings. If you are in the client's place of business and the client interrupts the interview, there is little you can do. Remain calm and professional. Remember where you were when the interruption occurred. Start at that point when the interruption is over. Do not give any sign that the interruption affected your train of thought in any way.

Second, consider the seating arrangements. The goal here is to be efficient while, at the same time, putting the interviewee at ease. Many interviewers simply place the interviewee on the opposite side of the table and begin asking questions. They do not realize that this arrangement seems very much like an interrogation to the interviewee. This is especially true if the interviewer is referring to notes or documents. Many successful interviews are conducted in this manner, but this technique is not appropriate for all situations.

Another technique is to forego the use of a table or desk and sit in a more conversational arrangement. This more relaxed approach can make the interviewee more comfortable and willing to talk. It is difficult to take or use notes when using this technique. For that reason, this technique is not well suited to lengthy interviews that cover a variety of topics.

A side-by-side arrangement is helpful if the interview will call for review of documents or exhibits. The questioner and the interviewee are both able to see the document without straining. Documents can be easily passed back and forth. This technique also provides space if it is necessary to spread out a series of exhibits.

Fact

Witnesses who allow constant interruptions when talking to their legal representative sometimes do so because they do not realize the importance of the information you are seeking. You can forestall this reaction by starting the interview with an explanation of the purpose of the interview, a general description of what you hope to discover, and why the witness is the appropriate person to provide the needed information.

Finally, consider issues of personal space. Some people require more space and find closeness intimidating. The appropriate amount of personal space varies with the circumstances. A discussion about a claimed breach of contract will not elicit a need for physical closeness. Physical distance during an interview with a battered spouse may, however, convey lack of empathy.

The Tone of the Interview

As important as the physical setting, the tone of the interview may vary with the purpose of the interview or the subject of the interview. The tone may even change during the course of an interview. In all cases, however, the paralegal should take the lead in setting the tone.

The vast majority of paralegal interviews are conducted to obtain information. This process is much easier if a friendly tone is established. The paralegal must be able to put the interviewee at ease before beginning questioning. This can be done in a variety of ways. Since most interviewees are nervous about meeting with a paralegal, an explanation of the purpose of the interview and how the information from the interview will be used is helpful. Allowing the interviewee to ask questions about the process before beginning the interview also relaxes the interviewee.

Always remember that the interviewee is doing you a favor. This is true whether the interviewee is a client, an employee of a client, or a witness. The interviewee does not have to talk to you. Acknowledge that by thanking the interviewee for their time. Promise to be expeditious in completing the interview. Be certain you know if there are any limitations on the availability of the interviewee and respect them.

Interviewing Experts

Many legal matters require the assistance of witnesses with specific expertise. Personal injury cases require information from doctors, a real estate valuation matter might require information from an appraiser, and a complex divorce might benefit from the assistance of an accountant. These witnesses with specific expertise are called expert witnesses. They are ordinarily hired on behalf of the client to provide information about the legal matter. Paralegals are often assigned the task of locating and hiring specific experts.

The initial interview with an expert is essentially a job interview. The paralegal should be trying to make a determination about whether this expert is right for this case. Although the selection of the expert is predetermined in many cases, the paralegal should still be on alert for signs that another expert should be considered.

Subsequent discussions with an expert usually involve exploring the factual underpinning for the expert's opinion. When an expert offers the opinion that an apartment fire was the result of arson, it is critical to understand the facts that support that opinion. Experts often make assumptions about the facts to reach their opinions. These assumptions must be examined as well to determine if they are justified and are consistent with other known facts. Effective interviewing of expert witnesses demands attention to detail.

Communicating Your Results

The end of the interview does not mark the end of the interview task. The information gleaned in the interview must be communicated to the supervising lawyer and to the client. An oral report about the interview is an effective method of passing along information, but it does not create a record in the file. To properly document the results of the interview requires an interview memorandum. The interview memorandum should have at least three parts: a description of the interview assignment, a description of the results of the interview, and suggestions for follow-up.

Description of the Interview Assignment

Always repeat the interview assignment at the beginning of the interview memorandum. When you begin working on multiple legal matters over several months and years, you will appreciate the need for a slight memory jog about why the information from this witness was important. This information also serves as a form of communication with the client; if the memorandum is sent to the client, the description of the assignment operates as an explanation of why the interview was necessary. Finally, including a description of the assignment helps direct your summary to address the important facts first.

Immediately after the description of the interview assignment comes the contact information for the witness. If it is necessary to locate the witness in the future, a quick look at the interview memorandum will provide the required information. Of course, the same information should be elsewhere in the file as well.

Description of the Interview Results

The results of the interview must be accurately reported. The extent of the reporting requires the exercise of judgment, but when in doubt you should err on the side of including more information. To be useful, the information must be properly organized. Your description of the interview assignment is a good starting point for organizing this portion of the memorandum.

Always begin your memorandum with a summary of the information initially sought. If more than one topic or issue was discussed, your memorandum should discuss each one separately.

After addressing these important facts, you may address any additional facts that came to light. It is not uncommon for witness interviews to reveal facts that were previously unknown. Part of your job is to recognize the significance of those facts and call them to the attention of the supervising lawyer. If the interview produced new documents, attach them to your memorandum or describe where they are filed.

Include your impressions about the witness. All witnesses are different. Some witnesses are tentative; others are too confident. How the witness acted is almost as important as what the witness said in evaluating the reliability of the information. Your observations can be an important factor in how a lawyer treats the information received from a witness.

 Fact

Suggestions for follow-up should be a part of your response to every assignment. There is always more to do. In the typical law office, assignments go to people willing to do them. If you express an interest in continuing to work on a client matter, you are at the top of the list for the next assignment. Even if your suggestions are not followed, the explanation about why they were not followed is an excellent learning opportunity.

Suggestions for Follow-up

The end of a witness interview should never be the end of the inquiry into the facts. There are always more questions and other things to do. As the interviewer, you should have some idea about what the next step should be. Make that suggestion—interview another witness, request additional documents, or perform legal research—to demonstrate that you are interested, concerned, and committed to using your legal skills for the benefit of the client.

Chapter 18

Legal Research

The law is tremendously broad in scope, and nearly every case requires some legal research. Legal research is the process of determining the law that applies to a specific legal question. For every legal problem, the paralegal must be able to locate the current law, verify that the law is applicable to the client's case, and analyze the effect of the law on the client's case. This process is known as legal research.

Why Assign a Paralegal?

There is a very definite split of opinion among lawyers about the use of paralegals for legal research. Some lawyers believe that legal research should only be done by lawyers. Others recognize that a properly trained paralegal can be of great assistance in performing routine legal research tasks and in performing preliminary legal research on more complex tasks. No matter which kind of lawyer you work for, the ability to do legal research is a critical skill for a paralegal. Even paralegals who are not assigned legal research tasks must know how to locate and analyze the law.

Effective legal research must be accurate and thorough. The results of any legal research are used to determine a course of action for the client. Whether the purpose of the legal research is advising a business on the environmental regulations governing a new real estate development or determining the necessary allegations in a breach of contract lawsuit, your legal research will have consequences for clients.

Fact

Some clients are reluctant to have a paralegal perform legal research. They think the complexity of the law requires the skill and training of a lawyer. In fact, the process of locating the law is often the most time-consuming aspect of legal research. The skill and training of the lawyer is needed most in the interpretation of the law. The task of *locating* the law can be delegated to a properly trained paralegal without any adverse effect on the representation of the client.

Types of Legal Research

In practice, there are three categories of legal research tasks assigned to paralegals. While each of these categories have different purposes, the legal research must be performed in the same manner for each of them. The three categories of assignment are legal research performed to obtain background in an unfamiliar area of the law; legal research in preparation for an upcoming meeting, hearing, or deposition; and legal research in preparation for writing a opinion letter for the client or a memorandum of law to the court.

Background Legal Research

Background legal research is the most general of the legal research assignments. It is research to determine what the law is in a particular field. The research is broad in scope and designed to determine the general legal principles that apply in that area of the law. In this sense, it is much like the law studied in paralegal education classes—very broad and not tied to any specific aspect of the client's legal problem.

Background legal research is performed out of academic interest. It is a necessary step in determining what advice to give the client if the field of law is unfamiliar to the lawyer. The lawyer must first understand the broad issues of the field before deciding on more specific legal research tasks. This may include gaining an understanding of the policies and goals underlying a particular area of the law.

Just because background legal research is broad in scope does not mean that you should not have a thorough grasp of the client's legal problem. Knowing why the background legal research is necessary helps narrow your research. An assignment to research the insurance requirements for registered vehicles traveling on public streets is more easily performed if you know that the client is charged with operating a moped without insurance.

Event-driven Legal Research

This type of legal research is performed because it is likely an issue will come up at a court hearing or client meeting. You will perform this type of legal research any time there is a discrete issue requiring a specific answer. A common example is an evidentiary question—you might be asked to conduct legal research to determine if a witness can testify about a conversation with your client. Event-driven legal research is designed to determine the answer to a very narrow and specific question.

Event-driven legal research requires detailed knowledge about the specific legal problem. The results of this kind of legal research are always determined by the facts of the client's problem. If your legal research discovers alternative solutions, these will also depend on the facts. It is imperative that the results of this type of legal research be placed in a specific factual context.

This kind of legal research is narrowly focused and looks for results. Your research should not address issues of policy or effects of other laws unless those questions are appropriate for the client.

Alert

Staying focused on the client's problem is essential when conducting legal research. The scope of the law is very broad—there is always another court opinion or another statute that might affect the results of your research. If you follow every trail, you will delay your conclusion and run up a big bill for the client. Be thorough, but do not overdo it.

Legal Research in Preparation for Writing

Lawyers often use the results of legal research to present written advice to clients or to prepare written arguments to a court on behalf of a client. The writing usually has a specific purpose. The opinion letter will discuss the effect of a contract provision so that the client can decide whether to agree to the provision; the written argument will support the client's position concerning enforcement of a settlement.

Since only lawyers can write letters to clients giving legal advice and only lawyers can file written arguments with the court, this kind of research is not a final product but is used to formulate a final product. The results may be supplemented or supported by other legal research as necessary.

This kind of legal research is somewhat broader than event-driven legal research. Although the result is important in this kind of legal research, it is often necessary to understand why the result was reached. Questions of policy and relationship to other laws are valuable context for the results of this type of legal research.

Sources of Legal Research

Because the law is so varied, there are many different resources available to help locate the law, each with a specific use and specific limitations. The major types of legal research resources are primary sources of law and secondary sources of law.

Primary sources of law are the actual law itself—constitutions, statutes, administrative regulations, ordinances, and court opinions. Anything that creates the law is a primary source of law. All legal research should rely on primary sources.

By contrast, *secondary sources* of law provide summaries and interpretations of the law. They are the result of what someone thinks the law is, not the law itself. Secondary sources are used to locate the law and to explain the law. Secondary sources are useful tools for finding the law, but they should never be relied on as stating the law.

Primary Sources

There are three main categories of primary sources of the law. They are statutory law, administrative regulations, and case law.

Statutory Law

Statutory law is any law enacted by a legislature and includes constitutions. It is also called *enacted law*. Statutory law is sometime contrasted with written opinions issued by the courts, called judge-made law (or common law). Statutory law can fill a void left by the common law, supplement the common law, or replace the common law.

Even though statutes are intended to be available to the public, locating the appropriate statutory law can be surprisingly difficult. There are several sources for locating statutory law; which of these sources you use will depend on the nature of the client's problem.

If the client's problem involves the application of a new law or a recent amendment of an old law, your legal research should begin with the most recent version of the statute. In most states, the earliest version of an effective statute is the *slip law*. The slip law is the version of the law presented to the executive branch of government. In the federal system, each slip law is assigned a unique number known as a public law number. In most states, the slip law number is simply the number the bill was given as it made its way through the legislature. Federal public laws are printed in the *United States Code Service*. State slip laws are generally available through legislative printing offices.

There are bound volumes of slip laws called session laws; compilations of slip laws in the order they were passed by the legislature. Each volume of session laws represents the work of one session of the legislature and will cover a myriad of topics. Many compilations of session laws use underlines and strikethroughs to show the additions and deletions in amended statutes. Session laws are the basis for the publication of official statutory codes.

Because session laws are not organized in a topical fashion, using them for research is difficult. To make locating statutes easier, the session laws are organized, or codified, for publication. A codified statute is assigned a number that follows a topical organization. While each state uses a different topical organization, the structure of most state codes follow a variation of the title (topic), chapter (subtopic), and individual statute hierarchy.

The government publishes official statutory codes. Typically, these official codes contain only the text of the statutes and the history of the statute as reflected in the session laws. In the event of a discrepancy between the official code and any other version of the statute, the official code controls. The official statutory code of the federal government is the *United States Code.*

E ssential

Legal research cannot be learned from a book or in a classroom. Go to a law library and take down a book. Begin reading. When you have a question, look for the answer to that question—either in the book you are using, or some other book. Begin your legal research in the library, especially in the early stages of your career. Know what the books are and how they are organized before you attempt any form of computer-assisted research.

Because official codes provide only statutory information, legal researchers have the option of referring to an unofficial code. These unofficial codes are published by private legal publishers and usually contain additional information not found in the official code. For example, West Publishing offers the *United States Code Annotated* as an alternative to the *United States Code.* The *U.S.C.A.* contains annotations that include summaries of court opinions that have addressed the statute; historical notes about the text of each statutes, including important statements about the purpose of the statutes or an amendment; and references to secondary sources. Annotated codes are updated frequently by the publication of pocket parts that include the most recent references to the statute.

Administrative Regulations

Administrative regulations are forms of law promulgated by administrative agencies. If the legislature has enabled the agency to make rules addressing a specific topic, the pronouncements of the agency have the force of law. Administrative law is found in two places: the statutes enacted by the legislature and the rules and regulations of the agency itself. The legal researcher must consult both sources.

There are two main statutes that govern the effect of an administrative rule or regulation. Most states and the federal government have an Administrative Procedures Act. This statute applies to all administrative agencies and sets forth the process the agency must follow in promulgating new rules and regulations. For each individual agency there is a specific statute defining the purpose and authority of the agency. This is known as the enabling legislation.

Some agencies require little in the way of specific rules and regulations to do their work. Other agencies have extensive sets of rules and regulations covering many topics within their authority. In all cases, these rules and regulations are usually found in an administrative code that contains all the rules and regulations of the agencies created in that jurisdiction. In the federal government, this administrative code is called the *Code of Federal Regulations*. It contains administrative regulations from the Department of Labor, the Department of Health and Human Services, and many others. The rules are organized according to the statutory title that created the agency. For example, the enabling legislation for the Occupational Safety and Health Administration (OSHA) is contained in Title 29 of the *United States Code*, so all OSHA rules are found in Volume 29 of the Code of Federal Regulations. State compilations have many different forms of organization.

Case Law

Case law is the record of the opinions of judges in deciding cases. Each jurisdiction has its own set of case law. The decisions of trial-level courts are seldom reported because they are not binding on any other court. Nevertheless, trial court opinions are sometimes useful where no other authority exists. For this reason, the federal court system and some state court systems make certain that written trial court opinions are available in electronic format. Use caution when referring to these decisions, however, as they are the least permanent of all court decisions.

The vast majority of reported decisions are written opinions from the appellate courts of the jurisdiction. Most states have one or two levels of appellate court—a state supreme court and an intermediate appellate court. In some states, such as New York and California, there are additional appellate levels. Each court has a specific abbreviation that identifies the court's position in the judicial hierarchy. These abbreviations are part of the citation to the opinion.

Fact

The standardized system of identifying the location of court opinions makes it possible to locate any reported court opinion in the United States. This system has become so much a part of legal usage that a major publisher of legal materials lost a lawsuit in which it claimed proprietary control over its standard pagination. Other legal publishers now use the same pagination system.

The opinions of each appellate court are published in bound volumes known as *reporters*. Some states have an official reporter that includes only the opinions for that state. In other states, the opinions published by West Publishing serve as the official reporter. West, the largest legal publisher in the world, publishes appellate cases for all states and the federal court system according to a regional system. For example, the *Northwestern Reporter* contains opinions of the appellate courts in Wisconsin, Minnesota, Iowa, North Dakota, South Dakota, and Nebraska. Specific opinions are referenced by the volume of the reporter, the abbreviation for the reporter, and the page number—the case of *Hagerty v. Hagerty*, 281 N.W.2d 386 (Minn. 1979) is found in volume 281 of the *Northwestern Reporter* on page 386. The Minnesota Supreme Court decided it in 1979. Similar reporters are available for the federal system.

Secondary Sources

Constitutions, statutes, and case law are primary materials. These items comprise "the law." All other materials are secondary legal sources. Secondary sources contain summaries of the law and commentaries on the law. Although they are not the law itself, they are valuable resources to the legal researcher.

Secondary sources often contain clearer descriptions and explanations of the law than primary sources. In addition, court opinions sometimes rely on secondary sources to help explain a particular interpretation of the law. For all this, secondary sources are not the law and should not control your interpretation of the law on behalf of your client.

Legal Encyclopedias

Legal encyclopedias are summaries of general legal principles. The publishers of legal encyclopedias organize the law by topics and provide an outline of the law on that topic with references to major case opinions and statutes explaining the topic.

The major legal encyclopedias are *American Jurisprudence* (*Am. Jur.*) and *Corpus Juris Secundum* (*C.J.S.*). Both of these encyclopedias are national in scope. Some legal publishers also offer state-specific legal encyclopedias that summarize legal principles in that state. Legal encyclopedias provide an overview of the law that is often a necessary starting point for legal research.

Treatises

Some of the pre-eminent legal scholars in the last century concentrated their legal studies in a specific area of the law. Their writings about that area of the law have been compiled into a treatise. A *treatise* is a combination of a summary of the law and commentary on the law. A legal treatise often summarizes a rule of law and describes the application of that rule of law in various jurisdictions. Treatises may also include a historical perspective on the development of the law and commentary stating the commentator's view of the rule of law. Treatises are often useful for providing the legal researcher with an in-depth understanding of a specific legal principle.

E ssential

Digests

When an appellate court decides a case, its opinion might address several legal principles. For example, an appeal from a criminal conviction can raise issues of interpretation of a statute, admissibility of character evidence, and the constitutionality of a confession. Not all of these issues are relevant to the legal researcher, so the publishers of legal digests provide indexes that reference the opinion under each topic discussed by the court. These indexes are organized by legal topic and include short summaries of the portion of the opinion that discusses each topic. The compilation of these indexes and summaries is called a digest.

A digest allows the legal researcher to locate topical case law quickly and easily. The most popular digest system is published by West and utilizes an index system developed by West called the key number system. Under this system, specific areas of the law are divided into topics (key numbers) and subtopics. The summaries contained in the West digest system also appear as headnotes, or topical summaries. Because the headnotes are not a part of the official court opinion, they are not primary law, but are an indispensable aid in locating primary law on a specific topic.

Restatements

Many areas of the law have deep historical roots. The law in these areas has expanded and developed over the years, sometimes resulting in confusion about the current state of the law. To help the legal researcher understand the legal principles that govern a specific area of the law, committees made of legal scholars, judges, and lawyers have prepared restatements of some areas of the law. These restatements summarize the rules of law and provide detailed explanations showing the application of the law to facts. Restatements also provide explanations about the historical development and policies behind specific legal principles. Restatements are considered so accurate that specific portions of some restatements have been adopted as rules of law in many jurisdictions. The publishers of the restatements include these references in separate volumes. There are restatements of the law of torts, product liability, contracts, property, judgments, and agency.

Annotations

Annotations are information about the interpretation of statutes. All federal and state statutes are available in an annotated version. The annotated version is rarely the official version of the statute, but annotated versions are commonly cited when it is necessary to refer to the language of a particular statute.

An annotation is supplemental information about the statute. Typical annotations contain the history of the statute, including the date of first enactment, dates and substance of any amendments, and the effective date of any changes to the statute. This information is important if the language of the statute has changed in a way that affects the client's legal problem. Annotations also include related statutes, references to law review articles or other commentary concerning the statute, and an index to various topics the courts have addressed in interpreting the statute.

The topical index to a court opinion interpreting a statute uses the same information contained in case headnotes. The summaries of court opinions referring to a specific statute are listed immediately after the statute in an annotated volume. These references are useful when the legal researcher is attempting to determine whether the courts have applied the statutory language to a factual situation similar to the client's.

Computer-assisted Legal Research

The legal research sources discussed so far are some of those available in book form. All together, the print volumes containing the law fill entire libraries. In fact, most law schools around the country contain all of the primary law of each state and the federal system, virtually all of the available treatises, restatements, digests, and annotations applicable to each jurisdiction, and many other legal resources for specialty practices such as international or patent law. These libraries are extensive, and it only takes one look to realize that it is impossible to master all of the law contained in such a library. It is quickly apparent that legal research by hand can easily be a massive undertaking.

Over the last several years, the burden of conducting legal research has eased somewhat. The presence of the personal computer in law offices led to the development of systems for electronic legal research. Today, computers can search all primary law, and an increasing number of secondary sources are available in electronic versions as well.

There are two kinds of electronic legal research sites. The first, proprietary legal research sites, or pay sites, have been available for a number of years. The two most popular—Westlaw and Lexis—are commonly used in law firms and legal libraries. These sites contain nearly all the legal research material these publishing giants have available in print. For a fee, the legal researcher can ask the electronic database to locate all cases that use a specific phrase or refer to a specific statute. A carefully phrased search request can quickly identify all cases that address a specific concept. The search request can be limited to the databases covering a specific state or extended to search all databases maintained by the publisher. The quality and ease of such searches has led smaller law firms to abandon any library of print media except for those publications not yet available in electronic form. Each publisher has its advantages and most legal researchers prefer one database to the other. In most respects, however, the databases maintained by Westlaw contain essentially the same information contained in a Lexis database. These days, the primary distinction between the two giants is pricing.

The second form of electronic research involves the use of free electronic databases. There are a number of specialized databases that a legal researcher can access. For example, most states and the federal government maintain electronic databases of the primary law in that jurisdiction. The information in these databases is often word searchable, making these sites a frequent starting point for a legal researcher who does not wish to use a pay site until the target of the search can be properly identified.

 Fact

Computer-assisted legal research can be very effective in the hands of a legal professional already familiar with the area of the law being researched. In the hands of someone unfamiliar with the area of the law, computer-assisted legal research can be time-consuming and frustrating. Both major legal research sites offer the assistance of research professionals to help you direct your research. The assistance is free.

In addition to governmental sites, several law sites maintain specialty sites for specific kinds of legal research. Cornell University maintains a Web site devoted to the Uniform Commercial Code mentioned in Chapter 14. The University of Washington in St. Louis also maintains a Web site with specific, topical databases that allow free searching.

Communicating Your Results

Once your legal research is done, you must report your results. In nearly every case this report will be in writing so there is a record of the legal research results. You may be asked to report on your legal research in the form of a memorandum to the court; more often, you will prepare an office memorandum addressing a specific legal issue for a client.

The first step in preparing a legal office memorandum is to state the goal of the legal research. The goal of the legal research is not the same as the legal issue. You may define the legal issue as whether a witness whose back was to the accident will be allowed to testify which car ran the red light. This legal issue can be analyzed in terms of the facts of the client's case and the applicable primary law. It does not tell you, however, what the goal of the legal research is. Obviously, the goal of your legal research will be different if your client is accused of running the red light than if your client is the driver who was hit. Knowing the goal of the legal research keeps you focused and lets the reader know that the research was intended to support a particular result.

After the statement of the goal of the legal research, you should state the issue addressed, including enough facts so the reader can easily see why the issue is important to the client's case. An issue phrased as "Whether a witness whose back was to the accident, but who could see the accident reflected in a plate glass window, should be allowed to testify which driver ran the red light" is far preferable to an issue asking whether a witness whose back was to the accident can testify as to which driver ran the red light.

A brief summary of the facts should follow the issue. It is not necessary to include all of the facts of the case. Instead, include only those facts that are important to the resolution of the issue. It is not important that one of the cars is blue unless the witness uses that fact to identify the car that ran the red light. Do not clutter your memo with unneeded facts. On the other hand, do not omit facts that are necessary to resolve the issue.

Include a statement of how the law applies to the facts of your case. This is called the *analysis* portion of the memo. Here you will explain the primary law you have located and explain why it applies to this issue. You must draw factual analogies between the facts of your case and the facts in a controlling court opinion. In many instances, you will find that several court opinions seem to be relevant to the client's legal issue. Each opinion must be analyzed on its own, but many cases can stand for the same legal proposition. It is up to you to find a logical structure to these factual analogies that satisfies the goal of the legal research.

A good legal research memorandum should end with a conclusion. Here is where the question posed in the issue is answered. Most conclusions will also include a statement about why the result is reached.

Chapter 19

Pretrial Preparation

Most law firms use paralegals to help trial lawyers prepare for and conduct civil trials. For legal matters that may end in a trial, preparation for trial begins almost immediately. The use of legal procedures to develop facts supporting the legal theories involved is a major area of paralegal responsibility. To be effective, the litigation paralegal must have a thorough understanding of the civil litigation process.

Why Assign a Paralegal?

The ordinary civil case begins with a dispute between parties. Whether the dispute is an automobile accident, dissolution of marriage, or a breach of contract claim, the management of the lawsuit will follow a similar path. The civil litigation process begins with the exchange of formal pleadings outlining the claims of the parties and proceeds through a discovery process designed to uncover the important facts bearing on those claims. Long before the lawsuit is ready to be presented to a judge or jury, the facts of the dispute must be assembled, examined, and thoroughly analyzed. Developing these facts requires the use of formal legal documents and procedures.

The pretrial phase of the modern litigation dispute is primarily the management of documents. Even an ordinary automobile accident involves several types of documents—police reports, witness statements, wage loss records, medical records, depositions, and medical reports. Most civil cases involve even more documents. The litigation paralegal is ideally suited to manage and summarize the important document in a civil case.

A trained paralegal can perform a variety of other tasks related to the development of the facts in a legal dispute. The paralegal can assist in locating the applicable law and evidence in a case. Each case is governed by certain procedural requirements that can be monitored by the paralegal. Paralegals often assist in locating and interviewing witnesses. In each capacity, the paralegal can perform the task more quickly and efficiently than a lawyer and at a lower cost.

 Fact

The progress of a lawsuit can be separated into several stages, but the stages are all interrelated. Thinking ahead is the paralegal's best strategy—an important fact is of no use if it cannot be produced when needed. A paralegal should approach any litigation-oriented assignment with the expectation that the work produced will play an important role at trial.

Pleadings

Before a legal dispute can be presented to a judge or jury, the parameters of the dispute must be defined. The opposing side must be informed of the basis for the lawsuit and be allowed the opportunity to contest the allegations. Once the issues are defined, either or both parties may wish to ask the judge to resolve certain issues short of trial. Near the end of the pretrial phase of the litigation, the judge will require the parties to file statements of their respective positions on a variety of issues. The documents filed with the court in the course of litigation are collectively known as pleadings. Paralegals are often used extensively in the preparation of pleadings.

The Complaint

All civil litigation is started by a complaint. In some forms of civil litigation, the complaint is called a *petition*. The complaint begins the litigation. It must contain several components. The form of these components varies from jurisdiction to jurisdiction, but each component must be present in every complaint.

The Parties

The complaint must identify the parties to the lawsuit. The party starting the lawsuit is known as the *plaintiff* or the *petitioner.* There may be more than one plaintiff listed in a complaint. The responding party is called the *defendant* or the *respondent*. There may be more than one defendant in a case. The plaintiff must state at least one claim against every listed defendant.

The names of the plaintiff and defendant are listed in the *caption* to the complaint. The caption also contains the name of the court where the complaint will be filed. The caption also contains a space for recording the court file number that will be assigned by the court clerk when the complaint is filed.

The complaint is always accompanied by a summons. The *summons* is an order of the court directing the defendant to respond to the complaint within a specific time. The summons is issued by the court in some jurisdictions; in others, the lawyer for the plaintiff prepares the summons. Both the summons and the complaint must be served on the defendant to begin the lawsuit.

The Jurisdictional Allegations

Each complaint must include a statement of the facts that give the court jurisdiction over the dispute. A court cannot decide a dispute if it does not have jurisdiction. A typical statement of jurisdiction identifies the facts that establish the jurisdiction of the court, such as the residence of the parties, the location of the accident, or the consequences of a breach of contract. A statement of jurisdiction may also reference the statute that gives the court jurisdiction over the dispute. If the complaint is filed in federal court, it must also contain a statement that the dispute concerns an amount of money over the minimum jurisdictional limit.

E ssential

Drafting a complaint requires a thorough understanding of the facts and how those facts relate to the legal claim. It is not necessary to include every fact in the complaint, but the complaint must contain enough facts to prove every required element of each claim.

The Basis for the Complaint

The purpose of the complaint is to notify the defendant of the claim. The complaint must identify the claim with sufficient detail so the defendant can prepare a response. If the plaintiff was injured in an accident, the complaint should state when and where the accident occurred. It should describe the conduct of the defendant that the plaintiff believes was negligent and it should identify the harm suffered by the plaintiff.

The statement of the basis for a complaint is called stating a *cause of action*. Causes of action are types of conduct that entitle the plaintiff to a remedy from the defendant. Each cause of action is comprised of several required parts, or elements. The complaint must state a factual basis for each element of the cause of action. Most law firms have form books or form banks containing model complaints for a variety of different causes of action. These resources can be useful in ensuring that the cause of action is correctly pleaded and that all elements of the cause of action are included.

The complaint may describe more than one cause of action. It must state at least one cause of action against each named defendant. Multiple causes of action against a defendant are allowed as long as each meets the necessary jurisdictional requirements and has an adequate factual basis.

 **Alert**

The requirements for what must be included in a pleading vary from jurisdiction to jurisdiction and from claim to claim. The minimal elements of parties, event, location, breach of duty of reasonable care, causation, and damages may suffice for an automobile accident claim. Considerably more detail is required for an employment discharge claim. Refer to similar pleadings in other cases to get a sense of the minimum requirements for pleading each kind of claim.

The Request for Relief

The plaintiff must *ask* the court for a remedy for each cause of action. The court cannot order a remedy the plaintiff has not requested. This specification of the type of relief requested is called the request for relief or, in more old-fashioned jurisdictions, the prayer for relief.

The plaintiff usually requests relief in the form of money damages. The amount of money specified in the complaint must only be a good faith estimate of what the lawyer thinks a jury will award the plaintiff. The jury is not bound by the amount stated in the request for relief. A jury can award a greater or lesser amount based on the evidence presented to it.

A plaintiff can also request nonmonetary relief in some situations. Nonmonetary forms of relief are known as *equitable remedies*. The court awards them when monetary damages are inadequate and it would be unfair to deny the plaintiff any relief. Injunctions and orders for specific performance are forms of equitable relief.

The Jury Trial Demand

Civil lawsuits can be decided either by a judge or a jury. Many states guarantee the right to a jury trial in most civil lawsuits. These states also allow the parties to waive their rights to have the case heard by a jury. Local statutes or procedural rules sometimes require the parties to specify whether the case is to be decided by a judge or a jury. In these states, a demand for a jury trial must appear in the complaint. The demand for a jury trial should appear prominently in the complaint—as a separate allegation at the beginning of the complaint, as a part of the request for relief, or in a separate statement in the caption or at the end of the complaint.

The Signature

The lawyer for the plaintiff must sign the complaint. All states and the federal courts have rules of court governing the effect of the lawyer's signature. By signing the complaint, the lawyer certifies that the facts in the complaint are true to the best of the lawyer's knowledge and that existing law supports the allegations of the complaint.

The court has the authority to punish the lawyer if a factual allegation proves to be untrue or an allegation is contrary to existing law.

The Answer

The defendant's response to the complaint is called the answer. The summons calls for the answer to be served within a specific time from the service of the complaint. This time is usually thirty days, but that can vary from court to court and from claim to claim. If the defendant does not answer the complaint, a judgment of default can be entered. This is a real judgment for the relief requested in the complaint. When a judgment of default is entered, the defendant is not given any opportunity to respond to the statements of the plaintiff.

When a defendant files an answer to the complaint, it will be in a form similar to the complaint. That is, it will have a caption with the same information as the complaint, a body containing the response to the allegations of the complaint, a request for relief, a signature, and a demand for jury trial. Each of these components serves a purpose identical to the purpose served in the complaint.

 **Alert**

The defendant's lawyer is often at a disadvantage when preparing an answer. The plaintiff's lawyer may have taken weeks or months to investigate the claim before preparing the complaint, but the defendant's lawyer only has twenty days. It is common to grant extensions of time to answer a complaint, but beware of the pitfalls of such an agreement. Certain matters may only be raised within a limited time from the service of the complaint, or they are waived.

The answer must respond to each cause of action stated by the plaintiff. The defendant may contest the facts of the allegation by denying knowledge of the accident. The defendant can deny liability for the conduct as when claiming that the collision was caused by another person. The defendant can contest the extent of the injury suffered by the plaintiff. The defendant can even contest the application of the law to the defendant's conduct.

When the defendant claims there is a legal reason the plaintiff's claim is improper, this is called an *affirmative defense*. An affirmative defense is a statement that there is no legal basis for the claim asserted by plaintiff. A claim that the court lacks jurisdiction is an affirmative defense. A claim that the plaintiff is not entitled to sue the defendant is an affirmative defense. Most affirmative defenses center on a defect in the cause of action, otherwise known as *failure to state a claim*. Each of these defenses requires the court to hear arguments and make a decision about the legal issues involved.

If the defendant has a cause of action against the plaintiff, it can be asserted in the answer. This type of pleading is called a *counterclaim*. The contents of the counterclaim must meet all the requirements of a complaint. An example of counterclaim is if the plaintiff sues a remodeling contractor for shoddy workmanship and the contractor counterclaims to recover the agreed fee for performing the work. Each is a separate claim asserted by a different party. The defendant becomes the plaintiff when asserting a counterclaim.

Motions

Motions are used to resolve the dispute between the parties without the need for a trial. A motion asks the trial judge to apply established principles of law to the cause of action stated by the plaintiff. *Dispositive motions* address issues that can dispose of the lawsuit. Common dispositive motions are motions to dismiss and motions for summary judgment.

The form of most motions is prescribed by court rule. While each motion addresses a different procedural matter, they have several common elements.

Notice of Motion

The notice of motion is simply the notice that the court will hear arguments on the issue raised in the motion. The motion is prepared after consulting with the court clerk about the availability of the judge. It specifies the date, time, and location of the hearing. The motion specifies the nature of the relief requested. In many courts, reference to the applicable court rule is required. Finally, the notice of motion must be signed.

 Fact

Some court rules allow the notice of motion and the motion for summary judgement to be combined. Others insist that they be separate documents. In either type of jurisdiction, parties commonly serve notices that specify "a date and time to be determined." These notices are placeholders, since the timelines for opposing motions are usually calculated backward from the hearing date, instead of forward from the service date.

Memorandum of Law

Each motion must be supported by legal argument. The memorandum of law states the legal basis for the motion and provides the court with specific authority supporting the position of the moving party. Most memoranda of law follow a traditional format of Introduction, Statement of Facts, Statement of the Legal Issues, Argument, and Conclusion. The structure of the memorandum of law is usually defined by court rule. If there is no applicable court rule, the paralegal should review other motions filed and received by the law firm to determine if the structure of the memorandum of law is dictated by tradition.

Affidavits and Exhibits

Dispositive motions often rely on information that is not contained in the complaint. The moving party may want the judge to consider additional facts. The facts may be documents, deposition testimony, documents from previous litigation, or any other form of demonstrative evidence not contained in the complaint. These materials are made a part of the motion when they are attached as exhibits. Again, court rules govern what kinds of exhibits are allowed.

In certain cases, the motion might rely on observations or affirmations of fact by the client or another witness. If those factual matters are not contained in a document that can be used as an exhibit,

an exhibit must be created. The typical method is to create an affidavit containing the necessary facts that is sworn to before a notary
public. The sworn statements in the affidavit are entitled to the same
consideration as any other fact.

Proposed Order

All motions require a decision from the judge. The judge communicates the decision to the parties in the form of an order. The court
rules governing motions usually require the moving party to prepare
a proposed order that reflects the relief the party is requesting.

Discovery

The commencement of a lawsuit creates an impediment to accessing
certain facts. Some impediments can be overcome by diligent investigation, but others require the cooperation of the opposing side. Once
a lawsuit is begun, the exchange of information between the parties
is governed by rules of civil procedure. These rules allow the parties
to obtain information from each other in several different ways.

Initial Disclosures

The requirement of initial disclosure only applies in federal court.
The premise behind the initial disclosure requirement is that the parties always seek certain facts—the documents supporting the claim
and the names of witnesses with information about the claim. Rather
than delay the exchange of information, the federal courts require
the parties to make an initial disclosure of this type of information
shortly after the lawsuit has begin.

A paralegal may be assigned to compile the information for an
initial disclosure. This can be a time-consuming task. All documents
should be categorized and indexed. The index serves as a record
of which documents were actually produced in the event of a later
dispute. The file material should be thoroughly reviewed for names
of witnesses—the rule requires disclosure of the names of witnesses with information, not those that are favorable to your side or
witnesses with information you think is important. In addition, witnesses known to the client but not listed in any document should be
disclosed.

Interrogatories

Interrogatories are written questions to the other parties in the lawsuit. The questions can address any subject matter relevant to the lawsuit. The other party must respond to interrogatories within thirty days by answering the questions or interposing objections to the questions. Objections are usually based on attorney-client privilege, the work product privilege, or the relevance of the requested information.

The proper use of interrogatories is an art form. Many legal practitioners attempt to use interrogatories to argue a case or to discover the legal theories of the opponent. Many of these questions are met with objections or vague and incomplete answers.

A better approach is to use interrogatories to obtain factual information. An interrogatory can assist you in identifying relevant witnesses and documents, and it can also ask for a summary of damages claims, or the date and time of specific events. This information can be used to develop an investigation strategy that expands on the basic information received in response to the interrogatories.

Many jurisdictions restrict the number of interrogatories. The interrogatories may be divided into separate sets, but the number is limited to fifty. This number includes question subparts, a distinction often overlooked by drafters of interrogatories. For example, a question asking for the name, address, and telephone number of a witness is really three questions. Because of these limitations, the astute drafter will limit interrogatory questions to information that is absolutely necessary.

 Question

How are disputes over discovery matters resolved?
The rules about what is discoverable and what is not are considerably less restrictive than the rules of evidence. A fact need not be admissible in evidence to be discoverable, and the courts tend to lean toward allowing the exchange of information rather than restricting it. For this reason, parties to a lawsuit often resolve discovery disputes through some sort of compromise to avoid involving the courts.

Demand for Documents

Documents in the possession or control of the opposing party may be requested. A party may also demand entry onto land for purposes of inspection. A typical assignment is for a paralegal to draft a request identifying the documents to be inspected and copied. The request should be specific and descriptive of the category of documents requested. The request should be as broad as possible without rendering the request meaningless. A request for "all documents supporting the plaintiff's claims for damages" is preferable to a request for "all documents related to plaintiff's claims."

Once the requested documents are produced, the paralegal is responsible for reviewing, summarizing, and reporting on the documents produced. The process of digesting will vary with the document. Medical records may simply be incorporated into a medical chronology, quality control documents might be placed in a database designed to show results in a timeline, and documents from various sources might be indexed in relation to the legal or factual issues in the case. Where the documents in a case are voluminous, the paralegal may be responsible for creating and maintaining a numbering system that allows quick retrieval of specific documents.

Requests for Admission

Requests for admissions are used to obviate the need for proof of facts that the parties agree on. One party makes a factual statement that the other parties are required to admit or deny. An admitted fact need not be proven at trial. Requests for admissions are often used at the end of the discovery process.

Admissions are often used to lay the necessary evidentiary foundation for the introduction of documents or exhibits at trial. A paralegal assigned to draft requests for admission should review the entire file to identify facts that are necessary to the client's position. These facts should be stated as clearly and succinctly as possible. A request for admission should not contain editorial comment about the fact.

Once responses to requests for admissions are received, the paralegal must keep track of the facts that are admitted and the facts that are denied. Facts that are admitted can simply be presented to the court at trial and need not be a part of trial preparation. Facts that are denied must be proved and should be incorporated into pretrial preparation efforts.

Depositions

A deposition is the process of orally questioning a witness in a case. The witness is placed under oath and the attorneys for all parties to the lawsuit are allowed to ask questions of the witness. Paralegals may not participate in the questioning, but they may be present to manage documents to be discussed at the deposition.

Paralegals are often charged with arranging the deposition. This process involves contacting the lawyer for the opposing parties to determine their availability. The availability of the witness must also be determined. A place for taking the deposition must be arranged—this may be a lawyer's conference room or another location. The paralegal will arrange for the presence of a court reporter to administer the oath and prepare a transcript of the proceedings.

When the deposition is concluded, the paralegal may be responsible for collecting and preserving the exhibits used in the deposition. A transcript must be ordered and paid for. The transcript should be reviewed and summarized for later use in trial preparation. Important passages should be marked for easy reference if the testimony of the witness changes at trial.

 Fact

A deposition is sworn testimony under oath, just like in-court testimony. Since the deposition is a preview of the testimony the jury will hear, the deposition transcript must be carefully examined for potential discrepancies that might cause problems for the client's case. The process of summarizing or digesting a deposition is not merely creating an index, but placing the deposition testimony in the context of other trial preparation efforts.

Disclosure of Expert Opinions

The proof requirements in some cases include the presentation of expert testimony. When expert witnesses are involved, special discovery procedures apply. At the least, a party who intends to call an expert witness at trial must disclose the name of the witness, the qualifications of the witness, the factual basis for any opinions held by the witness, and the opinions of the expert. In many cases, this information is contained in a formal report from the witness. A report is required in federal cases.

A paralegal may be involved in locating an expert witness for a case. The client will often have suggestions about potential expert witnesses. In some cases, however, the paralegal must track down any expert without assistance from the client. This process may include contacting other paralegals for recommendations of experts in a specific field. The paralegal may also contact expert referral services if no other source is available.

The selection of an expert requires the involvement of the supervising attorney. An expert must meet the legal requirements of the case, fit with the tactical position the lawyer wishes to take in the case, and be cost-efficient. The paralegal should gather as much information about the expert as possible to assist in making the hiring decision. A current curriculum *vitae* and rate schedule are critical. The paralegal should also try to locate prior reports or deposition testimony by the expert.

Once the expert is hired, the paralegal must ensure that the expert receives sufficient information to form an opinion about the case. This usually involves copying all pleadings, discovery responses, depositions, and other factual materials from the file. The paralegal can safely send the expert all information received from the other parties and any documents from the paralegal's client that have been produced to the opposing parties. Undisclosed documents should be carefully reviewed for claims of privilege. The disclosure of documents to an expert is a potential waiver of any privilege with respect to that document. All questionable documents should be reviewed with the supervising attorney before disclosure.

Once the opinions of the expert are received, the paralegal should prepare a draft disclosure of those opinions. In all cases, the opposing parties are entitled to a disclosure of the opinions of an expert witness who will be called at trial. Of course, the supervising attorney may decide that the expert will not be called at trial, making any disclosure unnecessary.

 **Alert**

The required contents of a disclosure of expert opinion are often governed by court rule or interpretations contained in published court opinions. A disclosure of expert opinion that does not include these items can cause serious problems for the progress of a case.

On receipt of a disclosure of expert witness opinions from an opposing party, the paralegal must investigate the expert thoroughly. The expert's background and qualifications must be checked, including membership in trade organizations and employment history. The materials reviewed by the expert should be verified. In general, a paralegal is entitled to review any materials the expert relied on in forming an opinion. The opinions of the expert should be checked carefully. Expert opinions that represent a substantial deviation from the accepted conclusions in the field may be subject to challenge. At a minimum, the expert's opinion should be reviewed by the client's own expert. Regular summaries of these efforts should be provided to the client and the supervising attorney.

E-discovery

The common use of computers has added a layer of complexity on the discovery process. A request for memos or correspondence may produce little from a party who communicates entirely through electronic means. Document retention policies may have resulted in the destruction of all paper records, but electronic backups may still be available. Companies that use a central computer or server for e-mail or voice mail may have a wealth of information in electronic backups.

To be useful, electronic information must of course be requested and it must be readable. Most form interrogatories and demands for documents do not address electronic discovery. The paralegal should modify these forms to include specific questions about the creations of electronic documents, the backup strategy used by the party and the names of persons knowledgeable about the software used to create documents and backups. This information can be used to follow up on requests for specific documents.

An understanding of electronic evidence is necessary to make an effective request for electronic documents. While the retrieval and viewing of the documents may require professional help, the paralegal should be able to understand the basics of electronic discovery.

First, every document created on a computer contains information about the date and time of creation, the name of the creator, dates of any modifications, and other document information. This information, called *metadata*, is useful in evaluating documents in relation to the events in the case. Metadata is not available on the printed version of any document.

Second, even when deleted, most documents can be recovered. In an organization with a regular backup strategy, any single document may be saved several different times. Deleting the document from the working computer does not delete the document from the backup. Even when the document is created on a single computer and then deleted, the file may not be destroyed. Experts have been able to recover electronic information from erased or damaged hard drives. Further examination of the computer is always warranted if the data is important to the client's case.

The law related to electronic discovery and electronic evidence is changing rapidly. If you become involved in a case where this type of evidence is important, read the current version of the court rules on the subject. A computer search of all cases in the jurisdiction dealing with the issue is also a good idea. There are many sources of information about the status of the law of electronic discovery and the current technical issues—both online and in print. These resources should be reviewed before embarking on a search for electronic evidence. As always, the costs and rewards of such a search should be carefully considered.

Communicating Your Results

When communicating the results of any discovery pretrial preparation assignment, the paralegal should remember two things. First, any summary should contain a scrupulously accurate summary of the facts and the law. Do not assume, embellish, or shade the facts. Pretrial preparation is only effective if it is clear, accurate, and dispassionate.

Second, the paralegal should approach each stage of pretrial preparation as if the information will be presented to the court. You should assume that every assignment has the ultimate goal of presenting evidence or an argument to the court. If you are not continually thinking about how the current assignment affects the case as a whole, your preparation will be unfocused and incomplete.

Assistance at Trial

There is a popular image of the lawyer at trial: cool, collected, with a witness always prepared and ready to be called to the witness stand, examining witnesses with a single legal pad or file folder, and always prepared for whatever tactic or argument the other side presents. That image belies the tremendous amount of work that goes into preparing a case for trial and managing the myriad elements of an actual trial. Much of this work is performed by paralegals.

Why Assign a Paralegal?

The role of the paralegal at trial is supportive. This support, however, is more than just drafting documents and performing research. A paralegal trial assistant must be intimately familiar with the client's case, the evidence that supports it, and the evidence against it. When a paralegal trial assistant is used effectively, the entire litigation team is organized, effective, and prepared.

Of course, cost is a factor in the choice to utilize a paralegal trial assistant. The same work could be performed by a junior associate lawyer, but at a much greater cost. Few cases require a team of lawyers; the vast majority of cases are handled by one lawyer for each party and a paralegal trial assistant.

Even without the cost factor, there are other reasons for using a paralegal trial assistant at trial. The paralegal trial assistant usually has been working on the client matter since it arrived in the office. That paralegal often has an established relationship with the client—keeping the client informed is a major part of trial management. The paralegal assigned the task of preparing summaries of documents and depositions used at trial is usually able to locate a particular document or passage with ease. The paralegal assistant is in constant communication with witnesses and can arrange changes in schedule or relay unexpected developments in the trial evidence. All of these efforts allow the lawyer to concentrate on the effective presentation of the evidence.

Types of Trial Assistance

The paralegal trial assistant can assist the trial lawyer in a number of ways. Depending on the needs of the case or the requirements of the client, the paralegal trial assistant may be present in the courtroom or provide support from the lawyer's office. Each form of assistance has its own challenges.

 Fact

> The role the paralegal plays at trial depends on the impression the trial lawyer wants to make with the jury. It is a fact of life that a jury often forms its impression of the client from its impression of the client's lawyer. Rich clients have many lawyers and paralegals; less wealthy clients make do with a single lawyer without any obvious paralegal assistance. The decision to have the paralegal present at trial could be a tactical decision.

Some lawyers have their paralegals close at hand to assist with locating a document or an exhibit. These lawyers may have the paralegal take notes throughout the trial and refer to these notes when questions arise. The paralegal trial assistant may be asked to keep track of important points the lawyer wants to cover in the trial to make sure they are not overlooked. In this role, the paralegal trial assistant must have an excellent grasp of the strategy of the client's case. The paralegal may be asked to anticipate the needs of the attorney by locating a document or assuring the presence of a witness.

Effective trial assistance does not always require the actual presence of the paralegal trial assistant in the courtroom. In some cases, the paralegal trial assistant provides the best assistance by working from the lawyer's office. This type of assistance can involve arranging the appearance of witnesses, talking with experts, researching points of law or evidence that arise in the course of a trial, or passing along progress reports to an interested party such as an insurance company paying for the defense of an insured.

Whichever role the paralegal trial assistant takes, there are several main areas of trial assistance. The need for paralegals in these areas will vary with the needs of the case, but every trial requires preparation in each of these areas:

- Witness preparation
- Exhibits and documents
- Pretrial conference
- Jury selection
- Trial motions
- Posttrial matters

Witness Preparation

The paralegal trial assistant is usually assigned the task of ensuring the availability of all witnesses needed at trial. Typical witnesses include the client, lay (fact) witnesses, and expert witnesses. Each of these witnesses must be prepared for their testimony at trial and their appearances coordinated to assure the most effective presentation of the client's case. How each witness is contacted and prepared for trial differs with the type of witness.

The Client

The client should be notified of the trial date as soon as the court assigns it. This trial date may be months in the future, but it is important that the client put aside the time needed to attend the trial. The impression the client makes with a judge or jury depends on the client's presence. If the client does not appear attentive and interested in the proceedings, as when the client is not present, the judge or jury will conclude that the client does not really care about the outcome of the trial. If the client needs to make special arrangements to be present at trial, it is better to make those plans well in advance.

The lawyer usually performs the task of preparing the client for testimony at trial. The client is often the most important witness supporting the client's case and most lawyers do not delegate the task of preparing this vital witness. On the other hand, paralegals often participate in the client preparation meeting and provide necessary support for the client prior to the actual testimony. The client should not be "rehearsed" but should be aware of the important points in the case and how the lawyer intends to bring those points to the attention of the judge and jury. In addition, the client should be instructed on possible objections and how to deal with them. The primary areas of cross-examination should be identified and addressed.

 **Alert**

> The task of preparing a client for trial presents many opportunities for the paralegal to commit the unauthorized practice of law by giving legal advice. Instructing the client about the effect of a specific answer, sharing the lawyer's trial tactics with the client, and even telling the client what approach the opponent is expected to take are all legal advice. Where possible, conduct client preparation in the presence of the trial lawyer. If that is impossible, be sure to tell the client that the lawyer must answer all questions about trial tactics.

The role of the paralegal trial assistant is to make sure the client is present for the trial and all preparation sessions. In addition, the paralegal trial assistant should provide the client with copies of all statements or depositions of the client; these prior statements may be used against the client if the testimony at trial differs. The client should be provided with all documents containing statements of the client, including signed discovery responses such as interrogatories or requests for admission. These documents are signed under oath and can be used to impeach the client. Finally, the client should receive copies of each document or exhibit that will be offered into evidence from either side. All of these items must be provided to the client in the weeks before trial even if copies were given to the client several months ago. In connection with this, the paralegal trial assistant should personally review the documents to identify discrepancies or other issues that should be brought to the attention of the client and lawyer.

Lay Witnesses

Lay witnesses are witnesses who do not have any particular expertise about the subject matter of the litigation. These witnesses are sometimes called "fact witnesses" because their testimony is limited to the facts they have observed or experienced that are related to the lawsuit. A witness to an accident is a fact witness, as is a friend who testifies in a custody dispute.

Lay witnesses are of three kinds: friendly, neutral, and hostile. A friendly witness is willing to testify for the client and is usually cooperative in providing information and arranging time for preparation meetings and appearance at trial. A neutral witness usually has no particular connection to the case and often does not know either party. This kind of witness is cooperative to a point, but seldom willing to be inconvenienced to help the client. A hostile witness is unwilling to help the client, usually because of an affiliation with the opposing party. These witnesses are uncooperative and provide the most resistance to testifying at trial.

The role of the paralegal trial assistant with respect to lay witnesses is threefold. First, the witnesses must be identified and contacted. Second, the information possessed by the witness must be verified. Finally, the paralegal trial assistant must secure the attendance of the witness at trial.

Identifying and Contacting Lay Witnesses

Lay witnesses are usually identified from information in the client file. The client may identify a person who can testify on a crucial issue, a police report might identify an eyewitness, or the author of a document may testify about the facts in the document. These witnesses are identified in the pretrial preparation phase—those who are needed at trial must be recontacted. As with any contact with persons other than the client, the paralegal trial assistant should check with the supervising attorney concerning the ethics of contacting lay witnesses.

A well-kept client file will contain contact information on each potential lay witness. If the importance of the lay witness was obvious from the beginning, the paralegal may have collected possible dates of unavailability and alternate contact numbers. In the weeks before trial, the paralegal trial assistant should renew personal contact with each lay witness. The witness must be advised of the date the trial begins and the expected day the testimony of the witness is needed. Potential conflicts should be identified and resolved if possible. The witness should be encouraged to ask questions about their role in the proceedings, but the paralegal trial assistant must never disclose confidential or strategic information.

Essential

If the client matter is a litigation matter or a matter that is expected to result in litigation, the work of formulating witness files begins when the client file is opened. A paralegal who works on litigation matters quickly learns to treat every assignment with an eye toward the eventual use of the work product at trial. If you organize the file with the trial in mind, the final creation of a "trial file" or a "trial notebook" is much easier.

It is useful to follow the renewed personal contact with a letter. The letter serves as a reminder to the witness, documents the efforts of the paralegal trial assistant, and offers the opportunity to address additional issues such as transportation and witness fees. When the witness is friendly or neutral, the letter may contain an invitation to contact the paralegal trial assistant with additional questions. When writing such a letter, the paralegal trial assistant must keep in mind that this letter may be produced at trial. It is common to ask witnesses if they have discussed the case with the opposing side. If the lay witness has discussed the case, the witness will be asked to describe what was said. Extraneous information can damage the credibility of a lay witness who is seen as influenced by the actions of the lawyer or paralegal trial assistant.

Hostile witnesses cannot be approached in this manner. Because they are uncooperative, the use of hostile witnesses is limited to cases where a fact cannot be proved in any other way. Because hostile witnesses are generally uncooperative and unwilling to appear voluntarily, the initial contact phase is often skipped with these witnesses.

Verifying the Information Possessed by the Lay Witness

If the lay witness has been interviewed, has given a recorded statement, or has been deposed, the paralegal trial assistant should consider verifying the important facts in those documents. Do not provide copies of those documents to the witness without express instructions from the supervising attorney. The rules of evidence governing the admissibility of evidence often depend on how a witness remembers a fact and these evidentiary distinctions may be a part of the trial strategy. If the lay witness offers information in addition to, or different from, the information in the file, the paralegal trial assistant should make a note of the discrepancy and report it to the supervising attorney as soon as possible. Seemingly insignificant variations of fact can have significant consequences for the conduct of a trial.

 Alert

Knowledge of the law of evidence can be extremely useful to the paralegal trial assistant. Knowing the law of evidence allows the paralegal trial assistant to avoid mistakes that can have adverse effects on the client's case. The law of evidence affects the admissibility of oral testimony and documents at trial. If you have any question about the admissibility of a particular piece of evidence, be sure to seek a complete explanation of the issue from the supervising attorney before discussing the evidence with anyone.

In most cases, the paralegal trial assistant can verify the information held by a lay witness over the telephone. In some instances, a personal interview may be required. Always verify the need for such and interview and the parameters of the need for the interview with the supervising attorney.

Securing the Attendance of the Lay Witness at Trial

Some witnesses appear at trial voluntarily. Others are reluctant or unwilling to appear. In each case, the use of a subpoena is advisable. A subpoena is an order from the court directing the witness to appear at a specific date and time. A subpoena must be personally served on the witness and, in most states, must be accompanied by the statutory witness fees and expenses. Any witness can be subpoenaed. All lay witnesses should be subpoenaed for several reasons.

 Fact

The best source of information on subpoena requirements is the court clerk. If you can, make a personal visit to the clerk's office the first time you use a subpoena. Ask the clerk what fees are necessary, what information is required, and whether the returned subpoena must be filed with the court. They will be happy to help and you will minimize the possibility of a mistake in handling the subpoena.

First, the subpoena guarantees the appearance of the witness at trial. If the witness is not present when needed, the trial judge will ask the parties to move on. Sometimes the trial will last long enough to make another attempt at securing the attendance of the witness. In others, this requires a delay in the proceedings. All the promises the witness gave you are of no avail if you have not made an effort to secure the attendance of the witness by subpoena.

Second, even if the witness is agreeable and does appear, the use of a subpoena is additional assurance. Everyone understands that a witness under subpoena must testify. Not everyone understands a witness who appears voluntarily. The use of subpoenas for all lay witnesses places all witnesses on an even footing.

Third, the use of subpoenas creates a kind of schedule for the trial. When a witness is subpoenaed to appear at 2:00 P.M., there is a tendency to make every effort to be ready for that witness at that time. Witnesses who are irritated because of long waits can be detrimental to a client's case. The subpoena for a specific time is a reminder of this fact.

Exhibits and Documents

Any fact that is not proven through oral testimony is demonstrative evidence. Demonstrative evidence can be a document, a piece of physical evidence, a drawing, or a model. Exhibits are often duplicated, highlighted, excerpted, or blown up for easy visibility. The paralegal trial assistant is in charge of handling the physical exhibits. These responsibilities include arranging for any special equipment necessary to display the exhibit—easels, overhead projectors, or VCRs. This equipment is usually available in the courtroom, but a simple telephone call in advance of trial can save substantial consternation and delay once the trial begins.

ssential

If your responsibilities include using technology to display exhibits at trial, practice with the technology before the trial. Do this even if it is not your primary responsibility. Technology that does not work at trial is worse than no technology at all. If the exhibits cannot be shown to the jury, you might as well have left them at home. If necessary, prepare a nontechnological backup for use if technology fails.

The paralegal trial assistant's duties also include managing the exhibits offered by the opposing side. A court scheduling order usually requires the parties to exchange witness and exhibit lists in advance of trial. The exhibits listed must be compiled and available at a moment's notice during the trial. The exhibit is usually accompanied by notes of questions to ask about the exhibit, any legal challenges to the admissibility of the exhibit, and any related exhibits. Because the opponent's exhibits can be presented at any time through any witness, the organization of these exhibits is crucial.

A final exhibit task often assigned to the paralegal trial assistant is keeping track of the evidentiary status of each exhibit. Some exhibits are admitted without objection; some are admitted over objection; some are admitted for limited purposes; still others are admitted on a preliminary basis pending additional evidence; and some exhibits are never admitted. Knowing the evidentiary status of each exhibit can be extremely important for a later objection, argument, or motion.

Pretrial Conference

Before the trial begins, the lawyers for each party meet with the judge to discuss several matters. The issues normally discussed in a pretrial conference include the number of witnesses each party will call, the management of jury selection, and the resolution of any pretrial motions about the admissibility of evidence. The trial judge will make rulings on disputed issues that will affect the management of the trial. In addition, the parties may explore the possibility of settling the case short of trial.

The paralegal trial assistant often serves as the recorder of events at the pretrial conference, an informal meeting of the judge and lawyers, usually without a court reporter present. It is up to the parties to maintain their own records of the topics discussed and decisions reached. Because of the wide-ranging nature of most pretrial conferences, the participating lawyers are not the best source of detailed information about the conference. The paralegal trial assistant serves as the memory of the events of the pretrial conference.

Jury Selection

All jury trials begin with the selection of the jury. A pool of potential jurors is assembled according to the selection process of the particular jurisdiction. The jury pool reports to the courthouse on a particular day and is divided into groups from which the jury that will hear the specific case is chosen.

The jury selection process begins before the jury pool is even identified. A trial lawyer creates a profile of a model juror when preparing a case for trial. This profile is simply a compilation of juror attributes the lawyer thinks will be favorable to the client's case. From this profile, the lawyer creates a list of questions designed to identify those attributes in each potential juror at trial.

Each member of the jury pool provides the court with certain information—name, address, employer, age, etc. This information is available to litigants in advance of the trial. The paralegal trial assistant should obtain this information from the court clerk. These jury lists are often circulated among firm employees to see if any jurors are known within the law firm. In some cases, the paralegal trial assistant will work with an outside investigator developing additional background information on the potential jurors. Where permitted by the trial judge, additional written questionnaires prepared by the parties are sent to the jurors in advance of the trial. The cost of these types of efforts is quite high, so they are only undertaken when the trial involves significant pretrial publicity, emotionally difficult issues, or may result in significant precedent.

When the trial commences, the lawyer for each party is allowed to question the prospective jurors. This process, known as *voir dire*, is an opportunity for the parties to select jurors that fit the profile of the ideal juror. Lawyers often use the *voir dire* process to introduce themselves to the potential jurors and to familiarize the jurors with the client's case. While the lawyer is asking questions, the paralegal trial assistant must take detailed notes, recording not only the answers of the potential juror, but also the paralegal's impressions of the potential juror. The lawyer uses these notes to determine which jurors to strike.

Trial Motions

Many trials present legal issues that cannot be resolved until some evidence has been presented. The most significant of these is a motion for a directed verdict (called a motion for judgment as a matter of law). Any party can make this motion, which is a request that the trial judge determine that there is only one conclusion any reasonable jury can reach. The motion is very similar to a motion for summary judgment because it allows the opposing party to present all its evidence before asking the judge to apply the law to the facts established by the evidence.

A motion for directed verdict is often a renewal of a motion for summary judgment. If so, there will be a prior decision on the motion for summary judgment that will identify those issues the judge felt presented a factual dispute. If the actual evidence is weaker than expected, the trial judge may revisit the legal questions raised in the prior motion.

The paralegal trial assistant should take meticulous notes on the factual issues involved in any anticipated motion for a directed verdict. The paralegal should have a detailed knowledge of the facts presented in the prior motion and the reasons the judge denied that motion. Evidence that has a bearing on the motion for directed verdict should be highlighted and separately summarized for use in arguing the motion. The paralegal may also be assigned the responsibility for researching and updating any memoranda prepared in support of the motion.

Other trial motions are handled in a similar manner. The trial might involve motions on the admissibility of evidence, the allowable scope of an expert's testimony, or legal arguments about the propriety of certain jury instructions or questions to the jury. In each case, the paralegal assistant should be aware of the possibility of these motions and be alert for events at trial that might affect the outcome of the motion. Although the paralegal trial assistant cannot argue these motions, the value of an accurate, organized summary of the events related to the motions can be invaluable.

Posttrial Matters

The trial proceedings are not complete when the jury renders a verdict. The decision of the jury can be challenged in posttrial motions for a new trial or for judgment notwithstanding the verdict. These motions usually focus on a claimed error at trial—a mistaken ruling on evidence, inadequate or excessive damages, or a mistaken interpretation of the law by the jury or the trial judge. In most cases, these motions are a prelude to an appeal that will ask an appellate court to review the decision of the trial judge and jury.

As with other motions, the notes of the paralegal trial assistant are very important in preparing these motions. The paralegal must accurately record the events at trial—what the witness said, the specific language used in ruling on the admissibility of an exhibit, the authority cited by the trial judge in making a ruling on the issues presented to the jury for decision. If the paralegal's record of the proceedings is inaccurate, the argument in support of the posttrial motion may be weakened. Incomplete notes may result in the legal team overlooking a possible basis for a posttrial motion. These motions are quite important—a party must give the trial court an opportunity to correct any alleged error before an appeal is allowed.

The trial process comes into play in all areas of legal specialty. A contested custody issue, a probate dispute, or a claim of breach of contract all require a trial or hearing to resolve. In each case, the trial process will govern the resolution of the dispute. All paralegals in all legal specialty fields should be familiar with the basics of assisting at trial.

Paralegal Information on the Internet

The Internet has a wealth of information about being a paralegal. Not all of the information is reliable, however, so be careful which sites you visit. Some of the best Internet sites follow.

The American Bar Association Standing Committee on Legal Assistants (SCOLA)

The ABA maintains a Web site dedicated to paralegal education issues. The site includes a listing of ABA approved paralegal education programs, a newsletter, and paralegal career information. The information on this site is intended primarily for lawyers and paralegal educators.

www.abanet.org/legalservices/paralegals/home.html

National Federation of Paralegal Associations (NFPA)

The NFPA Web site is devoted to information helpful to its members. If you are looking for practicing paralegals in your area, the NFPA site includes a listing of member associations by region. The Career Center provides links to articles addressing project management, networking, job searches, and how to ask for a raise.

http://paralegals.org

National Association of Legal Assistants (NALA)

The NALA Web site contains general information about the NALA and about the paralegal career field. Under the Articles of Interest link are descriptions of court decisions and ethical rulings concerning the rights and obligations of paralegals. The current NALA Compensation and Utilization Survey can be purchased from this site.

http://nala.org

American Association for Paralegal Education (AAfPE)

This site, designed exclusively for paralegal educators, contains a wealth of information for the budding paralegal. Topics addressed on this site include a discussion of "what is a paralegal," information on Agape's criteria for a quality paralegal education program, and the history of paralegals.

http://aafpe.org

Legal Assistant Today magazine

Legal Assistant Today is an independent magazine that addresses the concerns of practicing paralegals. Its Web site includes articles from the current and archived issues. Special topics include e-mail lists for paralegal students and a link devoted entirely to "Becoming a Paralegal." There is also a listing of paralegal schools that appears to be advertisement-based.

www.legalassistanttoday.com/profession

International Paralegal Management Association (IPMA)

The IPMA is an organization intended for the benefit of paralegal managers and supervisors. The site includes a job bank that lists paralegal openings across the country. These opening are often a good source of information on the duties of a paralegal in specific fields. There is also a section on how to find a job as a paralegal.

www.legalassistanttoday.com/profession

Resources for Finding a Paralegal Program

Web Resources for Selecting a Paralegal Education Program

"Guide to Quality Paralegal Education"—a joint paper of the AAfPE and the NFPA
http://paralegals.org/displaycommon.cfm?an=1&subarticlenbr=116

NFPA—suggested curriculum for paralegal studies
http://paralegals.org/displaycommon.cfm?an=1&subarticlenbr=115

Paralegal Education Institutions

AAfPE—searchable database of member institutions—allows searches by name of institution, degrees awarded, state, and region
www.aafpe.org/m_search/index.asp

ABA—state-by-state listing of approved paralegal education programs
www.abanet.org/legalservices/paralegals/directory/home.html

ABA—alphabetical listing of approved paralegal education programs
www.abanet.org/legalservices/paralegals/directory/allprograms.html

NFPA—downloadable list of paralegal programs showing ABA approval, AAfPE membership, and NFPA membership
http://paralegals.org/associations/2270/files/Listparalegalprograms_1.pdf

Legal and Paralegal Associations

American Association for Paralegal Education
2965 Flowers Road South, Suite 105
Atlanta, Georgia 30341
(770) 452-9877

American Bar Association
Standing Committee on Legal Assistants
750 North Lake Shore Drive
Chicago, Illinois 60611
(312) 988-5000

Association of Legal Administrators
175 East Hawthorn Parkway, Suite 325
Vernon Hills, Illinois 60061-1428
(708) 816-1212

Legal Assistant Management Association
638 Prospect Avenue
Hartford, Connecticut 06105-4298
(203) 232-4825

National Association of Legal Assistants, Inc.
1516 Boston Avenue, Suite 200
Tulsa, Oklahoma 74119
(918) 587-6828

National Federation of Paralegal Associations
2517 Eastlake Avenue East, Suite 200
Seattle, Washington 98102
(206) 652-4120

Index

N

National Association of
Legal Assistants (NALA),
18, 31, 81, 281, 284
National Federation of Paralegal
Assistants (NFPA), 18, 31–32,
81–82, 281, 283, 284
Negligence torts, 138–42
Networking, 37

O

Obligations, contract,
198–99, 200–201
Online job search, 38
Oral communication skills, 11
Ownership rights, 176–79

P

Paralegal careers. *See*
also Specialties; *specific*
law categories
applying for jobs, 39–42
in banking industry,
46–47
changing jobs/specialties, 43
compensation, 16–19, 116–17
in corporate legal
departments, 44–45
creating opportunities for,
42
enhancement
opportunities, 26–27
finding jobs, 26–27, 36–38
goals, 35–36, 42–43
in government, 45–46
growth potential, 1–2
in insurance industry, 47

job interviews, 40–42
job satisfaction, 2
in law firms. *See* Law firm(s)
planning, 35–36
preparing for. *See* Education
reasons for pursuing, 1–3
self-employment
opportunities, 48–49
skills for, 7–13
in title/mortgage
companies, 47–48
traits for success, 5–7, 219–20
Partnerships, 56, 205–9, 211–12
Paternity, 158–59
Personal injury law. *See* Tort law
Pleadings, 252–59
Posttrial matters, 278–79
Precedent, 91–92
Pretrial conference, 276
Pretrial preparation, 251–66
communicating results of, 266
discovery, 259–66
electronic discovery, 264–66
pleadings, 252–59
reasons for paralegals
handling, 251–52
Probate. *See* Wills, trusts,
and probate
Product liability, 144–45
Professionalism, 6
Property. *See also* Real
property practice; Wills,
trusts, and probate
crimes against, 125–27
marital, distribution of,
156–58
tortes against, 137–38
Prosecution/trial, 130–32

Q

Questioning clients. *See* Interview(s)

R

Real property practice, 175–84
  commercial transactions, 182–84
  ownership rights and, 176–79
  paralegal role in, 184
  reasons for pursuing, 175–76
  residential transactions, 179–82
Regulation, 19–20, 68–69
Remedies, for non-performance, 200–201
Res ipsa loquitor, 143
Research. *See* Legal research
Residential real-property transactions, 179–82
Resources, 281–84
Responsibilities. *See* Ethics/professional responsibilities
Restatements, 246–47

S

Salary/compensation, 16–19, 116–17
Sales contracts, 195–96
Self-confidence, 7
Self-employment opportunities, 48–49
Skills required, 7–13
Sole proprietorships, 56, 203–5
Specialties, 109–18
  bankruptcy law, 114–15
  changing, 43
  compensation and, 116–17
  deciding on, 110–12
  employment law, 113–14
  environmental law, 115–16
  future hot areas, 117–18
  intellectual property law, 115
  medical/health law, 114
  options, 112–16
  value of, 109–10
Stare decisis, 92
State courts, 103–4
Statutory law, 87–89, 120–21, 241–42
Strict liability, 143

T

Timekeeping, 57–60
Title/mortgage companies, 47–48
Tort law, 133–46
  defined, 133–34
  intentional torts and, 134–38
  Internet torts and, 142
  negligence torts and, 138–42
  paralegal role in, 145–46
  product liability and, 144–45
  strict liability, 143
Trade journals, 38
Traits, of paralegals, 5–7, 219–20
Treatises, 245
Trial assistance, 267–79. *See also* Court system
  exhibits/documents, 275–76
  jury selection, 276–77
  posttrial matters, 278–79
  pretrial conference, 276
  reasons for paralegals handling, 267–68
  trial motions, 277–78

types of, 268–69
witness preparation, 269–75
Trial courts, 95–97

U

Unauthorized law practice, 70–73
Undue influence, 195
Uniform laws, 88–89

W

Warranties, 197–98
Wills, 168–71
Wills, trusts, and probate
  augmented estates and, 166–67
  intestate property
    distribution, 166–68
  law of succession and, 165–68
  letters of instruction and, 170–71
  ownership types and, 162–65
  paralegal role in, 174
  probate process, 173–74
  property/ownership
    types and, 161–62
  trusts, 171–73
  wills, 168–71
Witness preparation, 269–75
Writing skills, 8–10

The Everything® Career Guide Series

Helpful handbooks written by experts.

Trade Paperback
ISBN: 1-59337-583-2
$14.95 ($19.95 CAN)

Trade Paperback
ISBN: 1-59337-432-1
$14.95 ($19.95 CAN)

Trade Paperback
ISBN: 1-59337-433-X
$14.95 ($19.95 CAN)